MORE PRAISE FOR DR. KARP AND

The Happiest Toddler
on the Block

"A joyous adventure . . . with pearls of wisdom on every page."
—Morris Green, M.D., Director, Behavioral Pediatrics, Indiana
University, Riley Hospital for Children; editor, *Pediatrics Diagnosis*

"Dr. Karp's approach is terrific . . . and fun!"
—Martin Stein, M.D., Professor of Pediatrics, University of
California at San Diego, Children's Hospital San Diego

"Parents will be delighted by this clever approach to
communicating with toddlers. It allows us to see the world from
our children's unique point of view."
—Janet Serwint, Professor of Pediatrics, Director of the Harriet
Lane Children's Clinic, Johns Hopkins School of Medicine

"Dr. Karp's new book is an innovative, unique, and thoroughly
enjoyable guide to toddler behavior!"
—Donald Middleton, M.D., Professor of Family Medicine,
University of Pittsburg School of Medicine

"Dr. Karp helps parents turn the 'terrible' twos into 'terrific'
twos. His work will revolutionize the way our culture
understands toddlers!"
—Roni Cohen Leiderman, Ph.D., Associate Dean,
Mailman Segal Institute for Early Childhood Studies, Nova
Southeastern University

"It really works! With great humor and a gentle touch,
Dr. Karp shows how to rai
His book
—Gabrielle Redford, Se
and mother of seve

The Happiest Toddler on the Block

The New Way to Stop the Daily Battle of Wills and Raise a Secure and Well-Behaved One- to Four-Year-Old

Harvey Karp, M.D.

with Paula Spencer

Bantam Books

THE HAPPIEST TODDLER ON THE BLOCK
A Bantam Book

PUBLISHING HISTORY
Bantam hardcover edition published March 2004
Bantam trade paperback edition / June 2005

Published by
Bantam Dell
A Division of Random House, Inc.
New York, New York

Illustration on page 33 from YOUR TWO-YEAR-OLD by
Louise Bates Ames, Ph.D., and Frances L. Ilg, copyright © 1976
by The Gesell Institute of Child Development, Frances L. Ilg
and Louise Bates Ames. Used by permission of Dell Publishing,
a division of Random House, Inc.

Library of Congress Catalog Card Number: 2003062786

Bantam Books and the rooster colophon are registered
trademarks of Random House, Inc.

ISBN 0-553-38143-1

Printed in the United States of America
Published simultaneously in Canada

www.bantamdell.com

BVG   10 9 8 7 6 5 4 3 2 1

To all my little toddler patients, who invite me into their prehistoric world every day!

Contents

PART ONE

Your Evolving Toddler

To best understand your little one, take a giant step . . .
backward.

Epilogue

Appendix

Index

Acknowledgments

"The more things change, the more they remain the same."

—Alphonse Karr, 19th-century French journalist

Ever since I was little, I have been fascinated by frogs and bugs and understanding how everything in our world . . . made sense! How all of nature danced and spun, pulled and pushed, and yet, in extraordinary and unexpected ways, always found its way back to a perfect harmony.

In my working with families for almost thirty years, I have come to understand that toddlers also always "make sense"! They dance and spin, pull and push, but they can quickly be led back to harmony if you know the odd and often unexpected path. I travel that path every day with the toddlers who visit me for their health care. And now, like an adventurer who has just returned from an unexplored land, I am very excited to share the secrets I have discovered about toddlers with parents, grandparents, health professionals, educators, and all lovers of young children.

I have many people to thank for shining their light on my explorations and helping me to see toddlerhood in all its funny and satisfying beauty. My embryology professor at SUNY Buffalo, Gordon Swartz, a brawny ex-boxer with a passion for teaching; Arthur H. Parmelee, Jr., my child development professor at UCLA, a kind and patient man with a deep compassion and understanding of children;

and the concise and insightful writings of Carl Rogers, Haim Ginott, Thomas Gordon, Frances Ilg, Louise Bates Ames, Adele Faber, Elaine Mazlich, Stephanie Marston, Hans Miller and many others.

Thanks to my soul mate and treasured wife, Nina, for her "perfect pitch" corrections to the manuscript and her constant love and patience during my long hours of distraction and absence; to my late mother, Sophie, who many years ago taught me Alphonse Karr's words and thus planted the seed for one of the pivotal underpinnings of this book; to the kindness and caring of my father, Joe, and the generous heart of my unofficial stepmother, Celia; to the superb organizing and writing talents of Paula Spencer; to the illustrious imagination of C. A. Nobens; to the support and peace of mind given me by my colleagues at Tenth Street Pediatrics and my associate Julie Carson May; to my agent Suzanne Gluck, who helped save this project when it almost foundered; and to the always thoughtful and honest feedback of my editor Beth Rashbaum, who endured my constant "what ifs" and "why nots" with considerable (and much appreciated) diplomatic aplomb.

My deep and heartfelt gratitude to the many child development experts who generously gave of their time and wisdom to help make this book clearer and more useful to parents: John Baranowski, Morris Green, Debbie Glasser, Barbara Howard, Lewis Leavitt, Roni Leiderman, Donald Middleton, Karen Miller, Arthur H. Parmelee, Kyle Pruett, Gabrielle Redford, Janet Serwint, Steven Shelov, Marty Stein, and Jim Varga.

And finally, the biggest thanks of all to the trusting parents who chose me as their children's doctor and allowed me to journey with them into the exotic and extraordinary prehistoric valleys of their toddlers' minds.

Without the help of all of you this book would not have been possible.

Introduction

How I Discovered the Secret to Successful
Communication with Toddlers

*"The real voyage of discovery consists, not in
seeking out new lands, but in having a new vision."*
—Marcel Proust

Where did your baby go? One day you're cradling a tiny newborn in your arms, all of parenthood stretched out in front of you. Then before you know it, you're living with an all-new creature—cuter than ever, but suddenly upright, opinionated, headstrong, and lightning fast. Welcome to toddlerhood!

Toddlerhood is one of the high points of parenthood. There's nothing like a one-, two-, or three-year-old to help you see the world in wonderful new ways. The bugs in the grass . . . the shapes in the clouds . . . the "castles" in a pile of sand. Toddlers brim with curiosity, excitement, and irresistible charm.

But as we all know, toddlerhood isn't nonstop fun. It's more like three parts party mixed with two parts wrestling match and one part jungle safari. Why so wild? Because during these three short years the most amazing, explosive developments in a person's life occur! From walking, to speaking, to making first friends, to solving problems, toddlers achieve all of the major developmental milestones that make human beings unique and extraordinary. It's no exaggeration to say that between ages one and four our children are transformed from wobbly, adorable little monkey-like infants into singing, joking, thoughtful young people.

Progress Has Its Price!

All that progress comes at a cost—mainly in wear and tear on your back, your patience, and your sanity. Anyone living with a toddler knows how quickly the emotional climate can shift. One minute all is bliss. Then bam! They grunt, cry, scream, and explode into a tantrum (often in the most embarrassing places). Despite your best intentions, it can feel like the only words you know are "No!" "Stop!" and "Don't touch!" And that's no fun.

No wonder pediatricians find that questions about toddler behavior top parents' concerns. And the dozens of books and thousands of articles written on the subject offer further proof that if you're having frequent struggles with your toddler, you're not alone.

For centuries parents have tried to figure out how to get their little kids to behave. Spanking, isolation, and strict limits were promoted as the only way to keep resistant toddlers from becoming disrespectful children and rebellious youths. Even during the last century leading authorities warned against the evils of "kissing and cuddling" and cautioned parents not to "spare the rod and spoil the child." When I was growing up, it was still common to hear parents yelling, "Shut up, or I'll really give you something to cry about!"

Fortunately the past fifty years have given us exciting insights into what makes children tick. Today we know the destructive effects of rejection and hurtful words, and we're taught to acknowledge our children's frustrations with love. Surprisingly, however, as helpful as patient explanations and discussions of feelings can be with big kids, that logical approach often fails to soothe agitated little toddlers.

Of course, toddlers are *small* children. But they aren't simply miniaturized versions of older kids. Their whole way of thinking is more primitive and rigid. This difference gradually became clear to me after years of practicing pediatrics. Early in my career I followed the advice in "the books" and patiently acknowledged the feelings of the kids I was examining. This worked fine with older children, but upset toddlers usually steamrollered right over me. I tried distraction ("Hey, look at this fun toy!"), reassurance ("See, it really tickles."), compassionate reflection ("I know you hate shots, but . . ."), and respectful logic ("May I check if your ears are healthy inside?"). But I might as well have been speaking Swahili for all the good it did. Despite my best attempts, most eighteen-month checkups would end with a *distraught* mom holding a *frantic* child being examined by a *flustered* doctor. Yikes!

Needless to say, many parents I spoke with were also frustrated by their communication failures. Stressed-out and weary, they would report that loving responses (that I had recommended during the last visit) did little to calm their toddler's outbursts!

Then about ten years ago it dawned on me—toddlers don't act or think like older kids, so why should we speak to them in the same way?

Yes! That was the big breakthrough! We all get more rigid when we're upset, but frustrated little kids become almost prehistoric. I suddenly realized that toddlers needed a *cavemanlike* style of communicating to fit their Stone Age passions, language ability, and view of the world.

A New Mindset: Your Sweet Little . . . Neanderthal?

In my first book, *The Happiest Baby on the Block*, I explain how calming even the fussiest infants is easy once you can see the world from their point of view. Inside the womb newborns are continually fed, shushed, jiggled, and cuddled (the sound our fetuses hear is louder than a vacuum cleaner—24/7). But once they're born, we leave them alone, in almost total stillness, for hours a day! No wonder so many babies have trouble adjusting during those first three months.

That essential insight led me to the discovery of the "calming reflex" (the off switch for crying that all babies are born with), which parents can learn to turn on by re-creating the coziness, the sounds, and the rhythmic motion of the womb.

Armed with this new perspective, parents become a hundred times more successful at baby calming. Similarly, *toddler* calming is also a hundred times more successful when you start from the right perspective.

The insight that makes dealing with toddlers so much easier is that they are, in many fundamental ways, little Neanderthals. I mean no offense by that. Really! But prehistoric humans had only very primitive language and were strong-willed, opinionated, negative, tenacious, distractible, and impatient . . . is this starting to sound familiar?

Let me reassure you that I love toddlers! They're my favorite of all age groups. They are curious, charming, and cute. However, the more I researched anthropology and the latest findings on brain function in children, the more correct the Neanderthal comparison seemed to me. Combined with what I knew about fetal and child development and my daily experiences in the office, I became convinced that "evolution" was the key to understanding and communicating with toddlers.

As I put these ideas into action, I began loving eighteen-month checkups! Once I learned how to speak the *ancient language* of toddlers, I was able to soothe most skeptical, frightened, and screaming little children in minutes . . . or less.

Part One of *The Happiest Toddler on the Block* explains the fascinating links between modern toddlers and prehistoric man. Of course, even the wildest toddler isn't really a Stone Ager, but this general idea is like a window through which you'll be able to view your child in a profound new way. Once you learn how your toddler is similar to a caveman, your true job will become clear—you must think of yourself as an ambassador from the 21st century to the Neanderthal people!

To do that job well, you need to know not only how your little Neanderthal thinks but also how to speak her lingo. Part Two teaches you this ancient "language." You will learn what to say and—more important—how to say it. It's not hard, just *different*. Once you understand the concepts the "Fast-Food Rule" and "Toddler-ese," you will be able to connect with your tantruming toddler and quickly guide her to peace and cooperation. Eight times out of ten, this approach, called Prehistoric Parenting, will work even when your child doesn't get what she's begging for. That's because you'll be giving her a gift that is even more precious to her than cookies and toys: love, respect, and understanding—in her language!

In addition, Part Two will teach you the tricks of successful praise, limit setting, and discipline. You will learn how to give nurturing messages through the "side door" of your child's mind, the importance of helping her feel strong and powerful, and the art of successful toddler negotiations.

Finally, Part Three will show you how to apply Prehistoric Parenting to specific problems you may encounter with your toddler, including sleep issues, toilet training, separation worries, and biting. This section is loaded with practical tips that I've accumulated during my quarter-century in pediatric practice.

Back to Your Future

I know how challenging these years can be for parents. You dream of having a peaceful, happy family. And then toddlerhood turns everything topsy-turvy! That's why I'm so excited about this new way of easing these roller-coaster years. Not only will Prehistoric Parenting make your child's toddler years more fun, they'll also help you guide your little time-traveler on her way to becoming a happy and secure child, teen, and adult.

Important note for harried parents: If you're crunched for time and feel overwhelmed by the here and now, please feel free to flip ahead to Part Two and start to learn these powerful techniques right away!

Most parents achieve a 50 to 90 percent reduction in their toddler's tantrums and a big jump in cooperative behavior after just a week of practicing the tips described in this book. The Fast Food Rule and Toddler-ese usually quickly defuse about 75 percent of squabbles and, when they don't work right away, adding a little ignoring (page 236) usually takes care of the rest. Furthermore, once you get really good at the fun techniques discussed in Chapters 9 and 10 (such as praise, "gossiping," "playing the boob," feeding time-ins, and teaching patience), you'll be able to prevent most tantrums . . . before they even happen!

Once your toddler's behavior has improved, you can always return to the first chapters of the book to learn the fascinating story about how your toddler thinks and the marvelous way she sees the world around her.

A Real-Life Tale of Two Toddlers

Karen, mother of two beautiful toddlers, was about ready to pull out her own hair. Her husband, a soldier stationed in Korea, was gone for nine months . . . her family lived far from base . . . and she felt as if her children, Kate, two, and Taylor, three, were "running the show"! Karen confided in me that her strong-willed kids were having up to twenty tantrums a day!

Karen and I spoke for thirty minutes on the phone and I had her review my book and DVD. As amazing as it sounds, within less than a week, her toddlers were happier, more cooperative, and having only one to two tantrums a day.

Over and over again I've seen this simple approach turn tornadoes into rainbows and help wobbly, whining children blossom into the happiest toddlers on the block . . . and soon you will witness this too!

So get ready to take a giant step—*backward!* I promise you'll discover that it's the best way for both you and your toddler to march ahead to a great new relationship.

—*Harvey Karp, M.D.*

The
Happiest Toddler
on the Block

PART ONE

Your Evolving Toddler

To best understand your little
one, take a giant
step . . . *backward*.

1

"Help! There's a
Neanderthal in My
Kitchen!"

"A first step is like watching the history of human civilization from small fishy things to Neanderthals unravel in one instant before your eyes."

—Anna Quindlen and Nick Kelsh, *Naked Babies*

Main Points:

- All parents find toddlerhood challenging.

- Parenting tips that work with older children often fail miserably with toddlers.

- As your toddler grows, you are watching five million years of humanity unfold before your very eyes.

- Toddlers pass through four stages of development that echo the evolution of our ancient ancestors.

- Prehistoric Parenting: How to become the perfect ambassador to your little Stone Ager.

In the Beginning . . .

Tara, 14 months old, is proud of her newfound ability to walk. She tries to practice it every chance she gets. But right now she's confined to an exam room with me and her mom, Simone. Tara toddles over to the door. "Unghh!" She grunts reaching for the doorknob. "Unghh! Unghh!" She pushes against the closed door. Now she turns a pleading eye to me and starts slapping the door. She wants out!

Simone responds, "No, sweetheart. I know you want to leave, but we have to stay here a little longer. Let's look at this pretty book."

Tara's mom has lovingly acknowledged her daughter's feelings (a common parenting tip) and tried a favorite distraction (another good idea). This time, however, her efforts are rewarded with a crumpled red face, an open mouth . . . and . . . a long shrill scream that could shatter glass!

Taken aback by the tantrum's ferocity, her mom tries to engage her by heartily singing "The Itsy Bitsy Spider." Tara screams louder. So Simone decides to set a limit. "Tara! No screaming! Shhh. Stop or we'll have to leave, okay?" But by now Tara is in a full-scale meltdown. Embarrassed—and annoyed—Simone offers me an apology and hoists her little volcano over her shoulder; avoiding the stares of the other parents in the waiting room, she hurries to the exit.

Have you experienced your toddler's first temper tantrum yet?

Has your child discovered the word "No!"?

Do you get ambushed by fights that rise out of nowhere?

Are you mentally exhausted from shouting "Don't pull that!" and "Stop, now!"?

Parenting a toddler is filled with thrills and simple joys, but for most of us, it's also filled with the most difficult challenges we will encounter until the teen years. (No wonder it's often called "the first adolescence.")

Loving parents just like you have been scratching their heads for generations, wondering (and asking their pediatricians): What makes toddlers act the way they do? Why are they so unreasonable and tough to discipline?

I'm going to answer those questions for you. Better yet, I'll show you the way to a calmer toddler and a less-stressed household. But first it helps to see . . . the big picture.

Ah-ha! A New View of Toddlers

"A mind once stretched to a new idea never returns to its original size."

—Oliver Wendell Holmes

Until recently people mistakenly thought that babies cried because of terrible stomach pain. Then my book *The Happiest Baby on the Block* came along and revealed that newborns really cry because they need help turning on their "calming reflex." (Ah-ha!)

With toddlers, the "ah-ha" realization that perfectly explains their perplexing behavior is that these sweet kids, the apples of our eyes, are actually little Neanderthals!

Okay, okay. I've had more than one parent look at me strangely when I've said that. Please don't take the comparison as an insult. Allow me to explain how this new way of thinking will become your magic window for understanding what goes on in your toddler's mind—and help you turn conflict into cooperation in minutes—or less!

"The Little Adult Assumption": A Common Mistake

Recently John, a dad in my practice, said to me jokingly, "My toddler is a completely different animal than she was as a baby!" John was more on target than he knew!

Parenting a newborn involves overcoming some initial potholes (like colic and lack of sleep). But after a few months, life proceeds in a sunny way as your baby grows ever cuter and more fun. Then with her first lurching steps toddlerhood is off and running (and so are you)! Within months or even days, your waddling wonder will start developing a new sense of power and defiance. And suddenly you may feel the need to learn how to discipline your little one without squashing her spirit—or losing your mind.

Toddlers make the job of parenting a notch more complicated.

During your baby's first year you happily gave her whatever she wanted (milk, a pacifier, a fresh diaper, a change of scenery). Now, however, you can only give her 90 to 95 percent of what she wants. The rest of the time you'll have to say no to her desire because it is dangerous, or aggressive, or not what you want to do at that moment.

And guess what? She's not going to like that!

So what do you do?

You try to lovingly "acknowledge her feelings." ("I see you're mad about leaving, but we really have to go. Okay?") You get a fit.

You try to reason. You get a fit.

You distract. You get a fit.

You give a warning. You get a fit.

You do a time-out. You get a fit.

Pretty soon *you're* having a fit too!

What happened?

Too often we make the mistake of speaking to toddlers as though they're small adults. They understand so much of what we say, it's sometimes hard to remember their limits. Psychologist Thomas Phelan, author of *1, 2, 3 Magic,* calls this "the little adult assumption." He's right. Toddlers aren't small adults. Toddlers are unique—no longer babies, but not quite "kids." That's why hand-me-down discipline ideas designed for older kids don't work for them. They require a special approach all their own.

People will tell you you need to be more strict or more lenient. But what you really need are skills designed specifically for impulsive, distractible, inarticulate, self-absorbed, primitive toddlers.

First Let's Back Up—*Way* Back

"The child is nearer to the savage than to the angel."
—C. Gasquoine Hartley, "Mother and Son," 1923

Usually when people say, "It's ancient history," they mean, "Forget about it. It's not worth thinking about." But with toddlers, knowing a little ancient history is *exactly* what will help you be a terrific parent.

The starting place is your child's level of *evolution*. If that word makes you think about dinosaurs and fossils, you're on the right track! In dozens of key measures of brain maturity, toddlers are really pint-size Stone Agers! I know that sounds odd. But the language and problem-solving skills of a 12-month-old have more in common with a chimpanzee than a Girl Scout. Two-year-olds use mental processes very similar to those of cavemen. And three-year-olds think more like the first villagers, thousands of years before biblical times, than like your neighborhood Little Leaguers.

At birth your child begins a dramatic journey to adulthood. Starting from total helplessness, she will end up with the ability to recite Shakespeare, create paintings, and offer compassion and care to those in need—things no other animal has ever achieved. And the turning point for this major transition from brutes to humanity occurs during the toddler years.

In fact, all five of the major feats that make human beings so extraordinary blossom during the three incredible toddler years:

- Walking on two legs
- Manipulating things with our hands
- Expressing words with our mouths
- Combining ideas with our minds
- Forming complicated social relationships

You knew your toddler was a busy bug, but that's *really* accomplishing things!

Mastering all those milestones requires a rapidly evolving brain—which is just what your toddler is blessed with. As the human race evolved, from knuckle-walking to using tools and words, brains got bigger and bigger. Up to a point.

Eventually the heads encasing our fetuses' big brains started becoming too large to slip through the birth canal. In order to get out our newborns had to develop smaller "no frills" brains equipped only to manage the bare necessities such as sucking, peeing, and keeping the heart beating. To make up for this "no frills" nervous system, Nature designed our children's brains to grow dramatically over the first year. By the time your baby's chubby legs take their first steps into toddlerhood, her big brain is off and running too!

A great way to understand this explosion of ability is to understand the biology behind it.

From Monkey Business to . . . Monkey Business?

Introducing "ORP": Sounds like something a baby would do, and it is!

> *"Our soul is full in all its parts of faint hints . . .*
> *flitting for an instant . . . and then gone forever, dim*
> *and scarcely audible murmurs of a great and*
> *prolonged life . . . of many generations."*
>
> —G. Stanley Hall, 1904

What comes out of a frog egg when it hatches? A little froggie? No! Out pops a little *tadpole,* more fish than amphibian, a small echo of the frog's evolutionary ancestry.

It's the same with humans. The entire history of humanity is encapsulated inside each developing fetus. How is that possible? Back in 1971, when I was a college student in Buffalo, New York, my embryology professor, Gordon Swartz, exposed me to a fascinating law of biology that has since become central to my understanding of toddlers.

This law states: *Ontogeny recapitulates phylogeny.* (Or ORP!)

Wait, don't run! I know this law sounds weird, but it's actually simple and very fun!

Let me translate ORP into plain English:

Ontogeny? That's your child's development. In short, her steady path of learning and growing, starting from the instant of her conception.

Recapitulates? That means "mirrors" or "repeats."

Phylogeny? That's the step-by-step process of our evolution beginning 1.5 billion years ago.

In short, *as your child develops, from conception to adulthood, she will mirror many of the characteristics of our ancient ancestors as they slowly evolved into modern humans.*

Here's a fun way to picture this in your mind: Imagine you could watch the growth of your baby like a time-lapse movie from the instant your sperm and egg met, all the way to her high school graduation. In a way, you'd also be watching how life on earth unfolded, a whirlwind tour of evolution, from worms to fish to rabbits to tiny monkeys.

Your fertilized egg, looking a bit like the first single-celled creature to appear on Earth (1.5 billion years ago), rapidly multiplies, morphing from a blackberry-shaped clump of cells to a tubular, worm-like embryo. At about five weeks your tiny fetus begins to rocket through a "fish" stage with flipper-like limbs and little gill-like slits on her neck (400 million years ago); then undergoes an "early mammal" stage with two lines of nipples on her chest and a tiny tail (180 million years ago); then several months before birth these disappear (leaving just the two nipples we're all born with and a few small tailbones at the bottom of the spine). As a beautiful newborn, your baby has tightly grasping fingers and toes, the ability to breathe and swallow at the same time, and maybe even some extra hair on her back, ears, and forehead—all characteristics of newborn monkeys (30 million years ago).

After birth this process continues to speed along. Once your child is able to pull herself onto two wobbly legs, she will have reached the evolutionary stage of the first teetering chimp-like steps (5 million years ago)! That's the starting bell that announces the arrival of toddlerhood, when even more tremendous advancements take place. Around her first birthday, she will be unsteady on her feet and her speech will be a jumble of grunts and gestures. Yet by her fourth birthday, her abilities will match what took the human race five million years to attain. She'll be able to run, speak, sing, and handily wield a fork or a toy hammer. She'll have a developed sense of humor and definite ideas about fairness, and her scribbled pictures will even become recognizable! In fact, by the end of toddlerhood, your child will have grown from just an adorable muffin to a smart little citizen able to start tackling reading and writing—tasks not achieved by even the brainiest adults until about eight thousand years ago.

Your toddler's development is not a perfect reflection of ancient evolution. She looks no more like a caveman or a chimp than a real Neanderthal looked like your 18-month-old tot. But her development does tend to echo the stages our ancestors passed through. That's why ORP is a fun way for you to picture your toddler's march to maturity, and a helpful guide for your communications with her.

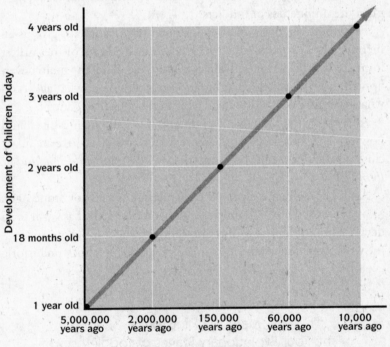

YOUR CHILD'S DEVELOPMENT ECHOES THE PAST

Development of Children Today

- 4 years old
- 3 years old
- 2 years old
- 18 months old
- 1 year old

5,000,000 years ago · 2,000,000 years ago · 150,000 years ago · 60,000 years ago · 10,000 years ago

Abilities of Man's Ancient Ancestors

Note: Those familiar with anthropology may be troubled by the license I take with nomenclature. Instead of *Neanderthal* I should have used the name *Homo habilis* and in place of *caveman* it would have been more accurate to say archaic *Homo sapiens*. Alas, those terms are a bit of a mouthful, so for the sake of simplicity, I chose names that were more familiar, albeit less precise.

Why It Helps to Think of Your Toddler as a Living . . . Fossil

"What's past is prologue."

—William Shakespeare, *The Tempest*

Over the past fifty years, research in anthropology and on children's brain function has been building a steady foundation of facts to explain the uniqueness of toddlers.

Fossil hunters, using the bones of prehistoric animals, give us an increasingly clear picture of what the life and culture of the earliest humans were like. Huge advances in studying children's brain development have taught us what brain centers turn on at what ages, and what parts of movement, language, and thought they control.

Amazingly, the more we learn about how early man evolved and how young brains develop, the more we discover that there are many close parallels between them. In other words, your *child is a kind of living fossil!*

Again, no toddler is a carbon copy of a chimpanzee or Stone Ager. (Not even when life with one seems at its rockiest!) But as I will soon detail, communicating with your child will be a lot more successful when you understand how her development echoes prehistoric evolution.

Meet the Flintstones: The Four Evolutionary Stages of Toddlerhood

Toddlerhood covers three years of exciting change that parallel five million years of human evolution. With so much happening, it's useful to see toddlers as falling into four distinct (but overlapping) phases:

The Charming Chimp-Child (12 to 18 months)

Some parents compare their wrinkled newborns to cute little monkeys, but toddlers? Developmentally, yes! To be more precise, by her first birthday your toddler has climbed the evolutionary ladder all the way up to the stage of the so-called Missing Link, between ape and man, who roamed the earth five million years ago.

Once early man began to walk on two legs, he was unstoppable (as the parent of any 12-month-old knows only too well!). With his hands now free, he used them morning to night to grab everything in reach. Wild chimps (the closest animals to the Missing Link living today) can communicate twenty to thirty words through signs and gestures. This closely parallels what an average child masters during the first six months of toddlerhood.

The Knee-High Neanderthal (18 to 24 months)

Midway to her second birthday your toddler will make a leap to the developmental level of a Neanderthal. When you watch your 18-month-old handle a spoon, drink from a cup without spilling, and try to toss you a ball, you are peering back about two million years into the past. Like apes, Neanderthals were consumed with moving and touching, and they were also ambidextrous, messy, and gawky (yes, just like your 18-month-old). But their balance was much improved over chimps', as was their ability to use their hands to twist, probe, and pick things apart. They could even make crude stone tools!

Neanderthals were more advanced than chimps because they could solve a few basic problems, like planning a simple hunt or selecting a good rock to use as an ax. These early sparks of ingenuity are echoed in your 18-month-old's ability to figure out how to use a wind-up toy, open a childproof latch, or use a stick to reach something that has rolled under the bed.

But as I mentioned earlier, progress has its costs. Along with the ability to use clubs and throw stones, ancient Neanderthals developed an attitude problem. They no longer lived in fear of the strong animals around them; now they could defend themselves with rocks and sticks. That made them more cocky, self-centered, and combative. It's no coincidence that the term "terrible twos" is used to refer to this stage. The period between your toddler's second six months of toddlerhood and her second birthday will probably be her most rigid, opinionated, and uncompromising.

The Clever Cave-Kid (24 to 36 months)

Around two years of age your toddler advances to the level of cave dwellers (150,000 years ago). Cavepeople turned their attentions to making friendships and alliances and entered the world of slightly more complex language, tools, and deal-making.

Most experts agree these ancient people had great manual dexterity. It is also believed they possessed a basic form of language that consisted of a scattering of nouns, verbs, and modifiers. They were able to communicate well enough to plan major efforts like hunting bear and mammoth using just spears and teamwork. Stone Age relics also reveal another type of planning—the emergence of a special corner of the cave reserved just for potty use!

Such developments parallel the world of your two-year-old. Now her hand is flexible enough for her to use more "tools" (toys), and she can finally make circular scribbles (another sign of control and planning). Also, a better attention span and growing interest in making friends increase your two-year-old's ability to take turns and be patient. But the flip side is that when frustrated by these new experiences, your uncivilized little creature may still resort to primitive responses like hitting or biting.

The Versatile Villager (36 to 48 months)

By her third birthday, your toddler zooms all the way to the level of the first villagers (sixty thousand years ago). Tens of thousands of years before the Bible was written, human culture suddenly mush-roomed. Evidence from across Europe, Africa, and the Middle East—art, tools, jewelry, and remnants of everyday life—reveals a village culture that was vastly more sophisticated than anything previously seen.

Many of these first modern men and women lived in groups of one hundred or more members, larger than ever before. Peaceful survival in these extended tribes required the invention of rules of politeness. The same increasing intelligence that allowed them to learn social rules and acquire sophisticated language skills enabled them to juggle ideas in their heads and master complicated songs, dances, and storytelling.

These developmental advances are almost exactly mirrored in older toddlers. After her third birthday your toddler's skills sky-rocket! She, too, now has the mental dexterity to juggle ideas, as shown in her love of making comparisons like "The ostrich is a giraffe bird" and "I'm not a baby. I'm big!" She works hard to figure out how the world works, saying things like "Why can't I?" and "Red means stop!" Like a prehistoric villager, a three-year-old freely embraces "magic" as a way to explain things that cannot otherwise be understood. And like early villagers, she too lacks the brainpower to turn her words into writing.

With her exciting new realization that she is bigger than a baby comes the unnerving realization that, compared to everyone else, she is vulnerable and small. No wonder three-year-olds enjoy stories about being big and strong and games where *they* get to be the big scary monster.

Once you begin seeing your child in this "evolutionary" light, your daily struggles and frustrations will make a lot more sense. The tantrums, the grunts, the bold disregard of your requests, and the desire to throw rocks at your cat—your toddler's whole lack of civilization—now all fit together. (It may even explain why little kids love Barney and little toy dinosaurs—but I will leave that to future generations of researchers to investigate!)

Remember, you know your toddler better than any book does. The age-based categories listed here are only rough guidelines. Every child is different and so is the pace at which they reach different milestones. Eventually, however, your toddler will progress through all these different stages and arrive, as a four-year-old, noticeably smarter and more civilized than she was when she started out a lightning-fast three years earlier!

See How They Evolve!

Increased brain growth fuels development. Let's look at the differences in maturity across two behaviors:

1. *How does a toddler use language to tell you she wants something?*

- A Chimp-Child just grabs it.

- A Neanderthal grabs it and says, "Mine!"

- A Cave-Kid wants to grab it but tries to please you by restraining the impulse and saying, "I want!"

- A Villager begins following the rule of politeness and says, "Please."

2. *How does a toddler use language to describe things she notices?*

- A Chimp-Child uses one word to describe a whole group ("doggie" for any small animal).

- A Neanderthal learns specific words ("bunny," "kitty").

- A Cave-Kid can compare two things ("big bunny" and "little bunny") and point to which is bigger.

- A Villager can compare several objects and can pick out which is the biggest, longest, etc.

"You Tarzan—Me Mommy!"

The first step to making your child the happiest toddler on the block is to think of yourself as an ambassador from the 21st century to a visitor from the Neanderthal people. Your guest doesn't know your customs and doesn't speak your language. But she's here to stay for the next year's term.

The goal of an ambassador is to promote harmony and avoid conflict. Top diplomats rely on respect, kindness, and lots of negotiation and compromise. (You'll have fun practicing your effective new skills, like time-ins, "gossiping," "playing the boob," and teaching patience.) Ambassadors aren't pushy (control freaks) or pushovers (afraid to take control). But when they need to, they must act firmly—along the lines of a time-out, *not a spanking.*

Naturally, your job as an ambassador will be much easier if you understand your guest's customs and speak her language. This is Prehistoric Parenting. Although it may sound a little strange, once you practice it, you will be amazed at how well it works!

Remember Tara, the little girl who wanted out of my exam room? Here's how another parent, already familiar with Prehistoric Parenting, handled a similar situation.

Prehistoric Parenting in Action

Mack, 14 months old, is normally fun and playful, but now he's focused like a bulldog on his immediate need: getting out of my exam room. Using his few words and whole body to communicate, Mack beats at the door and looks pleadingly at his mom, Kate. She kneels down and expressively mirrors her son's feelings with short, emphatic syllables to show Mack (in his own simple language—Toddler-ese) that she gets the message. "Out! Out! Out!!! Out!!! OUT!!!!!!!!!!!!" Kate says vigorously, pointing dramatically at the door with an earnest, concerned look on her face. "Out! Out! OUT! You go! You GO!!!! YOU want OUT!!!!!!!"

At first, Mack was so focused on the door, he seemed oblivious to his mom's words. But amazingly, after the sixth passionate "Out!" Mack suddenly turned to her. His eyes widened in grateful acknowledgment. Sensing the tide turning in her favor, Kate continued her energetic commentary of Mack's actions. "You are sooooooooo bored!! You want to go, go, GO!!!!!!!" Soon Mack takes a small step from the door toward his mom, momentarily satisfied—*Mom understands!*

Completing this perfectly executed Prehistoric Parenting maneuver, Kate finishes by sitting on the floor and inviting her son to play. Hey . . . hey . . . psssst," she whispers loudly, extending her hand and signaling him to come closer. "Come 'ere. Come 'ere. Let's dance!" Then she breaks into a chorus of her son's favorite song, "La Bamba." Kate claps her hands, and Mack toddles around happily, raising his hands in the air each time his mom does. In less than a minute the tantrum is forgotten, and he's happily mirroring her!

How to Talk So a Toddler Can Listen

Kate succeeded because she remembered how to be a good ambassador. She made sure Mack knew he was respected and understood. And, most importantly, she communicated that message in his language (with the right tone of voice and facial expressions) before presenting her message: "Let's dance, not hit the door."

"I feel kind of silly talking like a cave-mom, but it works," Kate told me. "What I really love is that instant when he pauses, and I know he's thinking, 'Hey! Mom gets me!' When we're on the same wavelength like that, it's magical!"

If you want to talk with a Swede, speak Swedish. If you want to make your point to a primitive toddler, you have to speak Toddler-ese.

Most parents are amazed to learn that the *least* important part of what we say to our upset toddlers is . . . *what* we say! *Our words are almost meaningless without the right tone and expression.* But this shouldn't really be a surprise. The same principle is true for communicating with adults. For example, if someone screams because she sees a spider, and you say, "Wow, that was scary" with a big smirk on your face, your caring words will be canceled out by your sarcastic look! The more upset adults are, the more we need those speaking to us to use the right tone *and the right gestures.* This is also true for our intense toddlers.

Kate connected with Mack by echoing his feelings by hammering out a short, expressive, "Out, out, *out!* You want to go OUT!" With toddlers this age, repetition and brevity are important. (I will discuss this in depth in Chapter 8.) Kate continued this until she caught the glimpse of comprehension in Mack's widened eyes: that's when she knew her message of respect and understanding had reached its target! Then as if by magic, Mack suddenly returned the favor. He focused his attention on her and listened to her message with respect.

That's what being an ambassador is all about. The language of diplomacy is rooted in respect. Like diplomats, we parents should always strive to use our words and actions to convey empathy and respect, rather than power and superiority. Not only is that more effective, it's far more pleasant for all parties involved.

2

12 to 18 Months: Your "Charming Chimp-Child"

"That's one small step for a child, one giant leap for mankind."

—Adapted from astronaut Neil Armstrong's
first words on the moon

Main Points:

- Developmentally, our sweet one-year-olds are not much ahead of chimpanzees.

- Your young toddler is thrilled by walking (but will still drop to all fours if in a rush).

- New fine motor skills like pointing, pinching, and grabbing let him explore in new ways.

- He says a little, understands more, and communicates mostly by gestures, grunts, and tone of voice.

- Like a cute little chimp, your one-year-old lives in the moment and loves "ape-ing" everything you do.

Ben had been cruising along the furniture since he learned to pull himself up at 10 months. The day before his first birthday he skipped his usual hold-on-to-the-sofa maneuver. Instead, he took off for the open terrain of the family room. Waddling like a duck, he plunked onto his bottom every few feet. But each time he crumpled, he'd crawl back to his starting point and start toddling again, determined to get it right.

Soon, look out, world! Ben was unstoppable.

"I couldn't believe how fast he got after just one week," marveled his dad, Sam. "Crawling had been a big accomplishment for him, but walking was a whole new ball game!"

Now when Ben doesn't want to do something, he wobbles away. When he sees something interesting, he toddles as close as he can and lunges at it! If he can't reach something, he points a chubby finger and holds out his hand. From the second he gets up to the time his eyes close at night, he's a lad on a mission!

In his own little game of "monkey see, monkey do," Ben follows Sam from room to room, pulling on every drawer he opens. Even though Ben's language is mostly made up of hoots and pointing, he seems to understand much of what's said to him.

Fortunately for Sam, he's fairly easy to distract. A fresh toy will keep him occupied long enough for a diaper change, and going to the yard makes him happily forget the cookies he demanded moments before.

Still, by dinner, Sam has begun fantasizing about bedtime. He's beat, bushed, and sometimes bonkers! But one look at Ben's sweet, sleeping face starts to "recharge his battery" and make him feel like the best dad in town.

How Is a Toddler's Development Like a Chimp's?

The first year of a child's life is called infancy. It comes from Latin for "without words," but I think a better description of this stage of life should be "in*foot*cy," for "without steps." A child's first words are unpredictable. They may start as early as nine months or not until three years. But around the first birthday, most children get up on their feet and toddle! That's why this period is called *toddler*hood.

With his first shaky steps, your toddler follows in the footsteps of the first ape-man (the so-called Missing Link) who gave up knuckle-walking five million years ago—and never looked back. He is definitely a little person, but he still loves getting into monkey business—yanking the tablecloth, dumping the dog food, or stuffing things into your VCR.

Humans and Apes: More Similar Than You Might Think

The difference between humans and apes is great. Yet genetically there is a surprising similarity between us. Believe it or not, our genes are about 98 percent identical to those of chimpanzees!

By one year of age, he is so smart that his behavior mirrors that of the most intelligent apes of them all—chimpanzees. Young chimps wobble around on two legs, understand some words, and can figure out simple things. They also love to go everywhere, touch everything, and play, play, play! (Sound like anyone you know?)

Now, I'm certainly not the only one who has noticed the similarity between young toddlers and chimpanzees. In fact, during the 1930s psychologists Winthrop and Luella Kellogg raised their one-year-old, Donald, with a slightly younger chimp, Gua. (Talk about a two-ring circus!)

Donald and Gua became buddies. They ate the same food, shared the same clothes, and learned the same things. In fact, Gua's brain power closely paralleled that of her "brother." They both loved climbing, though Gua was better. They both loved handling things: Donald did better with toys, while Gua was better with a spoon. And Gua even joined Donald in learning how to use the potty. In fact, Gua was toilet-trained faster than her human buddy!

Within months, however, Donald began outpacing the chimp. The Kelloggs noticed that both were curious, but Donald examined things to see how they worked, while Gua only held things briefly before discarding them.

Although Donald and Gua were equally good at following commands, Donald's ability to speak zoomed ahead while Gua's was stuck at grunts and gestures. And unlike Donald, Gua never brought toys to the Kelloggs to invite them to play, never imitated them doing chores or played games like pat-a-cake. While Donald kept on progressing, Gua was stuck in a five-million-year-old revolving door.

Indeed, more recent research has shown that human and chimp language development roughly parallel each other until about 18 months.

A Big Cerebellum—the Birthday Gift Mother Nature Gave Us Five Million Years Ago!

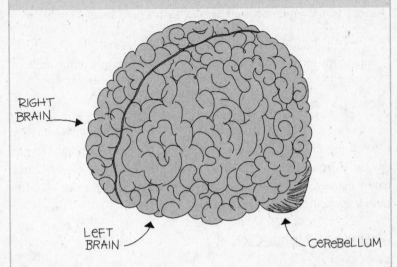

RIGHT BRAIN →

LEFT BRAIN ↗

CEREBELLUM

Cerebellum means "little brain." It's a part of the brain you probably didn't even know you had, although you rely on it every second. The cerebellum is the brain's balance and coordination center. It helps you walk straight, not fall off your chair, and ride a bike. In addition, this extraordinary "little brain" coordinates fast, tricky moves like writing, throwing a ball, and speaking, so that you can do them almost automatically.

What does this have to do with your toddler's development? A lot! As mentioned earlier, one to two million years ago, our newborns' heads became so big, they could barely be squeezed out of the womb. So in order to make the fetal brain a bit smaller, Mother Nature decided to give newborns a super-tiny cerebellum. That's why young infants have such crummy balance and coordination.

Once our babies' heads are out in the world and there's plenty of room for their brains to get bigger—*kaboom!*—the talented cerebellum starts growing explosively . . . and so does his coordination. By the age of one, your child is a virtual gymnast compared to where he was twelve months earlier. He can stand; he can reach out and grab a vase; and he can command his tiny mouth muscles to tighten and twist to make a zillion new sounds.

All of this is nonstop play for your 12-month-old! Now that's what I call a birthday present! No other gift you could give your child would entertain him as well as his own brain's cerebellar "fun zone."

Throughout your child's toddler years, his cerebellum will be one of his most important helpers. It will constantly refine itself, getting better and better at helping him move, climb, and speak.

One chimp raised by a human researcher was actually taught to recognize more than two hundred words! Yet even this clever chimp barely learned to put words together to make little phrases—a common achievement of 18-month-olds.

What Is a 12-Month-Old?

Of course, your cute little toddler isn't really a chimp, but he may often act like one:

C—Cute
H—Happy
I—Into everything
M—Monkey see, monkey do
P—Pushing the limits (at least beginning to)

Evolution Up Close and Personal: What's Your Toddler Doing Now?

The months after your child's first birthday are like his "on ramp" to the highway of top-speed toddlerhood. Your little child will gradually gain the confidence to stand on his own two feet and express his opinions. Thankfully, most one-year-olds are relatively compliant and easy to corral. But as the months go by, your toddler will increasingly push for independence and access to *everything*. That activity may start to make your house seem like a disaster zone, but to him, it's an enticing jungle to explore.

Gross Motor Skills Now

Discovering the thrill of walking. For most young toddlers, actions speak far louder than words. Although your one-year-old is working to master his first words, there's no doubt about what really makes his heart go pitter-patter—walking! To walk where he wants and touch what he chooses is intoxicating. These little primitives march around thinking, *Wow, I can do it! This is cool!*

Walking allows your one-year-old to test his confidence. Some kids are so self-assured that once they are on their feet, they waddle away and never look back. These kids rush for the nearest door as if they're ready to get their own apartment. Other more cautious children toddle a few steps, then turn to you as if to ask, "Are you still there, Mommy? See, I did a good job!"

The awkward way young toddlers walk with their feet spread wide and their hands held up for balance is very similar to the way chimps totter around, dropping to all fours when they want to get somewhere fast. And just as a baby chimp moves away from his mother to explore the world, your clever little creature will also begin leaving the safety of your side to tentatively start his own journey in life.

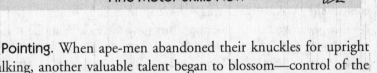

Fine Motor Skills Now

Pointing. When ape-men abandoned their knuckles for upright walking, another valuable talent began to blossom—control of the hands and wrists. This ability eventually allowed our ancestors to invent all sorts of clever tools, an ability that truly separates humans from other animals.

Perhaps the first tool of all was the pointing finger! Toddlers quickly learn to use their pointer to make contact with things that interest them. Just like a little chimp, your young toddler can point to pictures in books, push a grain of rice across a plate, and wiggle a finger up into his nose. (Pointing can also lead to accidents—a finger probing the jagged lip of an open tin can or touching the prong of an exposed electric plug. One of the great challenges of parenting is that with every developmental leap forward comes new hazards to watch for.)

Pinching and grabbing. After ape-men began to evolve away from chimps, they developed an extraordinary new tool that became even more important to their survival than their trusty pointer—the pincer grasp.

The fossil record shows that over eons of evolution, the thumb moved close enough to the other fingers to allow the tips of the thumb and pointer to come together—to pinch.

Chimp hands are perfect for swinging in trees, but not so great picking things up. Their thumbs are so low on their wrists that they have trouble grabbing morsels with their fingers. They can pick up big things like twigs by pinching them between their thumb and the *side* of the pointer, but for picking up tiny things, they rely upon their talented lips. Young toddlers, on the other hand (so to speak), are way ahead of chimps in their ability to grasp. Your child easily uses his thumb and the tip of his pointer like tweezers to pick up the teensiest crumbs and bits of lint.

Exploring by manipulating. The word *manipulate* comes from the ancient Latin word *manu,* which means "hand." Give anything to your young toddler, and he'll turn it over and over in his hands to examine it. As a baby, he might have immediately brought it to his mouth or banged it on the floor. But now the first thing he does is investigate it with his hands and eyes.

Ancient man's increase in dexterity is echoed in our toddlers. A 12-month-old is doing well if he can whack two little blocks together. But by 15 months his grasp and release are so precise that he can drop one block exactly on top of another to make a little stack.

A twist of the wrist. Toddlers can pinch with their fingertips better than any chimp, but they're a little slower than apes when it comes to complex movements of the wrist.

Twelve-month-olds can usually scoop up food with a spoon,

but they have real trouble swiveling it into their mouths. Suddenly at around 15 to 18 months they start moving their rigid wrists like the Tin Man in *The Wizard of Oz* after getting a shot of oil. That's when your toddler has the coordination to twist his wrist a smidgen to keep the food from spilling as the spoon approaches his mouth.

For your toddler, this is another moment of triumph and satisfaction! But once again this new skill creates the risk of new accidents. Now you must keep him from turning on the hot water, twisting stove dials, and getting into dangerous containers like perfume bottles, jugs of cleaning fluids, and thermoses filled with hot coffee.

Lefty? Righty? Which side of your toddler's brain is the boss? As shown on page 25, your toddler's brain is divided into two main parts: the right side and the left. Hundreds of millions of years ago Nature "realized" that brains were so important, they should be made in two identical halves in case one was damaged. It was like having a spare tire, or brain insurance. This is still true of most animals today.

But 50 to 100 million years ago, rather than waste half of that valuable real estate to just duplicate the other half, the brain's two sides gradually took on different functions.

The right brain became the seat of our emotions and our aggressive impulses. It also instantly recognizes faces, melodies, and places; and reads people's emotions, tone of voice, and gestures. All this helps us when we have to make snap decisions in our lives. The right brain also controls the left side of the body.

The left brain became the master of details, the nerd of the nervous system. It remembers and organizes information, putting together strings of notes to make songs, strings of ideas to make plans, and strings of words to make sentences. The left brain also controls the right side of the body.

In chimps and young toddlers the two sides are almost in balance, with the right side being a little more powerful. This explains why your 15-month-old is still aggressive and impulsive, better at reading faces than at understanding words and more tuned in to a song's melody than its lyrics.

When it comes to handedness, parents often notice that until age two or three, their kids may seem right-handed on some days and left-handed on others.

Language Skills Now

Like chimps, young toddlers use their mouths to hold things when their hands are full. But as the cerebellum develops it gives better control over the hand's tiny muscles. Within a few months you'll notice your toddler no longer uses his mouth as a "third hand." The "new improved" cerebellum also gives better control over the small muscles of the mouth. Soon you'll see him discover an exciting use for his mouth's new dexterity—talking.

Gestures speak louder than words. What was your child's first communication? "Mama"? "Dada"? If he is like most kids, it was more likely two arms held up ("Pick me up!") or a squawk plus a finger pointing to a milk jug ("I want that!"). When you think about it, it's hard to *say* words. You have to perfectly coordinate your lips, tongue, throat, and diaphragm. That's why kids are often able to wave bye-bye before their first birthday, but it takes them until 15 to 18 months to actually *say* "Bye-bye!"

The pincer grasp . . . of the mouth. The first "words" our children learn to say are single and double syllables like "ba" or "Dada." We don't teach these to them—they make them up! Just as your one-year-old practices the pincer grasp, repeatedly tapping together the tips of his thumb and pointer finger, he's doing the same tapping

The Finger That Talks

The fancy name for the pointer finger is the index finger. Interestingly, the word *index* comes from the Latin verb *dicere*, which means "to say." In fact, in Serbian, the pointer finger is literally referred to as the "talking finger."

with his lips and tongue. "Mama," "Dada," and "Papa" are the pincer grasp of the mouth!

And we are so eager to talk to our little children that rather than waiting for them to learn our language, we adopt *theirs*. We say, "Hi, Boo-boo! It's Dada!" and ask, "Do you want Mama to get your baba?"

All around the world the words used to mean mother and father are actually little double syllables taken directly from "the mouths of babes." Mother is *Mama* in Chinese, *Eema* in Hebrew, *Mama* in Swahili. Father is *Babbo* in Italian, *Ata* in Slovenian, *Papa* in Russian, and so on.

The game of "monkey hear, monkey say." If the first bunch of "words" your toddler learns are gestures and the second group are those he invents, the third bunch are definitely words he learns from you.

In the beginning he will learn to imitate a couple of your words a week. And his first words will have a bunch of different meanings. "Juz" may stand for juice, milk, water, bottle, or "I'm thirsty."

By 18 months he may be able to say twenty to thirty words (exactly the number of "words" wild chimpanzees can "say" through hoots and gestures). (Some 18-month-olds mutter only one or two words, while other clever little toddlers know up to two hundred words, roughly the same number mastered by specially trained chimps.)

A fun way to jumpstart your one-year-old's ability to get his message across is by teaching him sign language. It strengthens the exact same brain center used in speaking. Sign language can also lessen your child's frustration by helping him communicate and feel like he's part of the team.

Signing is easy. You can buy a book on sign language, but I recommend you just watch your child's behaviors and make up the signs from his gestures! For example, Jane noticed that her 15-month-old son raised his hands up over his head whenever he wanted to leave. So she started to use this sign to let him know when it was time to go.

Other signs that young toddlers in my practice have taught their parents include sniffing to mean "flower," putting a hand to the mouth for "eat," sucking on a fist for "drink," stroking the back of a hand for "doggie," wiggling a finger for "worm," patting the top of the head for "hat," and opening and clenching the hand for "breast-feed."

Social-Emotional Skills Now

Lives in the eternal present. Chimpanzees aren't known for sitting and pondering. They bounce from branch to branch, momentarily focusing on little curiosities, and then with a yelp they're off again. It's not that chimps don't have good memories—they easily recognize family members and familiar settings. But they have very short attention spans.

Our charming one-year-olds are impulsive and distractible too. Whether you live in Morristown or Minnetonka, your young toddler's address is a place called Here and Now. He has little awareness of the future and no interest in planning ahead. "Dat!" he shouts, lunging at the closest shiny object. Then seconds later, he's ready for something different.

This flitting from thing to thing is perfectly illustrated in a diagram in Louise Bates Ames and Frances Ilg's wonderful book *Your Two-Year-Old* (see opposite page). You can easily see in this diagram that as a toddler matures, he begins to focus his concentration for longer and longer periods of time.

Sometimes this shortness of memory can be a big help. You can toss out old toys, and they won't be missed. This handy opportunity to cut clutter gets harder when your child is four and can incessantly ask, "Where's my bottle cap collection?"

Like chimps, young toddlers also have excellent instant recall of people and places, especially if the memory is connected to an emotional experience. Countless parents have told me their child begins crying the moment their car pulls into my office parking lot. He's probably thinking, *Uh-oh. I know that big white building. It's where I got a shot!* In fact, some supersensitive young kids even start screaming several blocks away when they recognize a few familiar landmarks!

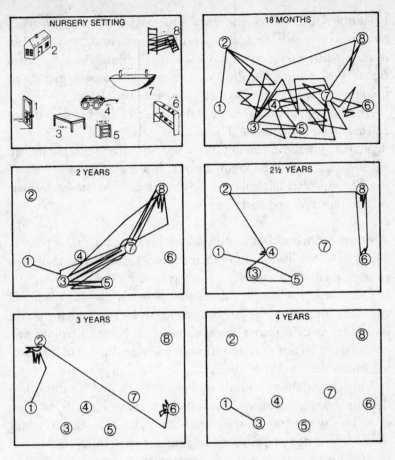

Seven Clocked Minutes of Nursery School
Behavior at Different Ages

The first "no." By 15 months a few storm clouds will be gathering on the horizon. That's when your toddler may start saying "no" to announce his increasing demands and opinions. By 18 months, however, his use of "NO!" is not just a word. It becomes a tiny verbal club that your prehistoric buddy pounds you with in your daily battle of wills (and won'ts!).

Many parents don't expect this phrase to begin until after their child turns two. But this surge in resistance and negativism actually begins around 15 months and usually fades shortly after the second birthday.

Heeding the call of the wild. Our uncivilized little one-year-olds are *oblivious* to the finer points of culture. They get so absorbed in eating that they don't notice that food is dribbling down their chins. (Real chimps actually have better table manners than young toddlers and may even wipe their faces clean with leaves.)

Another sign of the call of the wild is the fact that toddlers are fascinated by small animals. This natural attraction is so strong, he might roughly shove you out of the way so he can see a puppy better. It's as if he's found a kindred spirit. *Hey, look, I've found someone just like me!* After all, one-year-olds and baby pets are both small, cuddly, big-eyed, and frisky.

Aping Mom and Dad. Little chimps love watching their parents. That's how they learn most of their neat tricks, like banging on nuts to crack them open and then using a twig to pick out the meat.

Our cute little Chimp-Children rely on imitation too. Watch how your tyke loves to mimic you brushing your hair and talking on the phone. It's no coincidence we call this copycat behavior "aping." Imitating saves a lot of time and effort. It's a natural shortcut for learning things that are important.

Your child's ability to imitate, however, can lead him into new dangers. So, be careful what you do in front of him. If you don't want him to get into your vitamins, don't let him see you taking them. If you don't want him to figure out how childproof latches open, don't let him see how you undo them.

In general, though, when it comes to figuring things out, most young toddlers still have only a passing interest. They'd rather toddle, touch, and throw than think. Their focus is the thrill of exploring. The thrill of *understanding* will take just a little longer to emerge!

Just as the first walking apes marked the transition between chimps and humans, your child's first wobbly steps mark the shift from baby to full-fledged toddler. Now up the evolutionary ladder we go—and fast!

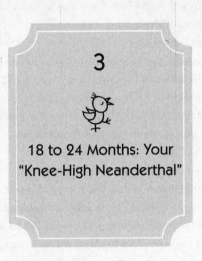

3

18 to 24 Months: Your
"Knee-High Neanderthal"

*"If a Stone Age man came and sat next to you on a
train, you would change seats. If a Neanderthal sat
next to you . . . you would change trains."*

—Paul Jordan

Main Points:

- Developmentally, your toddler is at a level similar to Neanderthals two million years ago.

- Neanderthals were smarter, more verbal, and more agile than ape-men but also more aggressive and stubborn.

- Your toddler is now faster on her feet and has begun to use her hands to scribble and throw.

- Your young child is getting better at forming words and phrases.

- She's intoxicated by her growing sense of independence. This is the age of "Me!" "Mine!" and "No!"

Twenty-month-old Paige has a winsome smile and a great chortling laugh. Her favorite part of the day is her afternoon visit to the park. She loves kicking the fallen leaves, watching ants, and zooming through the air on the swing.

Lately, however, Paige's mom, Joni, has come to dread when it's time to end the festivities and return home for supper. Paige now bursts into tears at the first mention that park time is over. Like a wild little Neanderthal she flails her hands and shrieks, "No go! No! No! No!" and tries to run away.

Once so easygoing that her nickname was "Sunshine," Paige now has three or four such explosions every day. She howls if her cracker crumbles. She hurls her cup in frustration when it's empty. And a loving reminder from Joni not to throw it is met with a mischievous grin and a second toss—right at her mother's head. What's worse, her aim is getting better!

The new Paige is busy following her own agenda. She rejects hugs. She scribbles on the table. She scratches her dad when he corners her at bath time. Yet once she's in the suds, she loves them so much that she throws a tantrum when it's time to come out.

"She's like the girl in the poem," Joni sighs wearily. " 'When she was good she was very good. And when she was bad she was horrid.' Well, 'horrid' is an exaggeration," she quickly adds. "But she's definitely a handful!"

How Is Your Toddler Like a Neanderthal?

Neanderthals might have been fun to party with, but you wouldn't want one as a roommate!

Life's a lark for a brand-new toddler, but by 18 months an unmistakable shift has taken place—*it's party time!* I'm not talking about a

polite little tea party—I mean a raucous, rollicking, full-tilt bash. The kind where furniture is thrown, the guests yell, and noise spills out the windows into the night.

Eighteen-month-olds are fun with a capital F! Compared to 12-month-olds they are livelier, sillier, and more curious. But they are also more demanding, rigid, and self-centered. They can be aggressive and tenaciously fight you, barking "Mine!" and "No!"

You may have expected to confront this wildness after your toddler's second birthday, but in my experience the "terrible twos" occur between 18 and 24 months. No longer like a wobbly little chimp, your incredible toddler has zoomed through three million years of evolution to the level of a Neanderthal, all in the space of about six months!

Sure, Neanderthals were still primitive. But with a brain twice the size of a chimp's, they were like college graduates compared to their ape-man predecessors. Two million years ago these ancient humans had long since left the protection of the dense jungle. Now they lived on the open plains, the dangerous world of lions and tigers and bears (oh my!).

Because these people lacked speed or sharp claws, you might think that was a dumb decision. But Neanderthals had two secret weapons that helped them fight off the other animals: big brains and agile hands. And the talented way they used their brains and hands closely mirrors many of the feats your little Knee-High Neanderthal will be mastering over the next six months.

Neanderthal Brains: New and Improved

The big Neanderthal brain contained several new and improved areas.

It had a spiffy thinking center that could sometimes figure things out. For example, these people invented the first simple stone tools. They probably realized that circling vultures indicated a recently killed animal they could eat. Similarly, your 18-month-old has now cleverly figured out that pressing the buttons of his pop-up toy makes a little figure appear. (A 12-month-old will jab randomly at the buttons, but an 18-month-old plans exactly which ones she wants to hit.)

In addition, the Neanderthal cerebellum, the brain center controlling balance and movement, improved by leaps and bounds (literally!). It helped humans run better to escape hungry animals. It also fine-tuned their ability to throw rocks and swing sticks to defend themselves against animals they couldn't flee from.

The appearance of stone axes more than two million years ago proves that these ancient people could whack things with precision—something your toddler is also getting good at. Whacking and throwing require the cerebellum to coordinate dozens of muscles with lightning speed and precision. Being off by even an inch when hammering two rocks together can severely injure a finger, something that toddlers learn when they accidentally whack themselves.

Despite all their achievements (running, making simple tools, tossing stones), it would be a mistake to treat Neanderthals like the folks next door. They had more in common with chimps than with today's most primitive tribes. The same is kind of true of your 18-month-old. She has more in common with a waddling one-year-old than a talking, turn-taking three-year-old. In fact, that's exactly what sets the stage for the upcoming struggles and battles of will. She is stuck between the dependency of infancy and her new desire to do everything herself.

What Is an 18-Month-Old?

Of course, your cute little toddler isn't really a Neanderthal, but she may often act like one:

N—Naturally curious
E—Emotional yo-yo
A—Acts before thinking
N—"No!"
D—Defiant
E—Energetic
R—Rough-and-tumble
T—Thin-skinned
H—Happy (mostly)
A—Attention is short
L—Language is limited

Evolution Up Close and Personal: What's Your Toddler Doing Now?

Once they were out of the jungle, Neanderthals no longer had the option of scrambling up into the treetops for safety. So to fight off threatening animals, they had to become aggressive, opinionated individuals with puffed-out chests, showy bravado, and displays of defiance. At the same time, being away from the jungle's safety may have also made Neanderthals more cautious and worried, imagining a lion around every bush.

It's no wonder, then, that your 18-month-old's behavior shifts so wildly. One minute she acts cocky and unintimidated by you, despite your much larger size. (Like a Neanderthal attacking an elephant, your toddler actually believes she can dominate you!) Yet she may act nervous and worried when you take her to new places.

Why Do Many Toddlers Seem to Bounce Off the Walls?

Spending all day inside four walls is a recent human experience. Buildings with four flat walls probably didn't exist before ten thousand years ago. And we've only lived in windproof rooms with good doors and windows for a couple of hundred years! So for 99.9 percent of human history, children lived mostly outdoors. No wonder they get antsy when they're cooped up for too many hours.

Gross Motor Skills Now

Picking up the pace. Every day your 18-month-old's muscles, bones, and brain grow bigger and work more like a team. Her wobble soon turns into a walk, and then into a teetering, headfirst little trot. Her hands, no longer held chest high for balance, are now perfect for carrying "tools" (or toys). This mirrors earliest man, who had to walk long distances, his hands free to carry weapons, berries, or babies.

Your toddler's awkwardness may make her walk like a mini-Frankenstein. Her ankles and feet are as stiff as her wrists were earlier. But her days of chimplike scrambling on all fours when she's in a hurry are over. By 18 months she's getting fast on her feet and is ready to scale furniture and tackle staircases.

Stair Safety

Stairs are as irresistible to toddlers as peaks are to mountain climbers. So use two gates on your stairs: one at the top, and the other two or three steps up from the bottom to allow some room for your tot to practice going up and down. It's also smart to put a soft rug beneath the last step in case a tumble occurs. Teach her to come downstairs by sitting on her bottom and bouncing down each step. If the steps are carpeted and not too steep, you might let her try sliding down on her belly, feet first.

Chopping, throwing, and hitting. More than two million years ago ancient people began being able to throw stones accurately to protect themselves. They learned how to repeatedly whack one rock against another to make the first stone tools. Your eighteen-month-old is also developing the ability to throw and whack things with some accuracy. Now when she throws a ball (or food), she may even be able to hit a close target. She has probably also started to hammer on a xylophone or toy cobbler's bench. And she can swing a stick like a weapon. Like the Neanderthals of old, your primitive little pal is definitely more dangerous now.

Fine Motor Skills Now

Getting a grip. As I mentioned, a Neanderthal's increasing hand dexterity was one of his secret survival weapons. Hand control still requires a lot of effort for your toddler, but she's getting the hang of it. She probably still grips spoons and crayons in tight fists. You can almost hear her brain shouting messages down to her uncivilized fingers: "Grab it!!! Hold it tight!!!"

But as the months pass, her wrists really start to loosen. She can now rotate her wrist to deliver a loaded spoon into her mouth and make fluid, circular scribbles, not just straight lines. Her scribbling, however, is still mostly long strokes coming more from the upper arm than from the wrist and fingers.

Language Skills Now

Stringing syllables into words. Neanderthals could probably make several dozen gestures, hand signs, and meaningful grunts. They had to be able to communicate well enough to hunt together and to pass a little information back and forth. Gestures and grunts may have helped Big Gorth teach Little Gorth how to make a stone ax, but they lacked the ability to discuss how to improve it.

Our toddlers have a real advantage over Neanderthals in learning words—if for no other reason than they hear us talking all the time! Your child may say ten, twenty, or up to fifty words at 18 months and many more by her second birthday. And astoundingly she will understand several hundred of the words you say to her!

A 15-month-old can string two syllables together creating names for the important people in her life: *Mama, Dada, Gaga* (Grandma), *Kaka* (the kitty cat), and *Li Li* (Lily, herself). Before 18 months much of what's said is parroting: you say "hippopotamus," and she echoes "pa . . . mus."

Increasingly after 18 months words become her tools. She realizes she can use them to tell you what she wants, thinks, or sees: *juice, bye, doggie, out, uh-oh, meow, quack, go,* and *cookie.* That's a lot easier than grabbing your wrist or pulling you into the kitchen! Your young toddler's speech is now made up of nouns, a few verbs, and power words like *mine, me, no,* and *more.*

She'll often use shorthand expressions like "Bobbi!" instead of "Bobbi's truck!" More and more she's training her mouth muscles to dance back and forth, stringing together several syllables into words like *applejus* and *elephant.*

Stringing words into phrases. Your tot's increasing memory and ability to wrap her tongue around a wide variety of sounds makes it easier for her to put words together. Her orderly left brain now helps her string words together in a line, just as she can put blocks side by side to make a little train. After months of storing up words, like ingredients in a cupboard, her left brain now begins pulling them out and combining them to cook up new phrases. As a result, your Knee-High Neanderthal can choose and mix her words to get her point across. New expressions usually include "More cracker," "Mommy, go," and "No, me!"

Social-Emotional Skills Now

"Neanderthals have a strong will and . . . a stronger won't!" There's little arguing with a tenacious 18-month-old. It's as if she's thinking, *My mind's made up. Period. End of discussion!* No tentativeness. No second thoughts. No wiggle room for negotiation. By two years of age, most toddlers have strong opinions about what they will wear, eat, and do.

Don't be surprised if your prehistoric buddy looks you right in the eye, smiling with irresistible charm, while her pudgy little hand reaches for a crystal vase she knows is off limits! She's a whirlwind of happy activity from sun-up to tuck-in, yet when you frustrate her—or she's tired or unsure—she may explode. Your gentle *no* is like cold water on a hot skillet, making her shriek, sizzle, and hiss.

A toddler's tantrum can be an amazing, even unnerving, spectacle. Sometimes they're so ensnarled in being negative, they even refuse the thing they want! I've seen 18-month-olds screaming for ice cream who continue to shout, "No!! No!!" even as they're reaching up for the cone in your hand!

> *Jeev, 18 months, is a gentle child, but he's still a bit of a Neanderthal. When his mom cut up a pear he wanted to eat whole, he picked up her generous gift and hurled it right at her! Then he rejected her offer of a new pear (even though it was whole) and just scowled.*

Your growing toddler will often feel pulled in opposite emotional directions. The best way to brace yourself for this unpredictable wild-child stage is to know it's coming. I can't tell you how many parents get thrown off-guard by a screaming meltdown simply because they thought that their cheerful baby would never do *that!* I encourage you to envision life with your eighteen-month-old as an ever-changing flow of push and pull, discipline and play, a daily dance that is sometimes a waltz, sometimes a wild watusi. Let your hair down, loosen your expectations, and don't be too tough on yourself. Parents and toddlers are constantly stepping on one another's toes, so please try not to take the tantrums personally! (To learn more about handling tantrums, see Chapters 8 and 12.)

I only have eyes for . . . me. The center of the universe would be a mild way to describe how your little Neanderthal sees herself. *Talk about me,* she thinks. *Then A TINY BIT about you. Then a lot more about ME!!*

It's a wonder that our tot's first word isn't usually *me me!* instead of *Ma ma!*

Between her strong sense of self and her poor sense of time, she wants everything—NOW! To get your attention, she will whimper, whine, tug at your clothes, and even grab your face with her hands, demanding a response. To your impatient toddler, when you say, "Just a second" it sounds to her like, "See ya next year."

Difficulty switching gears. Sometimes young toddlers are like little machines that have no off switch. They get wild or silly or furious and then have trouble settling back down. Even in play, once they start going they have a hard time stopping. They can whack a drum or push a noisy toy lawn mower for fifteen minutes straight. In fact, my office manager made me take all noise-making toys out of the waiting room—to preserve her sanity.

This same lack of an off switch also affects toddlers' fine motor skills. They have trouble making individual lines, and once they start drawing, they scribble and scribble right off the page.

A tiny attention span. An 18-month-old has the attention span of a—what was I saying? That's how lightning fast it can change!

Some will spend ten to fifteen minutes with a particularly interesting toy, but most get antsy a lot faster than that.

Having a short attention span was a survival asset for Neanderthals. It meant they were always alert to any new stimulus, such as a rustle in the nearby bushes, which could signal the presence of a tasty rabbit or a big bad wolf.

Similarly, a young toddler's focus tends to jump from one thing to the next. In fact, totally normal 18-month-olds are so distractible, impulsive, and active, they might even fit the diagnosis of Attention Deficit Hyperactivity Disorder (ADHD) if they were a few years older.

Order in the court: An important step toward civilization. Sometime between 18 months and your toddler's second birthday, she'll start showing interest in putting things in order. For example, she'll learn the names of body parts and begin to separate toys into groups: books in one pile, stuffed animals in another. Stacking is another fun way of organizing things. No longer does she randomly place those plastic rings on the stick; now she puts them on in order—biggest on the bottom, smallest on top.

Your little prehistoric buddy will also become interested in "helping" you clean up. She will imitate you vacuuming or loading toys into a box. (Help her help you by labeling each box with a picture to remind her what goes where.)

This new interest in orderliness also makes her suddenly interested in being neat. She now wants to wash her hands, though this may be only a couple of quick rubs. And she may begin telling you when she has a dirty diaper. This is one of five key signs of toilet-training readiness. (For more, see Chapter 13.)

> *Starting at 18 months, little Madeline began being interested in privacy. Whenever she felt the urge to poop, she would quietly sneak away and hide behind the sofa in the family room to "do her business" in her diaper.*

Despite this exciting new interest in putting things into order, your little Neanderthal is only a few baby steps closer to civilization.

It still may be hard for her mind to handle a puzzle with more than four pieces or a two-step command like, "Tina, get your ball and give it to Daddy." She may concentrate so hard on step one that she totally forgets step two.

Now you can understand why it's sometimes so difficult for your young friend to remember what she's not allowed to touch. She may get so excited about doing something, she forgets the rules. Even when she does remember your warning, it may interest her so much that she sneaks a touch anyway.

Happy but not yet friendly. Neanderthals weren't social butterflies. They sat together to share meals, but they weren't discussing the weather or waltzing cheek to cheek. Your little primitive may also like eating with others, but at the sandbox she may watch other children with keen interest and want to play near them . . . without actually playing *with* them. Toddlers this age prefer playing side by side, each with their own bucket and shovel—as unconnected as people sitting next to each other in a bus!

The dance of back-and-forth. You smile. I smile. You wave. I wave. After giving a little performance, your toddler will look around for applause and then return the praise with an encore.

Even as a baby, your child had little conversations with you. After you told her something she took her turn to release a joyous squeal, then once again paused—for your response.

This dance of back-and-forth will form the foundation for your child's learning about sharing, generosity, taking turns, and living together. There's no doubt that Neanderthals, too, practiced the game of taking turns when one had meat and the other had nuts.

This give-and-take may be a forced trade, as when your 22-month-old thrusts a toy at another child and grabs the one she wants away from him. Or it may be a step toward true bartering, as when she lets you tie her shoes after you give her a piece of fruit.

Often a young toddler will offer me a treasured doll but quickly pull it away when I reach to accept it. It's as if she wants to invite me into a friendly game of give-and-take, but at the last minute hesitates to part with such a precious possession.

As a pediatrician, I find these behaviors fun to watch and very useful too. During checkups I often offer toys to children who are unhappy. Having a toy to hold makes them think, *Okay, Dr. Harvey is a nice guy after all! He gave me a toy so I'll let him touch me.* Sometimes, however, even generosity fails to persuade skeptical 18-month-olds. They may accept the toy at first but thrust it back at me when I begin to get close, as if to say, "The deal's off!" Or they may refuse the toy from the outset, understanding on a deep, primitive level that accepting a gift from me would oblige them to cooperate in return.

This Neanderthal stage is one of the most challenging times of parenthood. Just a few months ago you could still expect your child to fit into *your* schedule. But now there's no doubt about it—you need to dedicate a big part of each day to meeting *her* schedule!

But take heart! All your efforts are like valuable seeds of love and respect. And as you will soon read, those seeds are just about to start bearing fruit.

4

24 to 36 Months: Your "Clever Cave-Kid"

"Faster, stronger, smarter."

—paraphrase of the Olympic Motto

Main Points:

- Developmentally, your toddler has a lot in common with ancient cave dwellers 150,000 years ago.

- His movements are smoother now, but he's even more accident prone, as he focuses more on where he's running than what's in his way.

- With greater patience and precision, your two-year-old will use his hands to examine and play with objects—and give you high-fives!

- Your toddler is now learning not just words but the rules of speech.

- Most two-year-olds love routines and order and increasingly want to do things to please their parents, relatives, and teachers.

Kyle loves to play with his growing collection of small metal cars. He likes to park them in separate little groups: red ones here, yellows there, blues on the end. Making zooming noises, he carefully "drives" them up a ramp to a play-parking garage.

His dad, Larry, recently gave him the cars on his second birthday. (Of course, Dad carefully checked to make sure that their wheels couldn't be pulled off and therefore weren't a choking hazard.) Kyle loved the cars, so last week Larry came home from work with one stuffed in his jacket pocket as a surprise.

"Which pocket?" Larry asked.

The boy spotted the bulge, and upon looking inside, he gleefully shouted, "Car! Daddy Ky-ky car! Zoom!"

For the next two days Larry brought a new car home every day, and Kyle quickly came to expect and love their little game. As soon as Kyle heard his father's footsteps, he shouted, "Daddy! Car! Car! Car for Ky- ky!"

But on the third night Larry had an apple in his pocket instead. Kyle looked confused. Apples didn't belong in pockets, cars did. Then Larry produced another car from behind his back, and Kyle roared with laughter.

How Is Your Toddler Like a Caveman?

Wow! What a transformation Kyle has gone through in just two years: from a tiny "smush" of a baby to a friendly little talking person able to figure out simple jokes and keep things in order.

Like Kyle, your child spent his first two years learning the basics. For a while he was an exploring machine, able to move, touch, manipulate, and taste everything. Now he's ready to do everything even better!

Remember those babbled words and strings of gibberish? They're developing into phrases that indicate exactly what's in that little brain of his.

The jerky walking? Soon he'll be running to you from across the room (although turning fast corners will remain a challenge).

He once bobbed rhythmically to music. But by the end of this year he'll belt out lyrics and know all the hand signs for "Head and Shoulders, Knees and Toes."

Your toddler is shifting from the "running-touching" stage (child specialists call this the "sensorimotor" period), where everything is about motion and grabbing, to the "figuring-out" stage. Friendships, language, order, and routine are the focus of this Clever Cave-Kid year.

The cave dwellers of 150,000 years ago had entered a "figuring-out" period too. They became better tool-makers, better communicators, and better friends. They were the first *Homo sapiens,* the same species we are.

They led a very predictable life. Their days were filled with the routines of hunting, eating, and resting. But they also began spending a little time wondering. They figured out how to improve tools that their ancestors hadn't changed for a million years. New language skills allowed them to work together to hunt bigger, more ferocious animals. There are even signs that they began to prefer order to chaos. Archaeologists studying their caves believe they put bones and eating debris off to one side. Sometimes they even designated distant cave crannies as the first indoor potties!

I call two-year-olds Clever Cave-Kids because they have these same inclinations. They're still kind of primitive, but now more than ever before they're starting to think and to get coordinated, organized. If your two-year-old had a motto, it would be "Faster, Stronger, Smarter" as in "I run *Faster.* My hands are *Stronger.* My brain is *Smarter.*"

Brain Update: Right and Left Sides Are Now Clicking on All Cylinders

What powers your two-year-old's developmental advances? The answer is found in an enormous explosion of new connections, making the brain much more complex and powerful.

After two years the left brain is finally getting in gear. The left half of the brain controls language, logic (figuring things out), and the right side of the body. Now your toddler is better able to make simple plans, express feelings with words, remember long strings of information (like all the words to "Happy Birthday"), and use his right hand with agility.

At the same time the right side of your child's brain is also becoming more powerful and sophisticated. It helps him better recognize your nonverbal messages (tone of voice, facial gestures, body language), endows him with the capacity for empathy, leads to improved impulse control, and helps him master the movement of the left side of his body.

All this means that pretty soon he'll start eating without throwing food, begin to be interested in toilet-training, and be able to narrate the events of his day. At last, patience is born. And just like a baby, it starts small, but it grows steadily.

You may notice a gradual fading of power struggles. Often within a few months of the second birthday, biting, scratching, and temper tantrums ease up as your toddler becomes better able to express his frustrations with words and as he starts wanting to live up to your expectations. (Of course, wild behaviors will continue to crop up frequently—two-year-olds are still just *two-year-olds,* after all!)

Your toddler's brain will also show a blossoming talent for making comparisons based on a fantastic new ability to keep two or three ideas in the head at the same time. Cavemen used this new talent to think about different ax designs. That helped them figure out that the best stone ax would be one attached to a wooden handle. (The invention of the handle allowed them to chop harder and protect their fingers better.)

Your little Cave-Kid is also becoming fascinated with comparisons. This year he will learn how to tell a fire truck from an ambulance and pick out which toy car is bigger or which pretzel is longer.

Despite all these mental improvements, however, this period for ancient cavemen and modern Cave-Kids is more about *fine-tuning* than innovating. (As you will soon see, next year will be the true dawning of invention and creativity.) These Stone Age men made their old axes better but didn't invent nets or needles or really new tools. (Their discovery of making axes with handles was the only "Nobel Prize–winner" they stumbled upon during the next hundred thousand years.)

Your two-year-old is probably not a whole lot better at innovation and problem-solving than those ancient people. If a box won't close because something is sticking out, his smart solution might be to just smash the lid down. He's unlikely to consider, *Hmmm. Maybe something's blocking the lid.*

What Is a Two-Year-Old?

Of course, your two-year-old isn't really a Cave-Kid, but he may often act like one:

C—Curiouser and curiouser

A—Attention increases

V—Very busy

E—Enjoys pleasing you

K—Kinder

I—Interested in order and comparisons

D—Determined to communicate

 Evolution Up Close and Personal: What's Your Toddler Doing Now?

The most common question I hear at the two-year checkup is "What are the 'terrible twos' going to be like?"

No wonder parents are nervous! They've just been through the most tumultuous, exhausting six months since their child's birth. What they're really thinking is, *How could this job possibly get any harder?*

Don't worry, it won't! As I mentioned in the last chapter, the rigid contrariness of one-year-olds usually peaks at 18 months. By age two, a toddler's "terrible twos" are almost over (although there may well be another rough spot midway to his third birthday).

Thank your child's amazing "new and improved" brain for making him less likely to pop like a firecracker at every little frustration.

As the year unfolds, you'll notice your prehistoric sidekick becoming more patient, agreeable, and open to compromise. And armed with the simple communication tips in Parts Two and Three, you'll be rewarded with a whole lot more of the fun and laughter that you hoped to experience with your toddler.

Gross Motor Skills Now

Less frenetic. After the second birthday most toddlers are no longer in constant motion (although there are many exceptions). Cavemen didn't spend a lot of time running wild. They had tools to make and sticks to sharpen. Your child may now sit with a book studying the pictures rather than randomly flipping pages.

Better stop/start control. Your child moves more fluidly and confidently. Clumsy running (he's still kind of flat-footed) gradually improves, and practicing going up and down stairs becomes an obsession. By the end of the year he will even be able to alternate his feet as he climbs stairs, and on the way down he will easily jump from the last step. He can walk backward for fun and even tiptoe, thanks to better ankle control.

He's learning to go fast or slow, stop himself quickly and dash off again, handle corners, and make sharp turns without falling. Toward the end of this year he may even be able to pedal a tricycle—a huge achievement! Why? Because pedaling requires one's feet to do opposite things: The right foot pushes down, while the left foot goes up. Most two-year-olds get confused and try to propel themselves by pushing with both feet at the same time.

Accident prone. You'd think that a good sense of balance and improved muscle control would make your toddler steadier on his feet. Surprisingly, as he becomes a better walker, he may begin having more accidents! This occurs because he's now so confident, he's concentrating less on what's in his way than on the thing he's running toward . . . CRASH!

Hands: Three things your two-year-old loves to use them for.
Two big things occur in your two-year-old that lead him to big
"strides" in hand use. Better patience means more time sitting and
manipulating toys. And his developing left brain means he has
started to have better control of his right hand. Soon his more nim-
ble right hand will permanently become his preferred hand. (For
left-handed people, the same process happens, but the right brain,
which controls the left hand, is calling the shots.)

Finger agility and wrist flexibility, so minimal during the first year,
are really increasing now. Cavemen put this ability to use fashioning
finer and finer stone tools. Your clever little Cave-Kid may want to
use this new ability to paint pictures and to give high-fives to
everyone he meets. He will also enjoy practicing three other rapidly
improving hand skills:

1. **Hammering.** Chimps (and one-year-olds) can crudely
   whack two objects together. But now watch your two-year-
   old using a mallet to strike wooden pegs through a hole in a
   toy cobbler's bench. His clumsy Neanderthal swings have
   given way to hammer strikes of nearly professional accuracy!

2. **Drawing circles.** He still has a fisted grasp of the crayon,
   and his movements come more from his arm than from his
   wrist; however, his wrist is loosening up enough to allow
   him to draw circular scribbles. (Making a single circle is
   still too hard because, as with running, it's easier for a two-
   year-old to start a movement than to stop it.) As the year
   progresses, your toddler will be able to stop right where he
   started, making a perfect circle. (A perfect example of his
   increasing impulse control!) This will be the beginning of
   his ability to draw a person.

3. **Throwing.** This became a caveman's best way to repel en-
   emies, catch dinner, and knock fruit out of high trees. Thanks

to your toddler's increasing wrist and finger coordination, throwing is becoming an art form.

The Fine Skill of Speaking!

Better muscle control brings one other huge breakthrough: speaking. It requires controlling the tiny mouth muscles. There's a huge difference in the lip and throat agility needed to say "baba" versus "Bobbie cookie, Mommy!"

Try saying those two things yourself. Feel your lips and the back of your tongue speedily hopping around. Your Cave-Kid's mouth dexterity is quickly maturing. And by the time he nears his third birthday, his tongue will be able to twist and twirl and imitate almost any sound you can make.

Language Skills Now

Behold! The word juggler cometh! By the end of this year, you'll hardly be able to remember a time when your "baby" couldn't talk! By two, he'll know from twenty to three hundred words. And over this next year he'll add three to ten new words every day! Your Clever Cave-Kid's left brain is neatly filing away all these words. And they aren't just a bunch of easy words like *book, car,* and *baba*. Now he's learning verbs, pronouns, and adjectives, which he'll juggle into hundreds of new phrases.

Once you have the tools, you can start to learn the rules. An emerging sense of order was a critical step for cavemen who organized grunts into simple language. It's an equally crucial step in your toddler's acquisition of speech. Have you ever tried to learn a foreign language? The nouns come quickly (that's pretty much how a one-year-old speaks). But other parts of speech, like verb conjugations, take longer to learn because they present so many more choices to sort through.

Of course, your toddler isn't just learning words, he's mastering *word rules* like adding an *s* to make a plural (*books*) or *-ed* to talk about something in the past (*kissed*). He's figuring out word order, too, for example, that in English we always say "big truck" not "truck big."

He's also learning which words mix well (like *Mommy* and *go*) and which don't work together (like *eat* and *shoe*). That may sound easy, but as you can see below, combining just three words (*Mommy, Daddy,* and *go*) creates twelve possible messages your little toddler's brain must flip through to find the one that best expresses what he wants to say.

"Go!"	("I want to go.")
"Mommy!"	("Mommy, come!")
"Mommy go."	("Mom's going somewhere.")
"Go, Mommy."	("Go away, Mom.")
"Daddy!"	("Daddy come.")
"Daddy go."	("Daddy's going somewhere.")
"Go, Daddy!"	("Go away, Dad.")
"Mommy! Daddy!"	("Hey, you guys!")
"Mommy, Daddy, go."	("You went somewhere together.")
"Go, Mommy Daddy."	("I want both of you to leave.")
"Daddy . . . Mommy go."	("Daddy, Mommy left.")
"Mommy . . . Daddy go."	("Mom, Dad left.")

Sorting through these word combinations takes lots of increased brainpower! Now, just imagine the amount of memory and planning your toddler will need for choosing the right words when he has *hundreds* to select from.

Here are some other hallmarks of a typical two-year-old's speech:

Confusing the words *you, me,* and *I.* Pronouns are tricky words because they constantly change! Even grown-ups misuse them. When you say "me," I think "you." (It's as confusing for me to explain as it probably is for you to follow!) That's why it's easier for a toddler to say "Jack running" instead of "I'm running."

Rigid rules, no exceptions. A two-year-old thinks of rules as things that should not be changed. That's why he may get so upset if you forget to say goodnight to some of his dollies. Likewise, your toddler will apply the rules of language he has learned to all words—without exception. For example, he'll say *goed* instead of *went* and *goodest* instead of *best*. These mistakes are normal. Right now he's working hard to learn the rules. It'll take him another year to start learning the exceptions to the rules.

> Twenty-four-month-old Zack was so tall he could reach the lowest buttons in the elevator. One day he and his mother, Julie, entered the elevator at my office, and she said to him, "Push the button, Zack, and the door will close." Zack looked thoughtful for a second. Then he hoisted up his shirt . . . pressed on his belly button . . . and waited expectantly for the elevator doors to close! Julie couldn't help but grin at her little boy's mistake. However, a second later, the doors actually did close! Julie laughed out loud, and Zack was very pleased with himself.

Describing things out of time sequence. This is an improvement over the here-and-now thinking of your younger toddler. Now he can easily refer to things that aren't there: "Where's Daddy?" or "All gone." And he can recount things from the past: "Daddy funny in store." But his concept of time is still murky. The word *yesterday* can mean "any time in the past."

The concept of the future continues to be almost completely beyond him. This makes sense when you consider how much easier it is to know what happened yesterday (only one reality) than to guess what might happen tomorrow (dozens of possibilities to choose from).

Remembering and understanding two-part commands. If you tell your two-year-old, "Go to your room and get your socks, then wash your hands and come to lunch," what do you think is going to happen?

Fifteen minutes later you'll find him in his room, with his socks on, playing with a stuffed animal. He remembered the first items on the list, but that was all his young brain could hang on to. Commands of more than two steps are a little too complicated to stick in his prehistoric memory.

Here's a tip to help your two-year-old remember what you ask: If you can make a little singsong rhyme out of your commands, you'll have better luck seeing them successfully completed.

The Priceless Language Course You Can Get for Free

Talk to your child!

Make each day a guided tour of the "national treasures" of your home. Point out interesting sights and sounds. Narrate the day as you do things together. Ask questions. (But don't push for answers.) Allow your toddler to overhear you talking to other people or to your pet, the birds outside, or his dollies! Even if he doesn't always appear to be paying attention it will really help him learn language and build his intellect.

Social-Emotional Skills Now

Law and order rule!

> Two-year-old Nina had a funny way of showing she understood order. She kept walking back and forth in my exam room, eyeing a toy giraffe. She had more than a passing interest in it. She was concerned because this poor toy was injured—it had one ear broken off. An hour after she and her mother left my office, I was amused to notice that mysteriously now both ears were broken off! That little Cave-Kid apparently took it into her own primitive hands to get that lopsided animal back in order!

Your two-year-old has gone from being a wild child to being a wild child with a plan! He increasingly feels safe and secure with rules and predictable events. Routines now become more important to him than ever as a way to organize his day into a predictable order. *Clean Up* becomes a favorite game. (Enjoy this while it lasts!) He may even demand that toys be stored in exactly the same place every time. And he may be able to say "poop" and want to be cleaned up as soon as he "makes."

Okay, some kids are still messy little Pigpens. Organization may never be their strong point. (I'm glad you can't see the towering piles of papers and books around me as I write this!) But somewhere deep in their brains, their sense of orderliness helps them start piecing sentences together, remembering songs, and noticing the patterns in the world around them.

> Twenty-five-month-old Jeremy screamed if his carrots touched his potatoes—or if there was anything green on his plate.
>
> Passionate little Eloise, 27 months old, got furious if she spilled a drop of water on herself.
>
> After seeing chicken kebabs at a family picnic, two-year-old Camille began refusing to eat unless the food was served on a little skewer or toothpick.

Yikes! I can't decide. Don't offer your two-year-old too many options. Imagine you have to select a preschool for your child and have twenty to choose from. Where do you start? Now imagine you only have one choice. Makes the process easier, doesn't it?

Choices require decisions, and making decisions can frustrate a toddler because he doesn't yet have the mental ability to compare more than two or three possibilities. Your child's immature brain can become overloaded with too many choices. Red cup, yellow cup, or blue cup? Barney pajamas, Pokémon pajamas, or Hello Kitty pajamas? Thirty-four flavors of ice cream? *Tilt! Tilt! Tilt!*

Caring and sharing: a new desire to get along. No longer is every exchange with your child like stepping into the ring for a fight to the death. Sure, your two-year-old may still hit and bite, but most parents report that between the second and third birthdays their toddler's frustration responses become much less primitive. More words, less whack. More wait, less wail.

Finally, the blessed trait of patience begins to appear! This allows your little child to delay his gratification (and also meltdowns) at least a bit longer than before. Like many of the developments that occur around age two, this is a reflection of the increasing maturity of his right brain, where his impulse-control center is forming.

Increasingly, your toddler *wants* to be your friend. He uses smiles, not shrieks, to get your attention. No longer a prickly little cactus, he may now rediscover how nice it is to nestle in your lap and cuddle. More and more he's willing to wait when you say "In a second" and "Almost done" as long as you respect him and follow through as soon as you can. The more you live up to your word, the better he'll be able to trust you and learn to wait patiently.

This new desire for your approval also announces the beginning of something else that's new: feelings of shame. Your toddler gradually starts following the rules even when you're not watching. Increasingly, he wants to do the right thing because he cares what you think about him. This is exactly why praise, criticism, and the technique of gossiping (all discussed in Part Two) suddenly become such powerful tools for improving his behavior.

"Dad's Home!": From Second-Class Parent to First-Rate Fascination

For a child's first two years Mom tends to be the star of the show. She's got the milk, the soft lap, and in most households, she's the one most likely to be there when he needs her. What more can a baby want? Moms are idolized, while dads are sometimes treated like strangers.

But now don't be surprised if you start noticing a shift in his affection. Dads score points by providing the exhilarating forms of play that two-year-olds love, such as tickling, pillow fights, piggyback rides, and wrestling.

At last your toddler's evolution has reached the stage of early civilization! He now shows the first inklings of manners, saying "please" and obeying rules like "We don't throw food on the floor."

Of course, sharing with Mommy is one thing, but sharing with a rival little child is much tougher. Such behavior will come, but don't be surprised if there's still a lot of grabbing and bossiness in the meantime. The good news is, it will take a different form now. Instead of giving his "friend" a hard shove to the ground, he may simply ignore him or nudge him with a shoulder.

Sweet empathy. In addition to developing a simple sense of order 150,000 years ago, Stone Age people also began exhibiting signs of real concern and love for one another. There is evidence that, for the first time, primitive peoples cared for their sick and injured, nursed their elderly, and even buried their dead, protecting them from the jaws of hungry scavengers. This means they had empathy—the ability to see things from other people's point of view, and to care about how they felt.

> When Sara's two-year-old Max saw her crying because of some bad news she'd gotten on the phone, he offered her his teddy bear and patted her back.

> Stephanie decided to use her 25-month-old's growing sense of empathy to help wean her from her breast. She came back from a weekend away with Band-Aids on both of her nipples. "They're broken," she told Kristi, who readily accepted this logical explanation and gave up nursing without a fight.

These seedlings of empathy are what grow into a person's willingness to donate a kidney to her sister or her life for her child. Your little toddler's desire to give a hug to his crying friend is an extraordinarily important step in his evolution from self-centered baby to compassionate child.

The delightful advances of this year put your two-year-old squarely in the middle of toddlerhood. Sure, he still has his bad moments, but once you know how to work with him, you'll be amazed at how quickly the dark clouds pass. It's a time to have fun—and catch your breath—before jumping into the amazing new accomplishments and emotional seesaws of the threes.

5

36 to 48 Months:
Your "Versatile Villager"

"Civilization is just a slow process of learning to be kind."

—Charles L. Lucas

Main Points:

- Developmentally, your toddler is a lot like the first truly modern people: the earliest villagers living 10,000 to 60,000 years ago.

- Her brain is making a great leap forward: her language, social, and intellectual advances are astonishing.

- She can deftly use her words to express ideas about almost anything.

- A growing interest in people sparks first friendships, pretend play, and new emotional attachments.

- Now that she knows the rules, she is beginning to learn how to bend them—both to get her way and to make you laugh.

■ Tantrums may explode again as your toddler realizes she's no longer a baby and not quite a big kid.

How Is Your Toddler like an Early Villager?

Since birth, your child's brain has been developing at a phenomenal clip, mirroring all the important evolutionary advances of our earliest ancestors. Your clever child has accomplished in a mere 36 months what it took prehistoric mankind millions of years to achieve. (She walks across rooms! She throws balls! She develops friendships! She can even say "Please!")

But, wait—hold your applause. The real show is just about to begin! About sixty thousand years ago something even more extraordinary happened. Man's ability to think, talk, and relate took off like a rocket. Archaeologists call this momentous advance in human evolution the "Great Leap Forward." Good-bye, cave life! Hello, Metropolitan Museum of Art and MTV!

No one knows for sure what caused this abrupt advance in brainpower. We know it wasn't an increase in brain size; brains had been big for 300,000 years. But whatever happened, people could suddenly combine more words into sentences, more strokes into art, and more ideas into inventions. They could now juggle concepts in their heads with ease. After millions of years of creativity increasing at a snail's pace, suddenly new ideas started popping up like weeds. And life on earth has never been the same!

The ability to walk and talk helped us cross the line into humanity, but the ability to create, understand, and explain was the evolutionary tipping point that led to the inevitable arrival of science, and art, and literature.

Thousands of years before the Bible, people lived in multifamily tribes. As communities grew larger, their citizens began to follow rules of behavior to prevent dangerous conflicts. They also divided up the work into specialized tasks. Adam made axes. Eve was the seamstress. Xerxes was the big boss. Splitting up the jobs led to increased productivity and more time for play. Music, dance, and storytelling flourished.

This great leap in brainpower made these ancient villagers very good problem-solvers. They developed tools like bows and arrows, nets to catch birds in bushes and fish in streams, and needles and thread. They invented painting, sculpture, modern language, and beautiful jewelry.

Perhaps most important of all, they gained the ability to think deeply. They became beings who spent much of their waking time asking "Why?" and "How come?"

If you have a three-year-old, this should sound astonishingly familiar. Your toddler's brain is now making a similar Great Leap. Almost overnight her mind is far more agile and powerful. What accounts for your little Villager's impressive burst of new skills? Her brain now has 50 percent *more* nerve connections (synapses) than even adults have in our brains! And her brain cells are working so hard, they consume twice as much energy as ours!

The huge surge in nerve connections occurring after birth gets organized into the information superhighways in the left brain (governing language and problem-solving), in the right brain (governing impulse control, memories of life experiences, comparisons, and nonverbal communication), and in the cerebellum (coordinating movement and balance).

Suddenly your Versatile Villager's inquiring little mind wants to know—*everything!*

What Is a Three-Year-Old?

Of course, your three-year-old isn't really a villager, but he may often act like one:

V—Verbal
I—Imaginative
L—Loving
L—Logical
A—Agreeable
G—Gives and takes
E—Entertaining
R—Ready for anything

 Evolution Up Close and Personal: What's Your Toddler Doing Now?

Another way to think of your child's brain is as a jet aircraft. At age one it took on fuel and passengers and fired up its engines. At two it taxied ever more swiftly down the runway. Finally at three, all systems are go. It's ready for takeoff.

Now your toddler is a constant fountain of creativity. From drawings to silly songs to castles made of boxes, blankets, and chairs, she can't stop inventing new things. The rigidity of her twos gives way to the flexibility of her threes. And her earnest love of rules is gradually transformed into a giddy pleasure in bending the rules and doing the unexpected.

Gross Motor Skills Now

"Look at me! I can do it all!" Your rapidly evolving buddy now walks like an adult—erect, shoulders back, head up. Her potbelly is fading fast.

During this year your toddler will learn how to jump like a frog, hop like a bunny, slither like a snake, spin like a waterbug, and balance on one foot like a crane. She'll delight in showing off her new control. You'll hear lots of "Look at me!" and "Watch this!"

Almost as amazing as all the things your child can now do with her body is what she *doesn't* do. She no longer flits from thing to thing. Instead she's able to sit still for long periods working on a puzzle, playing a computer game, or watching ants building an anthill.

(Take a moment to revisit the diagram on page 33 showing the activity levels of different-aged toddlers. You'll be amazed to see how much your little one has matured!)

Fine Motor Skills Now

Getting the hang of washing hands. Your child now uses her dominant hand to grab the soap. (For nine out of ten kids it's the right hand.) Instead of just rubbing her palms together under the water, your three-year-old can rotate her wrist and rub around all sides of her hands and really do a good job.

She has also developed enough wrist coordination to brush her teeth and run a comb through her hair. But she still needs help shampooing, fastening buttons and snaps, and tying her shoes. (No wonder some moms praise Velcro as their favorite invention, right behind the microwave!)

Putting ideas on paper. Small-muscle mastery also gives your child a new way to express herself. She can now comfortably control a crayon with her thumb and index finger. This advanced dexterity, plus her brain's improved ability to think ahead, allows her to draw neater pictures and keep her coloring on the page.

This same planning ability allows your little Villager to decide to make a picture of *something* specific. Endless streams of pictures of people, rainbows, and suns begin by the end of the third year. They may be undecipherable to you, but your toddler will beam as she tells you exactly what this red splotch and that black scribble represent. Before you know it, you'll be thrilled when she hands you a picture and you can make out—a face! You'll be as amazed as the archaeologists who discovered the Stone Age cave paintings in Europe— which, not coincidentally, were made between 15,000 and 30,000 years ago by prebiblical villagers!

Language Skills Now

Words for working with people. Your little child will talk so much, it's like having a window into her mind. She may be so chatty, she has running dialogues with you, her dolls, the dog, and even passing birds. Her vocabulary may be stupendous—more than a thousand words. She knows that words make the world go round, and she can deftly use and understand them.

It's a good guess that the first languages appeared sometime between 20,000 and 60,000 years ago—exactly during the time of the earliest villagers! Like those villagers who needed words to bargain, barter, and make friendships, your toddler's expanding social world also requires new language.

Take a simple thing like polite conversations. Most begin and end with a simple greeting. Your two-year-old could only say, "Hi" or "Night-night." Your three-year-old will add, "Good morning, Mommy" or "Let's go sleepy-bye."

"Goodnight, Tim," said his mom, Dora.
"See you later, alligator," added his dad, Frank.
"See you later, shark!" replied Tim, three.

In between those conversation openers, your toddler is now really talking! "Can I have a turn now?" she asks, or "Hey! It's my turn, please!" This is a definite improvement over her former rude demands.

Your Villager knows that finesse, not force, will help her get what she wants. A plea for fairness like "I need it" replaces the harsher "I want it." Persuasive excuses like "I'm scared" nudge out more defiant statements like "No, I won't." (Nonetheless, all bets are off when your toddler is tired, hungry, or stressed.)

Your three-year-old has also learned that praise helps build a relationship. She may cleverly toss out a compliment like, "Your hat is pretty" to build rapport with a friend before inviting her to join in a game. To increase the chance of success, she may soften a request by adding "okay?" as in, "Let's go to the sandbox . . . *okay?*" or "You can have a turn next . . . *okay?*" *Okay* is a powerful tool in the art of persuasion. It encourages the listener to agree and shows an interest in his point of view, even though it's still kind of pushy.

Questions, questions! When newspaper reporters write stories, they're supposed to tell readers the answers to the five W's. *Who? What? Where? When?* and *Why?* in that order. Interestingly, that's probably the same order in which our prehistoric relatives' ability to understand evolved.

By now it shouldn't surprise you that that's also the order in which your toddler learns to wonder about the world. *Who* and *what* questions ("Who is reading?" "What is Mommy eating?") are so easy that even an 18-month-old's simple mind can answer them. Telling you the answer to a *where* question ("Where is the teddy bear?") is the type of mental puzzle that two-year-olds can do. By age three, toddlers get good at replying to *when* questions. Finally, later that year they begin to crack that most complex of all questions, the one that demands all our intellectual skills: *why?*

Your toddler's first *whys* provide an exciting view into her developing intellect. "Why did the bird fly away?" And yes, even "Why is the sky blue?" Don't worry if you cop out by using that all-purpose answer, "Because . . .": "Because that's how God made them" or "Because that's how my mommy taught me." Sometimes it's the best you can do, and it'll often satisfy your toddler.

If all else fails, whisper, "I think it's . . . *magic!*" Older toddlers embrace the idea of magic for things you can't easily explain. They actually believe you can make a coin disappear, and they have faith in the magical protective power of *Superman Spray* (a spray bottle filled with water) to spritz away anything scary.

The idea of magic is a very creative approach to the unknown. Two-year-olds ignore what they don't understand, but three-year-olds believe there's an answer to *everything* and fully accept magic as a reasonable explanation for things that don't otherwise make sense to them.

You can also respond to questions by asking your three-year-old a question (and waiting patiently for the answer). This intellectual back-and-forth is as tasty and nourishing for her self-confidence as milk and cookies are for her body!

Words that put the world in order. Shortly after her second birthday your toddler may have begun making simple comparisons that fit her black-and-white world of rigid rules, like big/little, hot/cold, and on/off. But after her third birthday your smart little Stone Ager may be able to grasp more subtle comparisons and qualities such as *slippery, bumpy, worried,* and *excited.*

With each passing month her ability to attach these adjectives to objects in her world will increase astoundingly fast. You'll hear *ruby* slippers, *favorite* dolly, *peanut butter* sandwich, and *great big* truck. She'll conjure up poetic new words that even Webster's dictionary hasn't yet reported, such as *sugarish, prettyful,* and in the words of one of my patients, *ocean lotion* (suntan lotion). For the first time, her young mind can simultaneously compare four or five things at once and choose which is the biggest, tallest, or fastest.

She now loves words that stand for happy, exciting experiences. Words like *party, secret,* and *surprise* can trigger a cascade of joy and giggles just by whispering them.

Even though your Versatile Villager can now instantly choose from among hundreds of words, she still thinks each word has only one meaning. That's why she may be confused by phrases like "Daddy got tied up at work" or "Sally has a half-brother." It will take another year or two for her right brain to develop the ability to choose not just from among words but from among each word's most likely *meaning* in that context.

Discovering the time of her life. Your evolving toddler is also beginning to think about the passage of time and will use words about time to help her put the world in order. As an 18-month-old, she really only understood *now* and *soon*. However, around her third birthday, she will master more time-related words than at any other period in her life! Suddenly *now* and *soon* are replaced by dozens of shades of time such as *yesterday, today, tomorrow, next week, always, never,* and *once upon a time.* Your Villager's mind is now so agile, she may even create ingenious new words to describe the timing of events in her life, like *yesternight* and *bedfast*—which of course means breakfast in bed!

> Sophia remembers special days, like her third
> birthday two weeks ago, but she often has trouble
> remembering what happened on ordinary days, even
> the night before. She's starting to use the past tense,
> but when she's in a hurry she uses the tense she knows
> the best—the present tense. When asked, "What did
> you do at your birthday?" she replies, "I go down the
> slide!"

Putting two and two together. Do you remember in school having to practice new words by putting them into as many sentences as you could think of? This is probably the same exercise early villagers went through when they discovered something new. For example, they may have noticed that baskets could be woven from long grasses and then, using the same idea in different situations, discovered that they could also weave grass into clothing, fishing nets, and floor mats.

Three-year-olds also spend much of their day learning new *ideas* and practicing using them in as many new ways as they can think of. For example, the day after your older toddler learns that water makes plants grow, she may douse the puppy with juice, saying, "I want to make Fluffy grow faster."

This ability to use new ideas in many different ways is what the Great Leap is all about! Here are some of these three-year-old musings:

"Mommy, who was born first, you or me?"

"Is a knife the fork's daddy?"

"Do bad guys go poo-poo?"

"Lie on my pillow, Mom. We'll look at my dreams together."

"No wee-wee is coming out. I think the wee-wee is still sleeping."

"Your boobies are made out of pillows."

"Do kisses come off?"

"It's not throw up—it's throw down! Throw up would go into the sky."

"Who turns the dark off in the morning?"

Social-Emotional Skills Now

Making the first agreement: "You go first. Then it's my turn." As you can imagine, ancient villagers living in large groups needed rules to work and live together. The rules they developed helped them to avoid fights and be able to prosper and coexist. When arguments did arise, these people looked for compromises to settle them. One of the most delightful changes that occurs in older toddlers, a growing desire to make friends, mirrors the growing social skills of those ancient villagers. Three-year-olds begin to share, happily wait their turn, and work together. This is in large part due to the rapidly growing ability of the right brain to control primitive impulses.

Karen watched as Brandon, age three, handed his
12-month-old sister a second toy: "Here, Hannah, this
is for you." Before the surprised mom could
compliment him on the generous act she'd just seen,

> Brandon grabbed the toy Hannah was originally
> holding. Karen told him he was not being fair, and after
> a brief discussion Brandon gave Hannah her toy back
> and apologized for not following the rules.

"I'm big!" (But yikes, I'm little too!) One of the most profound comparisons your older toddler makes is between herself and others. These assessments help her see herself as a strong, independent person. But they can provoke some very troublesome feelings too.

> Dante, three and a half, sat in my lap, and I hugged
> him and jokingly said, "Ah, you're my baby." He
> frowned, got up, and asked his mom, "I'm not a baby,
> am I?"

Like Dante, your three-year-old is all too aware that she is no longer a baby. "I'm a big girl, and that's my baby," she'll say. But the recognition that she's bigger than a baby brings with it a potentially scary realization: Compared to everyone else, she's small and vulnerable. No wonder three-year-olds like to make big splashes in puddles and enjoy stories about being big and strong. (If you don't have any books about dinosaurs, superheroes, or giants, you will soon.) In their favorite games, *they* are the huge, fire-spewing dragon or the roaring Lion King.

"I'll be the teacher." Imagine how little time there would be to invent tools or language if you spent your whole day struggling to survive. Early on, villagers began to recognize that to get everything done, they had to divide up the work and help one another.

Gradually they organized themselves into soldiers and weavers and hunters and gatherers. Your little toddler may also start playing different roles. No longer is her interest limited to being Mommy, Daddy, or Baby. She increasingly embraces all sorts of new personas—princess, ballerina, firefighter, cowboy. Soon your toddler will spend hours in joyous pretend play wearing costumes and playing with dolls and action figures!

Bending the rules. At the start of the third year, your toddler may still prefer things to be predictable. But by the middle of the year, she'll give up her rigid rules and routines and start having hours of fun trying to *bend* the rules.

Rule bending requires her brain to consider several choices simultaneously and select an *unexpected* one. It's an ability that she will proudly notice makes her more clever than the little kids. This skill becomes the basis of limitless make-believe games. "Hey, I'm a giant, and I'll eat you," your son yells to your daughter. "No, no! You're my baby, so you're only allowed to eat milky!" she shouts back.

A sense of humor (even if the punch lines need a little work). Mix your three-year-old's ability to understand and bend rules, her desire to discover, and her increasing social interests and— *voilà!* You have the beginnings of humor.

Now she uses her brain's ability to compare several choices and select the funniest, most absurd one. She loves to make up silly words and little rhymes and to combine words that don't normally go together, such as *green elephant.*

> Little Jeffrey teased me, "Hey, I'm eating my cereal
> in my ear. Ha ha!" Abigail got into a giggly shouting
> match with me when I proclaimed, "My name is
> Daddy!" "No," she chortled, delighted to be in on the
> joke, "my name is Daddy!!"

(Potty humor, you'll be glad to know, comes well *after* potty training.)

The "terrible threes"? The first adolescence. When Trish joked to me that her daughter Courtney was three going on thirteen, she was pretty much on target! Just as teens struggle with making the transition from being kids to being adults, your toddler may struggle as she shifts her identity from being a "baby" to being a big kid.

The upsets that your toddler had during her "terrible twos" period may seem like brief thunderstorms compared to the tornadoes that now may roar through your house. One minute she wants to be carried. The next she's screaming to be put down. This year is a giant seesaw between wanting to be little again (when her life was easy and safe) and wanting to be big (when she'll be able to do all the cool things babies can't).

But—and this is a critical point—when you're feeling frustrated by your child's meltdowns, never forget *she's as much a victim of her own intensity as you are.* She may get so agitated, she paints herself into a corner. That's why fights with her end much faster if you help her find a way to gracefully back down. (Turn to Chapter 9 to learn about this tornado-taming skill.)

The span from 36 to 48 months is an intellectual bridge that your child is speeding across. Just as the Charming Chimp period marked the transition from infancy to toddlerhood, the Versatile Villager stage marks the end of the toddler years. After these last months, your child will finally set foot on the fabled shores of childhood!

But let's not rush ahead too fast. Toddlerhood may seem to pass in the blink of an eye—but you'll be packing plenty of laughs *and* tussles into these exhilarating months. Now that you know why your toddler acts the way she does, let's look at one more factor that can affect the tone and tenor of her behavior. It's another major part of who she is—called *temperament.*

6

Nature's Wild Card: What's Your Toddler's Temperament?

*"If I accept the sunshine and warmth, then I must
also accept the thunder and lightning."*

—Kahlil Gibran

Main Points:

- Knowing your child's temperament is as important as knowing his stage of development.

- Every temperament is unique; no two are alike.

- You can't change your toddler's temperament—but you can work with it.

- Temperament generally comes in one of three types: easy, cautious, and spirited.

- Be careful how you label your child's temperament— your words can nurture or scar.

You are the world's greatest expert on your child. You probably need to hear just one second of his giggle to pick him out from a hundred other kids! His face is unique, his voice is unique—even his personality is one of a kind.

Each child is born with a personality as matchless as his fingerprints. It's a smorgasbord of traits such as intelligence, sense of humor, integrity, and a fascinating quality called temperament.

Temperament is the way a person interacts with the world: his pacing, attitude, flexibility, general mood, and so on. Your toddler's developmental stages will march along exactly like all his friends; but his temperament, like each snowflake's design, is totally his own. Knowing your child's developmental stage tells you what milestone he's approaching, but knowing his temperament lets you predict whether he'll greet it with gusto or approach it with caution.

 ## Sun, Snow, Thunderstorm— What's Your Child's Temperament?

"Sunshine is delicious, rain is refreshing, wind braces up, snow is exhilarating; there is no such thing as bad weather, just different types of good weather."

—John Ruskin

Even among our primitive ancestors, I bet there were temperament differences. Each tribe likely had some bubbly Tarzans, some shy Tarzans, some mellow ones, and more than a few "punk rocker" Tarzans who were impulsive, impatient, and spirited! Scientists researching chimps even find distinct personality traits in wild apes.

Understanding your toddler's temperament is as important as knowing the temperature outside. Say you want to take a walk. Is it hot today or snowing? Either way, once you know what to expect, a little preparation will make your outing much more pleasant. After all, if you've dressed appropriately, even the winter can be glorious and beautiful.

Similarly, when you have to take your toddler to the store, knowing his temperament—whether he's prompt or tardy, afraid of new places or excited by them, easygoing about transitions or difficult to budge—helps you plan your errands with his personality in mind. And hopefully that will allow you to skip the tornadoes and head for the rainbows!

Exactly how temperament is passed down through the genetic code isn't fully understood. But for the most part, the apple doesn't fall too far from the tree. Shy parents tend to have shy kids; boisterous types have boisterous tykes. Every once in a while, however, two soft-spoken librarians wind up with a rock 'n' roller.

The nine main traits of temperament that your child is born with are pretty much the same ones you will be living with for the next eighteen years. If he is going to be a rose, he'll start out as a rosebud. That doesn't mean that what you do has no effect, though. With care that's tailored to his unique needs, you can help that rosebush grow strong, healthy, and full of blooms.

Variety *Is* the Spice of Life (and the Foundation of Society!)

It would be terrible if there were no doctors in the world, but it would also be terrible if everyone were a doctor. We need leaders and followers, thinkers and doers, and worriers, as well as those who throw caution to the wind. Different temperaments help fill all the niches of society.

So although it may have fallen to you to raise a saber-toothed tiger, remember that your little tiger has an important role to play!

The Big Three Temperaments

Not all parents have the same job. As soon as I became a pediatrician, it became crystal clear to me that some kids are much easier to parent than others. Your job is not to raise *a* child—it is to raise *your* child. To do that well, it helps if you can answer the question "What is *your toddler's* temperament?"

All nine traits of temperament (shown in the chart on page 82) are present in all kids. But pediatric experts have noticed that when

What "Weather Conditions" Are You Working With?

It's fun trying to figure out your child's temperament—kind of like taking the temperature of her personality. Temperament is a unique mix of nine basic ingredients of behavior (see below). Easy kids have more of the traits listed first, and cautious or spirited toddlers have more of the traits listed second. Where on each of the scales below would you place your child?

Easy, Cautious, Spirited

- **Activity** Enjoys quiet play . . . Fights, fidgets, is constantly on the go

- **Regularity** Naps and meals are pretty predictable . . . Routine is different every day

- **First reaction** Welcomes new situations . . . Sees new experiences as frightening

- **Adaptability** Handles transitions and plan changes easily . . . Has trouble with changes and the unexpected

- **Intensity** Is mild and gentle . . . Is boisterous and passionate

- **Mood** Is happy, easygoing . . . Is easily frustrated, discouraged, expects failure

- **Persistence** Easily goes along with others . . . Fights to the bitter end

- **Distractibility** Stays focused when playing . . . Is easily distracted, has short attention span

- **Sensitivity** Is unaware of minor changes around him . . . Is sensitive to noises, textures, smells, flavors

they carefully evaluate children's behavior, the mixtures of these nine often tend to fall into three major combinations:

- **Easy** kids (40 percent of children). These kids are flexible, active, not too intense, and open to new situations. They wake up on the right side of the bed in the morning, cheerful and ready for a new day.

- **Cautious** kids (15 percent of children) are also called "slow to warm up." Hesitant, sensitive, even fearful, they don't like changes and surprises. They tend to be peaceful but are easily frustrated. These are the kids who insist on watching the other kids go down the slide for twenty minutes before they get up the confidence to carefully try it themselves.

- **Spirited** kids (10 percent of children) are also called "challenging." These are the "more" kids: *more* active, *more* intense, *more* sensitive, *more* passionate, *more* inflexible, *more* moody, *more* impatient, impulsive, and strong-willed. They're a generous mixture of any (or all!) of those things.

About one third of all children don't neatly fit into any category. Will, for example, is generally easygoing and sociable but is extremely sensitive to itchy clothes and strong smells. He's also very rambunctious. Is he easy (due to his agreeableness), cautious (because of his sensitivity), or spirited (since he's so active)? Clearly, he's a little of all three.

If you're still not sure which category your child falls into, try this fifteen-second test: Wade into a noisy, crowded mall. Let go of your child's hand and turn your back for two seconds. What does he do? Start to cry? Just stand there? Blast off into the nearest shop and never look back? The answer will give you a pretty good idea of the temperature of your child's temperament.

Easy Toddlers: Mild and Moderate

"Not too cold, not too hot—just right!"

—Goldilocks and the Three Bears

Evan wakes up in a good mood and wanders into the kitchen for breakfast. A minor crisis appears when this 26-month-old's favorite cereal is "gone gone" (all gone) after only a few flakes have been poured into the bowl. "More!" he insists, his voice rising. His dad, Chuck, quickly takes another brand of cereal from the pantry and sprinkles it into his son's bowl. Evan stares down at the mixture of flakes with a cloud of disappointment passing over his face. "Mmm!" Chuck urges. "Your other favorite! Try it!" Evan plunges his spoon into the milk—and finishes the whole bowl!

Easy kids tend to bop through life on an even keel. They care, but they don't *care.* Bumps don't faze them much. They take frustrations in stride. That's not to say easy kids never have tantrums or act defiant. But when things do go wrong—as they inevitably will at times—easygoing children tend to shake them off and move on. They have resilience and balance.

An easy kid's first word is often *Hi!* (a great reflection of their cheerful, agreeable personality). Even during the wild Neanderthal period, kids with easy temperaments are like the elder statesmen of the tribe. They're impressively patient and reasonable. (But don't pat yourself on the back too fast; when push comes to shove, they're perfectly capable of behaving like the prehistoric creatures that developmental stage was named for.)

If you've given birth to an easy toddler, congratulate yourself on your good luck. But if you have a toddler who is slow to warm up, spirited, or challenging, give yourself even more pats on the back—you are a true parenting hero.

Cautious Toddlers: Slow to Warm Up

"Look twice before you leap."

—Charlotte Brontë

Eighteen-month-old Jess was a cautious guy. His mom, Jody, said, "He only speaks four words, but he's a thinker. He really assesses before he does new things. At the park he watched for weeks as kids went crawling through a little tunnel. Then one day he wanted to try it himself, and after he slowly made his way through, he was so giddy that he happily did it twenty times in a row!

Cautious toddlers live life in the slow lane. As newborns, their sensitivity often shows up as colic. By four months, when many babies hand out smiles like free samples, cautious infants frown with worry at the sight of a stranger (or doctor!) and retreat to their moms for rescue. This level of anxiety often pushes these toddlers into the rigid, stubborn Neanderthal stage a few months early and keeps their tenacious, demanding behaviors at a high level.

A cautious kid's first word is often *bye, go,* or *book.* (Not very sociable ideas, you'll notice.) They usually offer generous waves and bye-byes—only *after* the guests have walked out the front door.

Isabella, 15 months old, liked performing for strangers as long as they were a safe distance away. (Her mom, Meg, called it her "moat" of safety.)

Around age three their extreme shyness may decrease, thanks in part to their verbal abilities. (A few supershy toddlers stay in this fearful stage much longer.) Gradually these cautious toddlers gain confidence and become more open to new experiences.

It's easy to run out of patience with an overly cautious kid. "I want to yell at him, 'Snap out of it!'" one mother admitted. But impatience *always* makes these toddlers more reluctant. Fear is a primitive, deep emotion. It can't be just turned off and on. And once triggered, it starts an avalanche of reactions: fast pulse, panicky stares, wanting to run, and so on.

Cautious toddlers may also:

- *Be very careful when trying new things.* Their first reaction to something new is usually avoidance. They shy away from unfamiliar people, places, and things.

  > Emilio was so athletic, he learned how to ride a bike when he was three years old. However, he was also so cautious that when riding, he stopped every once in a while to look down and make sure his training wheels were still on!

- *Be ultrasensitive.* They'll often complain that the label on the back of their shirt (or even the shirt itself) is "scratchy." Food that's too lumpy, has an unfamiliar taste or smell, or has an odd color is usually rejected as "yucky."
- *Like to stay close.* These children are often clingy, trailing you from room to room.

  > Derek's dad, Tim, remarked, "Every morning at nursery school, Derek clings to me like plastic wrap for the first ten minutes. But once he gets engrossed in something, he kisses me good-bye without any

trouble." *Debbie's 18-month-old, Sophie, was so clingy she nicknamed her "Velcro."*

■ *Like rules.* Cautious kids are happy with routines and rules. Following them helps them feel safe and protected.

Handle with Care: Advice for Dealing with Cautious Tots

Your disapproving relatives (and your own worst fears) notwithstanding, your child's cautious temperament was not caused by you being overly protective or "giving in." Your child has been this way from birth, and he *will* get better and braver—as long as you are gently encouraging, *not* impatient and critical. Push too much, and his fears will only worsen and take twice as long to fade. (Did you ever try to talk someone out of his fear of flying? *Fugetaboutit!*)

There are many things you can start doing now to help your cautious child grow more confident. With younger toddlers:

1. Encourage the use of a lovey.

> *Fifteen-month-old Brandon was so cautious, he only crawled, rather than walk and risk falling. At my office his fear was kept in check as long as he had his blankie and thumb to comfort him.*

2. Weave lots of repetition and calming routines into your child's day. Special songs, familiar eating routines (his own plate and spoon), short massages, and Special Time (Chapter 10) can help build up his confidence.

3. Have more patience, not less. This is hard! But remember, your cautious toddler feels lost and vulnerable in a big scary world.

With older toddlers you can do the first three, plus:

4. **Avoid surprises.** Tell him what things are scheduled for later in the day. Some parents review the whole day's plans over breakfast. Give him something to look forward to after stressful situations. ("After lunch we're going to the doctor's, and right after that we're going to get some ice cream. Do you want sprinkles on yours?")

5. **Pump up his sense of confidence.** As will be discussed in Chapter 9, there are many ways you can build up your child's sense of confidence—for example, role playing: pretend *you* are a little child, and *he's* a big scary dog.

6. **Move ahead in baby steps.** Some days he may be more adventuresome and some days more shy. On a good day gently encourage him to make some small baby steps beyond his comfort zone. ("I know you don't like it here, so you hold Pooh's hand, and I'll be back in just one magic minute, and we will go home and draw a picture together! Now give me five. Ouch! You're strong! Don't let go of Pooh's hand, okay?")

7. **Practice relaxation.** Every day you can have your toddler practice taking deep breaths to learn how to calm himself (see page 189).

Spirited Toddlers: Little Tykes with Big Personalities

"In the middle of every difficulty lies opportunity."
—Albert Einstein

Fifteen-month-old Gina stays busy from dawn till dusk, flying from one activity to another. When she's moving, she's happy. But her constant motion means she's forever bumping into things and needing boo-boos kissed or getting into places she's not supposed to be. "If she can't open the door, she knocks it down!" says her mom, Olivia.

> *Laughingly, Elise said her fearless two-year-old,*
> *Spencer, was "a hundred percent ability and zero*
> *percent judgment. He would go straight up to an ax*
> *murderer and say, 'Nice ax you got there!'" Spencer*
> *was in motion every waking second. "I would jump*
> *every time I heard the loudspeaker at Wal-Mart,*
> *'Shoppers, we have a little boy . . .' His sister, Rosy, was*
> *so easy, she would just sit and study a toy for hours,*
> *but he immediately bounces it off the wall."*

"Spirited kids are the Super Ball in a roomful of rubber balls," observes Mary Sheedy Kurcinka in *Raising Your Spirited Child*. "Other kids bounce three feet off the ground. Every bounce for a spirited child hits the ceiling." Combine that trait with a Stone Ager's usual tendency to be rigid, active, opinionated, and self-centered—and you can see why spirited toddlers are particularly challenging.

Many parents of easy kids falsely believe that the tantrums they see in other kids are the result of poor parenting. Yet often exactly the opposite is true. Parents of spirited toddlers are often the best parents. But they have a super tough job.

Many moms tell me they knew their children would be spirited because they were so active in the womb. As babies, they can get themselves so worked up that once they start crying, they can't stop—even after you give them what they want! Of all our children, these would have the easiest time living a million years in the past—they're the alpha Neanderthals.

Spirited toddlers may also:

- *Show a range of personalities.* Spirited toddlers come in as many different variations as there are different breeds of wriggling puppies! Some are just incredibly active—never sitting still—but with happy, even tempers. Others are more moody, stubborn, cranky, and impatient. Generally, their highs are high, and their lows are low.
- *Be as active as a hive of bees.* These kids run farther, jump higher, and spin longer. Because they get so distracted and play so hard, they're accident prone.

- *Have trouble handling change.* Transitions from one activity to the next can be tough. They get so involved with one thing, they don't want to stop.
- *Steamroll right over the limits.* Their touches turn into pushes, and their voices rise into shouts. They run to the curb, look back (to make sure you're watching), and then proceed to step right into the street!
- *Easily get their feelings hurt.* They often have trouble bouncing back from slights or disappointments.

As you might imagine, during the toddler years these King Kong kids are the most challenging to civilize. They require consistency with a capital C and a steady supply of love, patience, and firm (but not rigid) limits. Fortunately, these children become easier to get along with as they grow more verbal and independent.

Roll with the Punches!
Tips for Helping Your Spirited Little Jumping Bean

Depending on just what variety of dynamo you have, you can pick and choose from the following ideas. Start with just a couple and see how they go. And most important of all—be patient!

With younger toddlers:

1. Get outside as much as possible! Frequent chances to burn up energy and play in the fresh air keep spirited Stone Agers in balance.

2. Rotate toys out periodically and store away a few. They'll seem more interesting if they haven't been seen in a while.

3. Make sure he gets his rest. Spirited kids often resist sleep because they are so excited by what they are doing. But overtired tykes get into much more trouble.

4. Make it fun. Begging and threats don't work. You'll get more cooperation by offering choices and requesting help rather than issuing orders.

5. Make your home toddler friendly. Move or remove breakables, valuables, and "tripables."

6. Make limits few but firm. Spirited kids have trouble with excessive limits, and they also have problems with inconsistency in enforcing limits. You can relax the rules—but when you do, make sure he understands that you're making an exception, not changing the rule.

7. Avoid overstimulation. For a few hours before bedtime, turn lights low, turn white noise up, and avoid roughhousing, loud music, and TV.

8. Try hard not to overreact to every hit or insult. Just because your child is acting like a primitive doesn't mean you should act like one too.

With older toddlers you can do the first eight, plus:

9. Have lots of backup plans to keep your child busy. For example, keep on hand quick, low-mess activities like crayons and paper, Nerf balls, and molding clay.

10. Tutor him in social skills. ("Bobby might let you share his ball, if you ask him nicely with one of your big smiles I love so much.")

11. Teach him the words to express his feelings: "You are acting the way you sometimes do when your body is telling you that you are hungry. Would you like a snack?"

12. Practice calming techniques to help develop the ability to bounce back. (See all the patience-building exercises in Chapter 9.)

13. Use "reverse psychology" to help your contrary toddler when he is intent on doing the exact opposite of what you want. (See Chapter 9.)

Labels Are for Cans of Fruit, Not Children

"I wouldn't have seen it if I hadn't believed it."

—Marshall McLuhan

"Keisha is a devil child!"
"Pete's so shy, he's almost frightened by his own shadow."
"Drew is so hyper all the time."

We've all heard kids being called names. *Obnoxious. Stubborn. Whiner. Wild. Demanding. Picky.* I am constantly amazed to hear parents refer to their children in words they would *never* allow someone else to call them! Although there may be a grain of truth in these words of criticism, negative labels are hurtful—even scarring. Calling a toddler a "devil child" focuses both you and him on his misbehavior. It makes you notice the five times he messes up (as you expected) and overlook the fifteen times he does something well.

Hmm, you may be thinking. But what if Keisha really does do bad things? Isn't avoiding a label that tells it like it is some kind of politically correct nonsense?

No, it's not! What you say matters. Many people go their entire lives waiting for their parents to praise them. Your little Neanderthal may fight you, but you're the one he'll run to when he's hurt or scared. You are the king (or queen) of the house and of his heart. Your loving words can build him up, and your criticisms can slowly shred him to pieces.

Hurtful names we've been called stick in our minds—often for life. Fortunately, kind comments also stay with us. So carefully choose the words you want your toddler to keep in his mind as his definition of himself.

We all will face many challenges in our lives, and those who believe in themselves will get through these difficulties most successfully. Use the power of your words to strengthen your child. It is one of the best gifts you can give him.

Besides being unkind, negative labels are also inaccurate! If you say, "You're lazy," of course, some days your child isn't. If you say,

"You're mean," later in the day he may be sweet. A better way of letting your toddler know when you're upset with his behavior is to comment about what he has done and how it makes you feel: "You broke my favorite picture frame, and Mommy is *mad, mad, mad* right now." This allows you to vent about what he did without applying an unfair, hurtful, and incorrect label.

Realize, too, that there's a positive side to all so-called "negative" traits that can become a great asset to your challenging child as he gets older. A "scaredy-cat's" fear may keep him from having unprotected sex. A "stubborn" child may resist peer pressure to experiment with drugs. A "whiny" boy may not allow himself to be taken advantage of by others.

Reframe That Name!

Replace labels that tear your toddler down with descriptions that build him up.

Labels That Hinder / Descriptions That Help

Nosy → Curious
Picky eater → Knows what he wants
Hyper → Spirited
Whiny → Speaks up for self
Shy → Careful
Wild → Energetic
Stubborn → Tenacious
Defiant → Courageous
Fussy → Selective
Slowpoke → Thoughtful and deliberate

7

The Clash of Civilizations: When Modern Parents Meet Stone Age Kids

"There are times when parenthood seems like nothing more than feeding the hand that bites you."

—Peter De Vries

Main Points:

- Parenting is a skill as much as an instinct.

- Feelings of frustration and failure, as well as unhappy memories from the past, can affect the way you parent.

- Your temperament may mesh or clash with your child's temperament.

- Compared to ancient human beings', our lives are busy, indoors, and isolated—not the best conditions for bringing up toddlers.

So here you are, an eager and caring ambassador to your pint-size primitive. Tell me, how much training did you get before you took this job? Diplomacy is a pretty tricky job, yet most of us get less training to be parents than we do to get driver's licenses! No wonder we often feel we're flying by the seat of our pants, doing what our parents did—or else exactly the opposite!

Even though most of us expect toddlerhood to be hard, few of us have any inkling of just how tough these three years can be. That rude awakening usually dawns the first time you and she get into an eyeball-to-eyeball conflict.

Boom! Suddenly you realize that while it's your job to give loving guidance, it's *her* job to scream, slap, and spit. That's the moment that really tests how civilized *you* are!

Just because your primitive little pal goes ballistic doesn't mean you should too! (One cave dweller in a family is quite enough.) Just keep repeating, "I am millions of years more advanced than she is."

The Apple of Your Eye—or the Pebble in Your Shoe?

Five good reasons why parenting is a challenge.

There are innumerable difficulties in being a parent, but here are five that often trip up even perfect moms and dads (if such people exist, which they don't!):

- Feelings of frustration—Your toddler's behavior may often frustrate or even anger you.
- Feelings of failure—Daily clashes may leave you feeling inept.
- Whispers from the past—Unresolved feelings from your childhood may come back to haunt you.
- Temperament—The personalities of some parents and children clash like polka dots and stripes.
- Modern life itself—Our modern lifestyle is not set up to help us with our toddlers.

What's It Like Parenting a Toddler?

"If at first you don't succeed . . . you're running about average."

—M. H. Alderson

Pick the statement that best describes how most parents of toddlers feel:

1. Some days I think I could take care of twins.

2. Some days I'm holding my own.

3. Some days I feel like I'm slipping.

4. Some days I'm overwhelmed.

5. Some days I feel like a failure.

No matter which answer you chose—you were correct!

Like most parents, I beam when my child is complimented, and I feel ashamed when she's rude. We naturally see our kids as extensions of ourselves. In reality, though, more than half of a toddler's behavior is due to her unique temperament and primitive state of development—factors totally beyond our control.

That's why the next three years will inevitably be filled with many yo-yo days and unexpected challenges. I don't care if you're a CEO or a four-star general, get used to the idea that as a parent you're probably going to fail a lot. Always try your best, but don't be so tough on yourself! Even the best baseball players get a hit only about a third of the times they go to bat.

Okay, get mad—then get over it.

How are *you* doing with all of this? Are you handling your raging little primitive with dignity, or have you let her drag you into the ring with her to trade punches?

If you've been duking it out, I can appreciate how that happens. We've all been there. Our kids learn how to push our buttons, and we *react!* But yells and threats only force your toddler to behave out of intimidation, not love. (I'll talk about spanking later, but suffice it to say that even the supporters of spanking usually warn parents *never* to hit their children when they're angry.)

> Peter, the dad of three-year-old Andrew, said,
> "There are days when everything my boy does pushes
> my buttons. I end up feeling like I'm one big button!"

What should you do when you're so mad your blood boils? Try seeing yourself as a bullfighter instead of a boxer. Step back, and watch her attacks slip right by like the bull's horns into the bullfighter's cape!

To help you emotionally back off, walk away for a minute (a little mommy or daddy time-out), and write about the day's ups and downs in a journal. Journal writing may help you see a pattern to the problem and strategies for overcoming it. For example, tantrums can often be avoided by giving an extra snack in the morning, ten minutes of backyard play after lunch, storytime before dinner, and so forth.

One thing I recommend you *don't* do is ignore your anger and frustrations. Stuffing feelings away is unhealthy. But that doesn't mean it's acceptable for you to explode in front of your child. Yelling is never okay! If she's sensitive and cautious, you'll frighten her. If she's spirited, you'll be making it extra hard for her to *gracefully* back down and cooperate.

When you're really furious, go away and scream into a pillow, punch the mattress, or (my personal favorite) dig deep holes in the garden. Displays you *can* use in front of your child include stamping your feet, clapping your hands, playfully barking like a dog, jumping up and down, scribbling hard with a crayon and then tearing the paper into little pieces. Also, any Neanderthal will understand you if you use Tarzan's old trick—beat your chest and hoot.

If you do accidentally lose your temper in front of your child, use it as an opportunity to turn lemons into lemonade. Apologize as soon as you cool down. Once both of you have recovered, take a moment to teach her that you've forgiven her and that love is stronger than anger. To a young toddler say, "You say 'No shout, Mommy! No, no, no—no shout. No, no, no!' Mommy loves you. Stevie want hug?" With an older toddler, try, "I'm sorry Mommy shouted. I felt mad. It was wrong to shout, but shouting doesn't break my love for you. I love you as big as a mountain! As big as an elephant!! Can Mommy give you a big hug? Boy, that feels good! Gimme five." Then after she slaps your hand, do a little dance in pretend pain, complaining, "Yikes, ow-ow-ow! You're strong!" She will laugh and feel relieved.

A Word About Child Abuse

Sara Jane said, "The other day, I got so mad, I threw the remote control and broke it. I had angry parents, and I'm so afraid of losing my temper with Kimmie. But something inside me just snaps when she looks right at me and disobeys. It's like she's daring me to do something!"

In his excellent book, *Understanding Your Child's Temperament*, William Carey says, "The child's temperament may be the spark that ignites parents' anger and pushes them over the edge." Feeling angry may be unavoidable, but *acting* angry can be stopped.

You must never lash out in anger with hitting or hurtful words. No parent *wants* to scream at her toddler, but if you lose your patience over and over, you need to make some changes. Here are a few things to try:

- Get more help at home or find a preschool.
- Don't spread yourself thin by trying to accomplish too many things.
- Find time to have some fun (and sleep).
- Ask your doctor about support groups and other resources or suggestions.

You may not be able to change the circumstances of your life, but you can change the way you see them. While you're totaling up all the troublesome things in your life, don't forget to take the time to count your blessings too.

Finally, you and your spouse should make time to give each other a little TLC. If your toddler could talk, she'd tell you, "Hey guys, don't burn out—I'm *really* gonna need you later!" If you're single, you're probably even more in need of a break, so be sure to get one whenever you can. Make every effort to get sleep, laughter, fresh air, and some time alone, and be sure to have someone who can listen to you without feeling the need to give advice, criticism, or pity.

What to Do When You Feel Like a Flop

The only place you find perfection is in a dictionary.

—Old saying

While talking to her mother on the phone, Lynne burst into tears. That morning her 20-month-old, Josh, bit a child at playgroup. It was the third time he had bitten, and this time he did it so hard, the leader asked Lynne not to come back. "When he was a baby, he was so perfect," she said, sobbing. "What am I doing wrong?"

We all proudly take credit when our children are well behaved, so it only stands to reason we would see their irritating behaviors as signs that we're bad parents—even though we know a lot of their behavior is a result of their temperament and primitive drives.

What about you? Do you think you are responsible for all your toddler's triumphs and failures? Do you hate it every time she has a tantrum? If so, please keep the big picture in mind. These years will be gone in a flash, and you'll miss them terribly, even the difficult moments that used to make you cringe: the constant thumb in the mouth, the screaming because her cracker broke, even her raging battles not to let go of her teddy at bath time!

Rather than getting down on yourself, I beg you to remember that your little Neanderthal is trying to master millions of years of development at almost the speed of light so that's bound to be hard on both of you. Not only is it a smart idea to tell your toddler all the good things she does, it's also useful for your mental health to remind yourself before going to bed of two or three *good* things that you did that day.

> The day after celebrating Sam's third birthday, Tracy confessed, "I was totally down on myself the morning of his birthday. He was acting up and ignoring everything I said. But once we got to Disneyland he was so happy and sweet. Then I saw all the other parents struggling to control their kids and I realized that everybody has ups and downs. That really helped me to lighten up on myself."

Of course, we *all* slip up sometimes. But failing every now and then does not make you *a failure*. The truth is that mistakes speed us along the path to success because they help us learn how to do things better. In fact, most of us learn more from our failures than from our successes.

Here's one more bit of consolation: Many toddlers save their biggest misbehavior for their mothers! They wait to let down their long Neanderthal hair with their moms because you're who they feel safest with. Consider it a primitive form of flattery.

Bad Day? No Place to Go But Up

Remind yourself that tomorrow, as Scarlett O'Hara famously said, really is another day! Dr. Seuss, America's most beloved writer of children's stories, was rejected twenty-eight times before a publisher finally realized how good his work was! Barbra Streisand's off-Broadway debut opened and closed the same night! A newspaper fired Walt Disney because he "lacked imagination and had no original ideas." Luckily parenthood is chock-full of second chances.

Whispers from the Past: Managing Intrusive Memories

"Happiness is good health and a bad memory."
—Ingrid Bergman

It's very common for our experiences with our little ones to bring up all sorts of childhood memories. Often these feelings are good. The smell of cookies may suddenly give you a warm, happy thought about cooking with your mom. But sometimes our toddlers shake loose memories in us that are troubling. For example, a slap from your little Stone Ager may unleash the angry memory of an unfair hit you received when you were young.

> Debby was proud to go out to dinner for Mother's Day with her husband, Andy, and their three-year-old twins, Sophie and Audrey. But her happiness suddenly turned to hurt when the girls started fighting over who would sit next to Andy. "I don't want Mommy! I want Daddy!" It reminded Debby of the painful feelings she had when she was little and kids on the playground rejected her.

It's amazing how hurtful memories from decades past can unexpectedly spring back into our hearts. Your child's laughing at you may suddenly trigger the recollection of sarcastic words of a deceased grandmother or the snickering of a schoolmate. These memories often make us overreact because of the waves of emotions that they trigger inside us.

Thoughts of your relatives can short-circuit your response to your child in other ways too. It's one thing to think your child has Uncle Phil's eyes or your mother's laugh. But when she shows a relative's darker traits—unfairness, a boiling temper, stony stubbornness—that can unleash unexpectedly strong and even irrational reactions, especially when we're stressed and exhausted. (And stressed and exhausted will frequently be the reality of your life as the parent of a young child!)

I always tell parents in my practice that when your toddler does something that makes you very angry, stop for a second, lift up your anger as if it were a lid, and look beneath it to see what's there. You may be surprised to find a totally different feeling, like hurt, embarrassment, guilt, or shame. Once you realize this, talk with someone you trust about those feelings. Allow yourself to experience them fully. Cry, yell, and spend a little time remembering those painful memories. Feeling is healing for you as well as for your toddler!

Even if your toddler wallops you in the nose, try to remember it's not really a sign of meanness or lack of love. It's just the primitive swing of an out-of-control Cave-Kid. (Why do you think the boy in *The Flintstones* was named Bam-Bam?)

 ## Temperament: Opposites Don't Always Attract

Is your child a chip off the old block—or a mutant from Mars? Are the two of you sparks and dynamite or peas in a pod? In the last chapter I discussed the large contribution your toddler's inborn temperament makes to her behavior. Now let's have some fun and look at *your* temperament. (Yes! You have one too!)

> *Judy lived in a "60 mph" world, but her little kids had a "meander-through-the-mud" mentality. In fact, Judy nicknamed Emily and Ted Speed Bump #1 and Speed Bump #2 because they forced her to switch from her normal fast pace to a turtle's creep.*

Few parents get along perfectly with their toddlers. Most of us clash with them on a regular basis. We're all different people, after all. Psychologists have a tailor-made term for how well a parent's temperament matches up with his or her child's: *goodness of fit.*

Do any of the following describe the match-up you have with your toddler?

- I'm neat and disciplined. My daughter is messy and disorganized.
- I'm a nurturer who loves to cuddle. My son doesn't like being touched.
- I'm athletic. My son is timid and refuses to try new things.
- I'm the life of the party. My daughter is sensitive and gets startled when I laugh.
- I'm respectful and fair. My son is opinionated, defiant, and wild.

Some passionate parents get bored with mild kids. Some soft-spoken parents get pulverized by their spirited Neanderthals. Sometimes problems even occur when children and parents are too much *alike*. Stubborn parents with stubborn kids can be an explosive mix, for example. In general, though, we have the easiest time getting along with children who are similar to ourselves.

Look at the list of temperament traits on page 82 and see how your toddler rates on qualities like intensity, mood, and so forth. Then see how you compare. Which of your own temperament qualities are you most proud of? Which would you most like to chuck out the window?

Of course, you really can't stop being intense or cautious, if that's your nature. You may be able to make some minor adjustments, but much of having a happy life is accepting yourself, warts and all, and playing the cards life dealt you with as much joy and integrity as you can.

Similarly, part of having a happy family is learning to let go of the "ideal" child you've been imagining and love your child for her own special mix of strengths and struggles! Love your girly girl, even if you wanted a tomboy, celebrate your shy guy, even though you had hoped for a class president. Nurturing your child with love and respect is exactly what she needs to grow up into the child you will be most proud of!

Modern Life: The Nuclear Family Is Normal— and Other Myths

"It takes a village to raise a child."

—African proverb

Did you know that the nuclear family (two parents and children to a household) is a recent invention? In fact, it is one of the largest, most unnatural human experiments in the history of mankind! We've only been living this way for the past hundred years—a tiny fraction of the sixty-thousand-year history of our most recent human ancestors! And every year we shrink family size even further: Many American kids today are only children, have just one sibling, and/or live in single-parent households.

Modern Western culture teaches us that it's "normal" to care for our babies without any help, locked up in our own little "huts" away from relatives and neighbors. Having a housekeeper or a regular babysitter has become a luxury reserved only for the rich. In fact, having other family members living with us is viewed as a misfortune of the very poor. Many of the women I know haven't cuddled a baby for twenty or thirty years! And for some moms in my practice, their own baby is the first they've *ever* held!

In other places around the world, people think all this is crazy. "You can't be serious!" they say. "How can you raise a baby without the help of your sisters, mother, aunts, grandmothers, and friends?"

I often wonder that myself. While we eat steak for dinner, the women of "primitive" cultures are eating only rice and beans. But while we are raising our babies in solitude (and some days going slowly crazy from it), they have a wealth of helpers to share the work and fun.

The Efé Pygmies of the forests of Africa pass their babies around like a bag of popcorn at the movies. More than twenty people may handle an infant in a day. Among the Navajo, sisters help care for each other's children. In Serbia first cousins are considered brothers and sisters. (It's an insult to call them "cousins.") My patients from India are often taught by their parents to call me "Uncle."

When you combine our shrinking families with other modern trends—living far away from our families, drive-through restaurants, online shopping—it's clear that we are spending less and less time in "touch" with other human beings.

This increased physical isolation is especially tough on new families. Caring for a young child is a big job. Thinking that we could, or should, do it all by ourselves is an unnatural departure from the whole of human history. You may have been eager to move away from your roots when you were a teen, but when young children come into your life, it's a time for families to reunite.

Raising kids does take a village—but where can you find that village when you live in mid-Manhattan (whether that's Manhattan, New York or Manhattan, Kansas)? Open your eyes, it's all around you:

- Find a friend with a toddler the same age as yours.
- Get to know your neighbors.
- Enroll your child in nursery school or preschool. (Age two is not too young.)
- Join a gym or activity group targeted to parents and toddlers.
- Join or start a playgroup or babysitting co-op.
- Invite an older neighbor to visit with your child.
- Attend a church or synagogue.
- Move nearer to your family or move them nearer to you.

PART TWO

Now You're Talking!

To help your toddler understand
you, try speaking his language.

8

How Do You Say That in Toddler-ese? Communication That Really Works!

"When people talk, listen completely. Most people never listen."

—Ernest Hemingway

Main Points:

- The Fast-Food Rule is the best way to talk to any upset person: Before saying what *you* think, repeat what *he* said—with sincerity.

- If you skip the Fast-Food Rule, your irate friend may not be able to listen to you.

- When you speak to someone who's upset, it is critically important to remember: What you say is not as important as the way you say it.

- When your child is upset, it helps to translate what you say to him into Toddler-ese (his native language).

- Toddler-ese takes some practice—but it will help you be a better, and happier, parent.

You are about to learn a new and highly effective way to defuse your toddler's outbursts with love and respect. It's based on understanding how his prehistoric mind works.

First, let's do a little quiz. Which best describes a toddler's mind?

1. A neatly manicured park

2. A rolling green meadow

3. A jungle

If you answered (3) "A jungle," you're absolutely right! Toddlers are sweet and fun, but they're also wild and disorganized. This is especially true when your child gets emotional (angry, frustrated, hurt, etc.). In fact, we all get more "primitive" when we get upset; that's why we say a person who is angry "went ape!"

As ambassador to your little jungle pal, your job will be much easier once you learn to speak *his* language (complete with grunts, gestures, and short phrases)! Becoming fluent in his language is nothing less than your ticket to a fun, wonderful relationship. But before being trained in Toddler-ese, you must first master the number-one law of speaking with *anyone* who is upset—the Fast-Food Rule!

Okay, I know that burgers and fries are not very prehistoric. But I hope that this funny name will help you remember this important concept forever! Once you've learned it, I'll show you how to translate the Fast-Food technique into Toddler-ese. Together they will be your miracle potion for quickly calming your toddler.

The Fast-Food Rule: The Golden Rule of Communication

In conversations you have to take turns—and whoever is most upset goes first!

—Karp's rule of communication

The Fast-Food Rule is simple: Before you tell an upset person *your* concerns, you must repeat back *his* feelings—echoing his words *and* (even more important) sincerely mirroring his level of emotion in your voice, face, and gestures.

Here's how it works (and why it's called the Fast-Food Rule):

The Fast-Food Rule, Step 1: REPEAT the message you hear

Burger joints have their problems, but they do one thing incredibly well: taking customers' orders.

Imagine you're at the drive-through. A voice crackles over a speaker, "Can I take your order?"

You reply, "I'd like a burger and fries."

What does the order-taker say back to you?

"What's the matter? Were you too lazy to cook tonight?"

"Do you realize how much fat is in that meal?"

"That will be four dollars."

The answer is none of the above!

No. The first thing she does is *repeat your order back to you!*

She knows she can't do a thing until she totally understands what you want. So, what she actually says is, "Okay, that's a burger and fries. Ketchup? Salt? Something to drink?" Only after she is sure she's got it—and you know she's got it—does she finally "take *her* turn" and say, "That'll be four dollars. Please drive forward."

Now let's apply this rule to a typical real-life situation. We'll start with one involving adults, before moving on to its application to toddlers.

You are terribly upset because you lost a purse. You're frantic because it contained important papers you've been working on for two weeks, and you're afraid that when your boss finds out, he'll fire you. Weeping, you begin telling a friend what happened, but your friend cuts you off and wraps you in a big warm hug, saying, "It's okay! It's okay! Don't worry, you can write another report. I love you no matter what you did. Hey, this will make you laugh; did I tell you what happened to me yesterday?"

How would you feel? Although she only wanted to ease your pain, her reaction probably made you feel interrupted, disrespected, and even *more* upset!

A much better response would have been for your friend to listen carefully, every once in a while letting you know she understood your feelings, before offering her solution or distraction.

Let's replay the conversation and imagine how you would feel if she had listened and reflected your feelings before giving her opinions:

"I went to a restaurant and left it on the seat!"

"Oh, no!"

"And my boss is so rude, I know he'll scream at me again."

"No wonder you're so upset."

"Yes, I'd been working on that report for two weeks!"

"Oh, no! All that effort!"

"Thanks for giving me a shoulder to cry on. I'll get through this somehow."

"You know I'm always here for you. What can I do to help? Can I give you a hug? Hey, did I tell you what happened yesterday? This may cheer you up a little . . ."

When you're upset, you want your friend to listen and care! Of course, suggestions can be great, but they're not what most of us want first. The best communicators show they truly understand someone's feelings before expecting that person to be able to hear their advice. They don't want to be like the waitress telling customers how much they owe—before they've even finished giving their order!

Do You Ever Get to Give Your Message First?

The Fast-Food Rule says that whoever is "hungriest" for attention gets to go first. Most of the time crying toddlers are so upset they need us to deal with their messages first before telling them what we have to say. But you can proceed immediately to your message if your toddler is being aggressive, doing something dangerous, or is breaking an important household rule. In those cases, *your* feelings take top priority.

The Fast-Food Rule, Part 2: Repeat the message sincerely, using your face, voice . . . and heart.

We're used to thinking that *what* we say is the key to good communication, but that's not always true. In fact, when talking to a person who is really upset . . . *what* you say is **much** less important than *how you say it!* Just parroting back a friend's complaints, with a blank face and a flat tone of voice, will make her feel even *worse,* no matter how accurately you repeat her words! That's why this second step of the Fast-Food Rule is so critical.

The Fast-Food Rule works only when you give your unhappy

friend your full attention and closely mirror her words, tone of voice, and gestures.

Once again, imagine you were just fired and are meeting your friend for tea and sympathy. Which one of these two responses would make you feel really cared about?

Using the Fast-Food Rule with Toddlers

When talking to upset children many of us are so impatient, we would never make it as order-takers at Busy Burger. We try to squelch our kid's protests (regardless of whether they're legitimate or hyped) with comments like "Be quiet" or "Stop that" or "Not now."

We defend ourselves by saying we're busy or just wanting to make everything better. But that doesn't give us the right to try to shut down a child's comments right in the middle of "his turn!" We don't *mean* to be rude and disrespectful. But that's exactly the message we send.

Here are some of the ways we "cut in line" ahead of our toddlers and interrupt their cries and complaints:

- Reasoning: "See, honey? There are no monsters in your closet."
- Minimizing feelings: "Oh, come on, it's not so bad. That didn't hurt."
- Distracting: "Hey, let's look at this book."
- Ignoring: Turning your back and leaving.
- Questioning: "Why did he hit you?"
- Threatening: "Stop now, or you'll get a time-out."
- Reassuring: "Don't cry, it's okay. Daddy's right here."

Please don't misunderstand me: all of these responses have their place—*but not until it's your turn!!* Farmers must plow before planting, and parents need to patiently reflect their toddler's feelings before getting to their own agenda.

Oops! Some Parents Do the Right Thing at the Wrong Time

Two ways parents push their child's feelings aside instead of showing them respect via the Fast-Food Rule are by rushing in to use distraction and by being too quick to say, "It's okay." Let me explain.

Why Distraction Backfires

> *"It ain't over till it's over."*
>
> —Yogi Berra, former New York Yankees star

Imagine if every time you tried to discuss your concerns with your doctor, she immediately pointed out the window, saying, "Look, there's a new building over there." You'd probably soon decide to switch doctors.

Toddlers also hate it when we answer their protests with irrelevant distractions. However, they don't have the option of switching moms, so they either become more defiant (to *make you* listen to their message) or more withdrawn (thinking you don't care how they feel). Either response can lead to physical/emotional ill health.

Why "It's Okay" *Isn't* Okay

> *"Putting a lid on a boiling pot doesn't stop the boiling."*
>
> —Stephanie Marston, *The Magic of Encouragement*

It's natural to want to soothe your crying child, but interrupting him to say, "It's okay" (over and over again) may accidentally backfire. He may think you're saying that he's wrong to feel upset or that you no longer want to hear about his feelings. So save your loving reassurance for *after* your child starts calming down—when he really *is* beginning to feel "okay."

Monica was preparing a snack for 20-month-old Suzette. On the plate was her daughter's favorite—a face made out of grapes, little cubes of mozzarella cheese, and crackers.

As a surprise, Monica decided to be even more creative than usual. Instead of whole crackers for the body, she broke them into strips to make arms and legs. Suzette reacted as if she had just been forced to watch <u>Friday the Thirteenth</u>—pure horror!

Monica skipped the Fast-Food Rule, and instead tried to calm Suzette by repeating, "It's okay. It's okay," over and over—about twenty times.

What was her little Neanderthal's response to this "reassurance"? She screamed even louder! Suddenly snack time disintegrated into chaos, with Monica saying, "It's okay. It's okay," and Suzette wailing as if to say, "No! It's NOT okay! It's NOT okay!"

I sometimes think of the Fast-Food Rule as a rescue mission. Your toddler is stuck deep in the jungle of his Stone Age emotions. The only way you can rescue him is by finding him in his jungle. And the only way to find him is by mirroring his feelings.

Now that you understand the Fast-Food Rule, you need to do one more thing to make it work perfectly with your toddler. You have to

learn how to reflect your child's feelings back to him *in his own language*—an ancient lingo I call Toddler-ese.

Toddler-ese: Your Stone Age Friend's Native Tongue

Imagine that a woman is visiting a country whose people speak a different language. She suddenly needs a bathroom. She stops someone on the street and politely, but urgently, asks, "Bathroom?" The foreigner replies, "Wjoorkt," which means "I don't understand." "What?" the increasingly desperate woman says, and she loudly repeats, "Bathroom! BATHROOM!" The stranger, hurt by her tone, yells back, "Wjoorkt! Wjoorkt! WJOORKT!!!"

Pretty soon they're both red in the face with frustration! And neither feels heard.

Even the most caring stranger would have trouble helping you if he didn't speak your language. The same is true for caring parents. The Fast-Food Rule works best with toddlers *when it's translated into their native tongue,* as this loving mom found out one afternoon in my office:

> The moment I took out my flashlight to look
> in Shannon's ears, the 23-month-old began to
> cry with worry. Her mom, Mary, responded with
> a respectful, calm voice, saying, "I know you
> don't like it, sweetheart. You're afraid and think
> it's going to hurt, but the doctor will be gentle. It's
> important to know your ears are good so you don't
> need to take that yucky medicine again, okay? It's
> almost over."

Do You Ever Get to Speak Normally?

You don't have to speak Toddler-ese to your child all the time. Usually you'll talk in your normal way. But when his mood turns stormy, you'll discover that regular talking is much less effective or even counterproductive.

"What we have here is a failure to communicate."
—Chain-gang warden to convict
Paul Newman in *Cool Hand Luke*

I am all for being caring and reasonable, but there are some good reasons why logic, distraction, and even loving acknowledgment often fail to help *irate* little primitives, when they're in a frenzy.

- *Your toddler can't really "hear" you.* All of us have more trouble seeing (and hearing) straight when we're upset. That's especially true for toddlers whose prehistoric brains don't handle language well to begin with.
- *Your toddler is not good at logic yet.* Reasoning requires parts of the left brain that are still very disorganized in children under four.
- *Your toddler is focused on what he wants—not what you want.* Can you imagine your fuming toddler saying, "You're so right," or "I never thought of it that way before"? Don't expect your prehistoric pal to be reasonable and compromise when he's livid. (He has a hard enough time being that way when he's happy.)
- *Your toddler thinks you didn't get his message.* How could your toddler yell his complaint at you—twenty-five times—and still think you didn't get the message? As odd as it sounds, it's probably because you never answered him in his language! Usually, once you tell him in Toddler-ese that you understand and respect him, the badgering and whining quickly get better.

So did Shannon calm down? *NO!* She yelled even louder! Why? Wasn't Mary using the Fast-Food Rule? Well, here's the problem. There were too many words, and the way Mary said them didn't accurately mirror her daughter's panic!

Angry, fearful toddlers quickly become intense and rigid. (That's even true for older kids—and for adults too!) When young children are upset, our gentle words just sound like a jumble of noise. Poor Shannon! She was worried and scared and felt that even her mom didn't understand her! So she yelled louder—like the tourist at the beginning of the chapter who thought that screaming would help people understand her!

How could Mary have better helped her frightened little daughter? What should she have said? Easy! All she needed to do was translate her loving words into Toddler-ese. But how do you do that?

 ## The Four Ingredients of Toddler-ese

"When in Rome, do as the Romans do."

I first learned Toddler-ese in my office, where I serve as an honorary ambassador to Toddlerland! I gradually mastered it by handling twenty tantrums a day. Eventually, I could take most crying two-year-olds and have them laughing and playful (or at least cooperative) in minutes.

Sound too good to be true? Actually, Toddler-ese is easier to learn than French, Chinese—or even pig latin. You may feel a bit self-conscious when you start trying it out. But please stick with it, and within days your little time-traveler will look up at you with big appreciative eyes, as if to say, "Hey, you understand me! Thanks, you're awesome!"

Here are the four simple steps for converting any messages into Toddler-ese:

1. Short phrases

2. Repetition

3. Correct tone of voice

4. Facial expressions and body gestures

These four steps break your communication into small, easy-to-understand pieces that allow your toddler's stressed-out brain to realize you "get" his message. Repeat his words (or what you think he would say if he could), but also use your tone of voice and gestures to mirror his feelings. Remember, with upset toddlers, the way you say something is a hundred times more important than the words you use!

1. Short Phrases

> *"Brevity is the soul of wit."*
>
> —William Shakespeare, *Hamlet*

Now I'd like you to read this as fast as you can: Imaginereading somethingwithnopunctuationorcapitalizationorevenanyspaces betweenanyofitswordsitwouldbehardwouldntit

Okay. You may have figured out what that sentence says, but would you have had the patience to decode it after drinking a pot of coffee and spilling nail polish on the carpet?

When you're talking with an upset toddler, words are not your friends. Long sentences are even tough for children to understand when they are calm and happy. Words require lots of attention from the left half of the brain, but that side totally falls apart the moment your toddler enters Tantrumland.

Of course, toddlers aren't the only ones who get more and more un-civilized the more upset they get . . . so do we! That's why we describe a really angry person by saying, "Oh, my God, she went . . . APE!"

Even adults descend an evolutionary elevator and get more primitive when our emotions get the better of us: "Ding! Going down!"

Toddlers are especially short on patience when they're fuming, that's why Toddler-ese works so well. It breaks our message into tiny phrases that even little children can handle . . . even when they are in a frenzy.

So, the first step in speaking to an upset child is to use very short phrases. For young toddlers, make them one to three words long. For older toddlers, you can stretch them to three to five words. (As I mentioned earlier, Toddler-ese is for unhappy, frustrated children. Once your toddler recovers, just return to your normal way of speaking.)

Toddler-ese—It's Better Than Magic, It's Real!

The Fast-Food Rule and Toddler-ese are not magic cures to all struggles. When your child must do something he hates or when he's hungry, sick, overstimulated, or overtired, he may get stuck in his tantrum for a while (and need you to try other skills, like ignoring and time-out, which are discussed in Chapter 11).

But with a little practice, you'll find that tantrums can be defused most of the time. Clare, the Toddler-ese fluent mother of Georgia, said, "Of course, there are occasions when nothing works with my two-year-old, like after the birth of her little brother, but my 95 percent success rate is nothing short of amazing!"

Even if you don't turn the situation around completely, your toddler's distress will lighten, and his behavior will grow less wild as a result of your loving, respectful Toddler-ese message.

Here's an example. Your bored 15-month-old child toddles over to the front door, bangs on it, and screeches to go to the yard. Whether you intend to go out or not, the first thing you should do is reflect his message by energetically and lovingly saying, "Out! . . . Out! . . . Out! OUT! You are bored . . . bored . . . BORED! And you want OUT!! You say, 'Go, Mommy . . . go, GO!!!!'" Once your son calms a little, then you can go out with him or offer some options or a distraction.

2. Repetition

> "If at first you don't succeed, try, try (and try and try) again."
>
> —Adaptation of an old saying

While anger can make an adult "blind" with rage, strong emotion virtually makes a toddler "deaf." That's why repeating is a key part of Toddler-ese. As you could see in the example above, "Bored!" is a short sentence, but by itself it's just not enough. Your frustrated toddler needs you to repeat it. *"You are bored . . . bored . . . BORED! And you want OUT!!"* If your child is screaming because you took away the lipstick he was using as a crayon, passionately echo his feelings by saying, "You want! YOU want!! You want it nowwww!! You want! YOU want!! You want it NOWWWW!!" Notice the repetition, the short phrasing, and the way the sentence builds up to the final emphasized word. You should be enthusiastic, but not to the point of shouting.

Don't be surprised if it takes four or five repetitions before you even begin to get your little buddy's attention! You'll know you're making progress when he suddenly looks up, as if he's thinking *What? Did you say sumptin'?* But don't stop then. When he's really upset, you may need to repeat his feelings another five to ten times before he realizes that you really "get it."

For example, when I'm examining the ears of a crying two-year-old, I emphatically proclaim what I think he would say if he were older: "Steven says, 'No ears!! No, no . . . NO ears!!! No, NO . . . NO ears!!! You stop! You STOP!!!! I don't like it!'" This makes many children relax, and those who continue resisting do so less vigorously *even though I'm still doing the thing they're upset about!*

When I'm finished, I show them my respect with more Toddler-ese Fast-Food statements, "You say, 'No, no, NO!' YOU don't like that! YOU say, 'Don't touch me!' You say, 'Don't look!!' You're mad!!!" Then I retreat across the room with my head down to show my submission and apology. Finally, when the child has begun to calm down, I reassure him in more mature words and a happier voice, "Bye-bye! Bye-bye! It's all over, sweetheart. It's done, done, DONE! YEAAAA!!! You did a good job! Bye-bye! Bye-bye! You hold Mommy. I'll go far away."

> Jack, 20 months of age, reached for scissors that his
> mother, Ann, left on a table. When Ann snatched
> them away just in time, Jack burst into tears. Seeing
> his distress, she instantly wanted to tell him that
> scissors are dangerous, but she postponed the
> lecture and instead launched into a vigorous stream of
> Toddler-ese, saying, "You want . . . you want . . . you
> want it now, now, nowwwww!!!" Jack paused.

Ann continued, "You want. YOU want! But noooo! No, no scissors! No scissors, Jack. No scissors!!!!" Only when his tears slowed to a trickle did she offer an enthusiastic distraction. "Hey!! HEY!!!! LOOK!!!!!!!! Here! BIG truck, Jack! BIG truck!! Let's play . . . truck!"

If you're starting to feel like this is a strange way to speak, you're right! It's strange, but extremely effective! And, after you practice Toddler-ese a little, it will start feeling as natural as riding a bike. So don't give up! You're halfway there!

3. Correct Tone of Voice

> *"All the world's a stage."*
>
> —William Shakespeare, *As You Like It*

This next part of Toddler-ese requires you to be a little *dramatic*. A key part of the Fast-Food Rule is to mirror someone's feelings through your tone of voice. Of course, I don't recommend that you scream or shriek even if your toddler's doing it. Toddlers feel such intense emotion that you won't always want to build up to their level of intensity. But when your child is wailing, your voice should not be calm and measured . . . it should be emphatic!

The tone you choose carries your main message. When your toddler is upset, his brain may not recognize your words, but he will easily understand your tone and gestures. Unfortunately, parents often pick the wrong tone. Rather than reflecting their little Neanderthal's powerful emotions, they choose a soothing tone to try to nudge him into feeling better.

A parent who is good at Toddler-ese always starts by mirroring her child's level of intensity. She only softens her tone after he begins to calm.

Silvia tried speaking Toddler-ese to her frustrated three-year-old, but her singsong voice made Carla even madder! Silvia then realized that rather than honestly reflecting her daughter's feelings, she was parodying them. She was trying to make Carla laugh rather than make her feel heard and respected. Amazingly, as soon as she changed her tone to sincerely match her toddler's level of upset, Carla quieted in seconds!

Imagine that your 26-month-old toddler is in the sandbox howling because he tried to grab his friend's shovel, and she resisted and moved away. Describe what happened using a frustrated tone of voice that matches what your toddler feels. Say with heartfelt empathy and respect for his irritation, "You're mad. You're mad. Mad. Mad. MAD!!!! You want Susie's shovel. You say, 'Give me the shovel!! I WANT! I WANT! I want it NOOOOOW!!!!!!!!!!' "

Why Toddler-ese Works for Toddlers of All Ages

Is the Toddler-ese that is spoken to the youngest toddlers different from that used for the oldest? Yes and no. Certainly a calm three-year-old can handle longer sentences and less repetition than a one-year-old. However, the more upset a child gets, the more primitive he becomes. So during your child's meltdown, start by using the most simple-sounding Toddler-ese, no matter what the age of the child. Then as he calms, return to the more mature language he usually understands.

---

4. Facial Expressions and Body Gestures

"One picture is worth a thousand words."
—Fred Barnard, "Printer's Ink," 1927

If you feel like you're talking to your little toddler Cave-Kid until you're "blue in the face," it may be because you're making your words do all the work and forgetting to use your body language. Oops, big mistake! Just like your tone of voice, the gestures of your

Kids listen to our faces more than our words.

Make your tone and words consistent.

body and face carry more meaning than the string of syllables coming from your mouth. *For upset toddlers, a gesture is truly worth a thousand words.*

By one year of age, your child is already an expert at reading your face. Your grimaces, sighs, and clenched fists mean much more to him than your words. That's why you shouldn't smile when saying something serious to him. (Even if he's doing something cute.) Toddlers believe our nonverbal messages more than our words, so if you smile when you say something serious, your little one will "listen to your face" and ignore your request!

Practice using your face and body to show your interest and respect. Nod your head, lower your face with humility, and kneel or sit down so you're just *below* his level. Gently touch his arm or sit right next to him. Let your face show your empathy. It can be like a big billboard saying, "I know exactly how you feel!"

If you do accidentally smile, look away for a second to regain your composure. Even bite your lip hard if you have to. Then turn to face your child again and, if he's a young toddler, say, "No, no!" with a little low growl. (To learn more about growling, see Chapter 11.) If your toddler is older, say something like, "I know my face was smiling, but I'm *not* smiling inside."

> When one of my young patients is about to do something dangerous, like leaping off my exam table, I don't just say, "Be careful, don't do that!" I put on a horrified, alarmed look. Then I g-r-o-w-l my warning deep in my throat while I wag my index finger at him, knit my eyebrows together, shake my head no, and turn my face of alarm into a serious scowl.

Many toddlers cry and thrash when they're upset. How do you mirror that back in Toddler-ese? Well, I don't recommend you get down and kick and scream. You'll do fine if you passionately announce the words you think your irate little child might say if he could.

Here's how Terri, mother of a three-year-old Stone Ager named Billy, describes putting Toddler-ese to work in her home:

"Despite my initial embarrassment about looking silly, I have been using Toddler-ese to calm Billy's tantrums almost every day since I learned it six months ago. Now I've gotten so good at it that I can quell most major meltdowns in seconds.

"His tantrums usually follow this pattern: He starts to scream and cry at the top of his lungs. I jump in, almost matching his feelings with words and emotions. If I stop talking too soon, he starts crying again, and I restart the Toddler-ese. 'Billy is still mad, mad, MAD!!!! He's ANGRRRRRRRY!!!' Billy says, 'No, no, no . . . NO!!!' If he stops screaming and looks puzzled but remains calm, that's my signal to go to the next step and start distracting him or offering some solutions.

"Initially, his tantrums would last two to three minutes. Now Billy still needs two to three minutes of my attention when he's upset, but as soon as I start talking Toddler-ese, he usually stops the tantrum right away!"

Respect—Something More Precious than Jewels . . . or Toys!

Many parents ask me, why would an angry toddler calm down when you're not even giving him the thing he's fussing for?

Have you ever noticed that your child may cry nonstop to get a toy but toss it aside a few seconds after you finally give it to him? That's because he doesn't want the *thing* as much as he wants to be understood and responded to.

Throughout our lives, there will be thousands of *things* we desire—that we will not get. We can all live with that disappointment, but what we *cannot* live without is the respect of those we love!

Even when you can't give your child what he's screaming for, the respect and caring you show him by speaking to him in Toddler-ese will help him calm down.

It's the message of caring, attention, and love that you convey that's the true magic behind this simple technique. By translating the Fast-Food Rule into Toddler-ese, you should be able to quickly settle your upset toddler 80 to 90 percent of the time!

These steps may sound like a lot of effort, but with a little practice they actually *save* you a ton of time and aggravation.

Exceptions to the Rule—Sometimes Even Toddler-ese Can't Do the Job

When you do Toddler-ese correctly and it doesn't work quickly, it's usually because your child is tired, hungry, sick, bored, or stressed by some other special situation. (There's more about this in Chapter 11.)

If your child can't stop crying:

1. *Offer a hug.* He may need physical help to release his anger.
2. *Solve the problem if you can.* If you think your child is upset because of hunger, being overtired, or boredom, offer the appropriate solution (a snack, a back rub and rest, a different toy) while speaking Toddler-ese.
3. *Walk away for a minute.* Occasionally, you may have to respectfully leave for a minute to remove the "spotlight" and allow your child to calm down without an audience. (Some kids are too "proud" to give up their tantrum when they're being watched.) So, if a minute or two of Toddler-ese is not helping, you might change your approach and say, "You go ahead and cry, my angel. Mommy has to check something in the kitchen. I'll be right back—I love you." Return in thirty to sixty seconds, and try Toddler-ese and the Fast-Food Rule again to see if he's now ready to settle down. (Really tenacious toddlers may need you to repeat this technique three or four times before giving up their struggle.)

Toddlers have a sense of fairness. They think, *You give to me respect, and I will give it back.* So not only will your respectful communication make him feel better, but in turn he'll give you more respect too. Additionally, you'll build into your child's mind the image of the treatment he should expect from the people who love him. This lesson will serve him well later in life as he picks his long-term friends and companions.

Leslie's Story: Toddler-ese in Action

"Last night at a restaurant, Nathan, 15 months, pooped, and I had to take his flailing little body out to the car to get a fresh diaper on him. As he screamed in protest, I tried acknowledging his feelings: 'I know you don't want to leave the restaurant. I know you don't like it.' But he was so mad and squirmy that I couldn't even change him. I gave Toddler-ese a try. I made fists and started to beat the air, echoing what I thought was in his mind: 'You hate it. You hate it. You HATE it! YOU HATE IT!! You HATE being here with your pants down. It's COLD!!! And you hate it, hate it, HATE IT! You're mad, mad, MAD!!' I wasn't shouting but I showed him I really got his message.

"Then the coolest thing happened. He suddenly looked at me with a face that was half amused and half mischievous, and he started to play with the mobile hanging from the ceiling light. (I had earlier tried to get him to look at it, without success.) As I cleaned up the poop and put on a new diaper, I kept up a dramatic narration about what he was doing. He stayed happy, and then I sang a little song as I danced him back to the restaurant—feeling like a perfect parent!"

"But, Dr. Karp, I Sound Demented!"

> *Todd and Birgitte are the tender and loving parents of two-year-old Oona. They live part of the year in Denmark. A few months after explaining Toddler-ese to them, I asked Todd if he and Birgitte had had an opportunity to try it. He said, "Toddler-ese feels funny for us—almost like we're upset with her. The Danes don't like to go 'over the top' like that."*

Don't be surprised if you feel a bit uncomfortable—okay, a little *weird*—when you start using Toddler-ese—*wherever* you live. At first most parents hesitate to speak Toddler-ese in front of other people. "It's too *embarrassing!*" they tell me. "It feels *unnatural!*" (A few even feel shy rehearsing it in the privacy of their own bathroom—although practicing before a mirror is a great way to improve your technique.)

As I explained to Todd and Birgitte, speaking calmly is fine for gentle, mild-mannered toddlers. But reflecting a child's emotional intensity is usually necessary to help an upset child feel respected and heard. Certainly most parents feel quite comfortable applauding and jumping up and down to mirror their toddler's enthusiastic joy. Your animated response helps him know you approve of him and his feelings. Similarly, mirroring your toddler's upset feelings gives the message that you love him, even when he's angry.

Aside from feeling self-conscious, here are some other concerns parents occasionally bring up about Toddler-ese:

- *I feel like I'm teasing him.* The goal in Toddler-ese is to show love and respect. In the past, you may have seen people using mirroring to taunt or parody someone, but here it's being used as the opposite of teasing! It's the best way of acknowledging your frenzied little primitive child's feelings in an accurate and genuine way, so that he'll feel like you really get what he's "saying" to you.
- *It feels like I am encouraging bad behavior.* Reflecting his message does not give him permission to act badly. It

merely lets him know that you understand he has strong feelings about something. It helps him learn the important difference between feelings and actions. It teaches that angry feelings are allowed. (Bottled-up emotions can lead to loneliness, stress, and more tantrums!) But it also teaches that angry actions, like hitting, biting, scratching, saying hurtful words, are never allowed no matter how mad he feels. (More on this in Chapter 11.)

What if I disagree with his feelings? Just because you see his point of view doesn't mean you share it. Toddler-ese merely lets your child know you understand him and respect his right to have his own feelings. After he settles down, you can be as strict or permissive as you think is appropriate. But wait until later in the day when he is calm and receptive to teach him why you had a different view of the situation.

It feels like baby talk—like I'm "talking down" to my child. This speech style may sound juvenile, but hey—your toddler *is* a juvenile! And when he's upset, he slides even further down the evolutionary ladder. You will decide how to talk once the tantrum is over, but your toddler's behavior shows you how to begin!

It would be exhausting if I had to talk like that all day. Of course no parent speaks Toddler-ese 24/7. It's a tool to use only when your little one is having strong feelings (happy or sad). Toddler-ese may require a little more talking at first, but within days you'll actually be saving lots of time (and wrinkles and gray hairs).

Sometimes I don't know what I'm supposed to say. This is where the Fast-Food Rule comes to your rescue. You'll never make a mistake if you simply start by narrating what your toddler is doing, feeling, and saying. *First repeat his agenda, then you can state yours!*

Is it possible to be too respectful? Can your husband or wife be too respectful to you? I doubt it. Respect doesn't mean caving in or being wimpy. It's a sign of love, and that's something everybody needs.

"Learning Toddler-ese was simple. The real challenge was letting go of my self-consciousness to get the best results. I used to only use it at home, with no one around, but now if there's an audience—so be it. I figure I'm going to get the dreaded stranger looks when he cries anyway, so I might as well help my child!

"Of course, there have been rare occasions when nothing has worked (mostly when he's overtired). But in general the Fast-Food Rule falls into the category of 'the best advice I ever got.' Thanks!"

—Mari, mother of Aidan and Nate

The Fast-Food Rule, Continued: You Heard His Message—Now It's Your Turn!

"To every thing there is a season."

—Ecclesiastes 3:1

As you've discovered by now, you can't teach much to an upset toddler. Emotions and lessons mix as poorly as oil and water! Your little primitive isn't terribly logical or reasonable, even when he's happy. So when your tot is frustrated, don't teach, just reflect his feelings.

However, after you've used Toddler-ese to help him out of his emotional tangle, he will be able to listen—*a little*—to your message of reassurance and love. It's still best if you save your important teaching for later, when he's recovered from his tantrum. But as he's calming down, here are some great ways of helping him bounce back:

Be physical. See if he'd like you to hug him, rock him, or quietly sit next to him.

Offer options. "Would you like a big glass of apple juice or a magic back scratch?"

Teach other ways of showing emotion. Say "Show me with your face how mad you were!" or "Let's draw how mad you were!" or "Come on, let's punch pillows together!"

Teach words to express emotion. Tell him, "Wow! You were so mad, your blood was boiling!" or "You looked like you were scared. When I'm scared, my tummy sometimes feels like this [make a fist], and my heart goes *boom boom boom* like a drum."

Give him what he wants in fantasy. This is one of my favorite toddler tricks. Tell him you wish you could give him everything he wants and even more!

Use the power of a whisper. Whispering is a great, silly way to change the subject and be friends again.

Catch him being good. Comment on any little baby steps of cooperation you see. For a young toddler: "Hey . . . ball . . . ball . . . you have ball!!! GOOD! . . . Roll it to ME!" For an older toddler, say, "Good listening to my words—it was hard not touching. Let's go find your dollies and see if they're hungry!"

Share your feelings with "you-I" sentences. Once the dust settles, and it's your turn to talk, *very briefly* share your feelings using a "you-I" format. For example, make a big frown and shake your head, saying, "Mommy says, 'No, no!' When *you* pinch, *I* get mad, mad, MAD." That will help him to see things from your point of view.

Patty's Story: A Parental Triumph

"The Prehistoric Parenting model resonated with me and my husband. We'd already noticed the gradual transformation in our 26-month-old daughter from delightful to Neanderthal, replacing her coos with yelps of 'Me do!' and 'No!'

"One day, when I told her that her shower was over, she went ballistic! I love warm showers, so it was easy for me to sympathize. 'I know! I know! I KNOW!!!!' I said, jabbing my finger at the shower head. Using a serious but loving face with wide-open eyes and lots of nodding, I added, 'You want shower! You want shower! You WANT IT!!! You WANT IT!!!'

"Kira responded immediately! She stopped crying and looked at my face with a hopeful glance. I shared a few more 'you want its' with her, and then I said, 'You want to stay, stay, STAY!!! But, no, noooooo. I'm so sorry, sweetheart, we need to go, go, go and get dressed! And your dolly wants some yummy breakfast.' After a fake cry, she allowed me to dry and dress her, while I discussed the exciting plans for our day.

"Now when I try to dress Kira, and she shouts, 'No! Me do!' I am more apt to respond with understanding Toddler-ese. I say, 'Okay! You do! You do! You do! You do!!!! You want to do it yourself, right?' Kira typically smiles sweetly, with apparent relief, and says, 'Yes.' As she's struggling with her shirt, she puts up no resistance while I slide on her pants and socks! I feel like a genius!

"An unexpected gift that I've gotten from using Toddler-ese is that I actually feel closer to her. Now when Kira makes an impossible demand, my Neanderthal empathy magically makes her feel my love, and we enjoy a very special moment of connection."

9

**Respect and Rewards:
Ways to Encourage
Good Behavior**

*"You can catch more flies with honey than you can
with vinegar."*

—Old adage

Main Points:

- Six great ways to nurture kids and get cooperation.

- Respect: Share a power as nurturing as love. (Try It: Saving Face)

- Praise: Give your toddler a word hug. (Try It: Believable Praise)

- Side-Door Messages: Find the secret way into your toddler's mind. (Try It: Gossip, Fairy Tales, and Reverse Psychology)

- Confidence: Give the gift that keeps on giving. (Try It: Strength-Builders)

- Patience: Inch your toddler toward civilization. (Try It: Baby Steps)

- Rewards: Grease the wheels of cooperation. (Try It: The Hand Check and Star Charts)

Tools for a Loving Relationship

Now that you can speak Toddler-ese, you're ready to be the perfect *ambassador* to your prehistoric friend. Like all wise diplomats, sometimes you'll need to be tough, but fortunately you'll spend the bulk of your time nurturing your relationship and encouraging cooperation.

There are six basic "tools" that can make your job as a parent/ambassador a hundred times easier. These tools will help prevent blow-ups, increase self-confidence, and help you form a bond with your child that all your friends will want to copy!

The six tools are:

- *Showing respect.* Next to your love, it's what your toddler wants most.
- *Offering praise.* Praise helps you gently steer your child toward better behavior.
- *Talking through the secret "side door" of your child's mind.* Toddlers hate lectures, but they're all ears when it comes to things they overhear.
- *Boosting confidence.* Games to build your tot's confidence.
- *Encouraging patience.* Teaching your toddler how to wait—bit by bit.
- *Offering rewards.* Sometimes it's the perfect grease for the wheels of cooperation.

Now let me show you how these diplomatic tools will help you build love and cooperation between you and your pint-size Neanderthal so you can become the best ambassador on the block!

Respect: A Power as Nurturing as Love

"All I'm askin' is for a little respect."
—Otis Redding, "Respect"

Some parents think of respect as a modern, "airy-fairy" concept, but it's as old as mankind. Respect is the glue of all of our good relationships. Respect is not just important—it's essential. It says to your child, "You are valuable in my eyes. You matter." In fact, from the ancient past to the present, *disrespect* has been one of the main triggers for war and aggression.

What does respecting your toddler mean? Letting her do whatever she wants? Giving her an equal vote in the family? Of course not! Respecting her means giving her your genuine attention, valuing her opinion, and meeting her desires when they're reasonable.

As I mentioned earlier, your child can live quite happily without many of the *things* she craves, but what she can't be happy without is your love and respect.

How Do You Show Respect?

Here are a few of the many ways to show a toddler—or any person—your respect and interest:

Showing you care with actions:
- Smile, nod, make eye contact, and then look down for a few seconds.
- Sit, kneel, or lean so that your face is slightly below your child's level.
- Lean forward, in the direction of your little one.
- Listen with interest, and without interrupting.

Showing you care with words:
- Respond promptly.
- Repeat back. (See the Fast-Food Rule in Chapter 8.)
- Ask permission to give advice. Do this even with your young toddler. She may not understand your words, but she will understand your respectful tone of voice.

Try It: Saving Face—a Graceful Way Out

Saving face is an old term that means maintaining dignity. It's much like our modern warning not to shame your opponent by "rubbing his nose in it."

Top ambassadors want to help their defeated foes save face. It allows the enemy you're struggling with today to become your partner tomorrow (exactly what you're hoping for!). You'll win most of the time, so the least you can do is let your little child lose gracefully. Show her some mercy. Shame or loss of dignity only brings scars and the burning desire for revenge.

Here are some ways to let your toddler escape from the corner she's painted into—with her self-respect intact:

- *Use the Fast-Food Rule.* Listen with interest and repeat back—in Toddler-ese.
- *Give options.* Toddlers two and up feel respected when given a couple of options to choose from. For example, if whining is a problem, you might say, "Hillary says, 'Mommy . . . Mommy . . . listen, listen . . . Listen Now!!' I know you want Mommy to listen, sweetheart. So you can choose. Use your big-girl voice or your baby voice. But my ears won't listen to that yucky whining voice."
- *Let her win some little battles so she can let you win the others.* We're all willing to "win some and lose some," but no proud person wants to lose *all* the time. If you let your tot win some little battles (of your choosing), she'll be more likely to concede when a battle comes that you really want to win.
- *Meet her halfway.* Offering a fair compromise is not a sign of weakness. It shows your toddler you value her desires as well as your own. Very competitive toddlers often need you to give in a little more than halfway.
- *Don't mock or berate.* The worst thing you can do when your toddler whines is to make fun of her. It will either shrivel her self-confidence or make her dig in her heels and become even more defiant.

■ *Have a win-win mindset.* Just because you can win doesn't mean you should. You could easily dominate most struggles, but you're trying to win something much more important than a fight. Your real goal is to build a relationship of mutual love and respect that will last through a lifetime of pressures and conflicts. So even if you disagree with what your toddler wants, try to understand her point of view, and find a way you *both* can end up feeling like winners!

Respect: Real-Life Questions

What if my child fights the car seat? Is there a respectful way to put her in it?

Occasionally, for safety's sake, you'll need an iron fist inside your velvet glove. However, even when you're forcing your toddler—do it with respect! When you have to put your crying child into the car seat, use the Fast-Food Rule: "You say, 'No, no, NO!!' You say, 'No car, Daddy. No, no, NO!!!'" Wave your arms and sincerely shake your head no. Then say, "You hate it, hate it! You say, 'No, no, no, NO!!!' I'm so sorry, but Daddy has to put you in the seat." (Skip the lecture about highway safety for the moment.) "So you go ahead and scream, and in a minute Daddy's going to put on your singsong tape."

What do you mean by "let my toddler win some battles and she'll let me win some"?

Even our youngest toddlers have a natural understanding of the idea of give-and-take. You smile, and she smiles back. The same is true for settling power struggles. You can help her to avoid "hardening of the attitudes" if you let her win a few skirmishes.

For example, when I examine a worried 18-month-old, I often take five or six *boring* little toys out of my bag and offer them one by one. Most kids snub me. And as a child rejects each one, I say in Toddler-ese, "No, no, NO! You say, 'No, no, NO! Throw that away—NOW! I don't like you!'" Then I toss the toy down onto the exam table, mirroring the child's disdain. Finally, I offer a much more interesting toy. If she takes it (and most do at that point), I still say,

"No, NO! I'll take this toy, but I don't like you right now!" so that she knows I don't take her acceptance of a toy for granted. But it is a signal that I can start doing my exam and expect some cooperation.

What about when she's disrespectful and hits me? Should I spank her?
That's like thinking it's okay to bite a 15-month-old because he did it to you. You're the ambassador, the mature grown-up. You should expect her to be unreasonable and primitive. That's about the best she can do, but you can do better.

Spanking may make you a short-term victor, but it plants the seeds of long-term problems. (See Chapter 11 for more reasons not to spank.)

Praise: Giving Your Toddler Word Hugs

"A child is fed with milk and praise."
—Charles and Mary Lamb, *Poetry for Children*, 1809

No matter what shirt you're wearing, if people smile at you and genuinely compliment your taste, you're more likely to wear it again. We're social animals, and our brains (even the brains of toddlers) make us want to repeat whatever brings us compliments. That's why praising your toddler's efforts—"catching her being good"—is so effective at preventing problems.

Try It: Believable Praise

Here are three ways to use praise to boost your toddler's confidence and spirit:

1. **Give your toddler a balanced diet of big and small praise.**
   Praise is as nutritious as food, so naturally you'll want to *feed* it to your child many times a day. But using too much extravagant praise ("You're the best girl in the world!") is like

filling her with doughnuts—it's way too rich! Think of praise as a delicious, nourishing casserole. It's mostly made up of plain noodles, with a tasty handful of cheese for flavor, and a dash of some wonderful, exotic spice to finish it off. Likewise, your praise should mostly be made up of lots of attention, gentle smiles, quiet compliments, brief descriptions of her activity; a handful of stronger, bigger praise; and an occasional over-the-top celebration to spice up the mix.

A perfect example of the first kind of praise for a 24-month-old is for you to sit down, with an interested look on your face, and narrate her activity for thirty seconds: "Hmm, you're pushing the truck! Bang! Right into the teddy bear." Then give her a little compliment about how well she entertains herself, then you can go about your business while she happily continues to explore.

Note: An exception to my advice to use "big" praise in small doses is with younger toddlers (up to about two years of age). These little ones feel life so intensely that you

should supplement all your attention and understated praise with a generous amount of cheering and applause.

2. Compliment the action, not the child.

If you just baked a cake, would you rather be told "Wow! You're a fantastic cook!" or "Wow! That's tasty!"? They both sound good, but only the second is totally believable. We all know that baking one great cake doesn't make you a great cook. You may think I'm just being picky, but it's usually more accurate to praise the act rather than the actor. "You're such a big helper" may be true one minute but totally false later on when your child refuses to help. On the other hand, saying, "Wiping that spill really helped," is true forever—*and* it tells the child exactly the behavior you want to see more of, while boosting her self-esteem.

3. Never spoil the praise.

Some parents give praise, then immediately take it away. For example, they say, "Good girl! You ate all your peas. . . . Now, why did it take you so long?" Remember, praise is like food. Don't give it and then pull it out of your child's mouth just as she's savoring it. Parents who "praise-spoil" take all the fun out of being complimented and teach their child to be mistrusting of praise from others.

Praise for the Ages and Stages
Your child's evolutionary stage influences the way you should offer praise.

- *Charming Chimp-Children and Knee-High Neanderthals* (12 to 24 months) see themselves as the center of the world. After doing a little trick, they swivel their head to see if you're watching. It's as if they're proudly saying, "Look! See what I did! Isn't it great?" These prehistoric party animals love enthusiastic praise like applause and big grins. (Many, like 18-month-old Alex, even clap for themselves when they do something they're proud of!)

Don't flood your toddler with too many words. Keep your praise short and sweet, but accompany it with generous dollops of loving body and facial gestures, and a happy tone of voice.

■ *Clever Cave-Kids* (24 to 36 months) love applause but do best on a diet balanced toward understated praise. When praise is wildly enthusiastic, these kids start taking it for granted. Lovingly watching your child, smiles, head nods, and saying, "Hmmm . . . I like that," are perfectly satisfying little morsels. For fun, sometimes try whispering your praise. After two, your toddler knows that this change in tone means what's being said is extraspecial.

■ *Versatile Villagers* (36 to 48 months) are much more interested in your responses and feelings. Your toddler will love hearing, "Thanks for carrying that heavy box. It really helped me." Around her third birthday, when she starts comparing things all the time, it will be fun for her to be told, "You did that *super*fast! As fast as a tiger!" But telling her over and over, "You're the fastest little girl in the world," soon becomes unbelievable, even to a toddler.

A Dozen Little Word Hugs That Speak for Themselves

Here are twelve easy ways to praise your child without saying any words at all:

■ Silently watch—with interest.
■ Smile.
■ Nod.
■ Give a hug.
■ Tousle her hair.
■ Pat her on the back.
■ Raise your eyebrows in pleasant surprise.
■ Give a thumbs-up sign.
■ Say "Hmmm" and "Wow" and "Uh-huh."
■ Wink.
■ Shake hands or "high-five."
■ Tape her drawings on the wall.

Praise: Real-Life Questions

What if my two-year-old is doing so many things wrong that I can't praise her?

Your praise is not only a reward for good behavior, it's also a powerful tool for encouraging your child to do more of the things you want. Here's a way to start finding little actions you can encourage:

Think about a goal you would like your child to achieve, such as not fighting with her sister. Break it down into little steps she'd need to reach that goal: (1) play quietly; (2) entertain herself; (3) share more; and (4) use her words when she's angry.

Now take a step back, put on your ambassador's hat, and try to catch your toddler accomplishing the first of these baby steps. As soon as you see her playing quietly, give her a thirty-second reward of your attention. If she starts to squabble, come in and with a sour face growl, "Grrrrh!!! No! No fight . . . NO fight!!" Then ignore her briefly. As soon as she's playing quietly again, return and give her a little more attention. Try to give tidbits of attention several times an hour. It won't take long to see the difference. Once she's doing well with the first step, start paying a little less attention to that step and start focusing on the next baby step you've decided on (in this case, entertaining herself).

Will praising my child make up for all the critical things I say when I'm angry?

It will help, but it takes an awful lot of praise to make up for harsh words. As nurturing as praise is, criticism is much more destructive. According to Karp's Law of Praise: *It takes five words of praise to cancel one single word of criticism.* But don't try to overcompensate with extravagant compliments. After a person has been criticized, the only words of praise that are really credible are little loving comments about small accomplishments.

Side-Door Messages: The Secret Way into Your Toddler's Mind

"You never know till you try to reach them how accessible men are; but you must approach each man by the right door."

—Henry Ward Beecher, abolitionist (1813–1887)

Here's a curious fact of human nature: We believe the things we accidentally overhear more than the things we are told to our face! For example, if your friend says, "You look beautiful today," there's a good chance you'll think she's just being polite. However, if you overhear her telling *someone else* how good you look, you'll probably think it's her honest opinion. Even toddlers (over 18 months) pay more attention to what they overhear us say than to what we say directly to them.

Our focus on what we overhear reminds me of the side door of the house where I grew up. My parents locked the front door, but they always kept the side door open to let the kids run in and out. Well, in a way, we're all like that house. We often stand guard at the "front door" rejecting compliments as being excessive or insincere. Yet our "side door" happily lets in messages that we just happen to overhear.

There are three easy ways to foster good behavior by sending messages through the secret side door into your child's mind:

1. Gossiping—saying something that you intentionally wanted to be overheard.

2. Telling fairy tales—wrapping a message to your child in the disguise of a story.

3. Using reverse psychology—encouraging cooperation by telling your defiant child to do the opposite of what you truly want her to do.

Try It: Gossip ("Psst . . . hey—hey, teddy bear, let me tell you the great stuff that Lauren did today!")

You know how we spell words so that we can say things without our children understanding us? Gossip is the flip side of that technique. It means speaking our opinions in a whisper to make our children pay *more* attention to them.

Amazingly, the more we think we're not supposed to hear a message, the more interested we are in listening to it and the more we believe what's said. (This is true for toddlers, adults—even national governments!)

Here's how to do it:

With your toddler close by, loudly whisper some praise about her to someone else (your spouse, a bird, her teddy bear, Grandma, or pretend you're talking to someone on the phone). *Don't look at your child when you do this.* Gossiping only works if you seem to be telling a secret that you don't want her to hear. Begin with a loud whisper to get her attention, but as soon as you notice her getting quiet and starting to eavesdrop, lower your voice and cup your hand alongside your mouth—*like you're telling someone a secret.* (For older toddlers, an extra trick is to make some mumbling sounds during your gossiping to make it sound like there are some words you're saying she can't quite hear. It's fun and it adds to the appearance that this is an important secret.)

Later in the day repeat the same compliment, but this time say it directly to her. She will think, *Wow, that* must *be true. I'm hearing it a lot lately.*

Gossiping starts being effective at 18 to 24 months. That's when toddlers begin to understand the rule that people whisper when they're saying something important!

Gossip for All Ages and Stages

Here are some ways to use gossip that work great with toddlers:

■ *Compliment something your toddler has done.* Whisper to your pet parrot, "Hey! Psst—hey, Mr. Birdie! Yes, Selma ate *all* her peas. I said, 'Good, peas, good peas, good girl.'

Hey . . . Mr. Birdie, pssst—then, Selma said, 'Thank you.' I really like it when she says, 'Thank you, Mommy.' It makes me happy!" Even at two years of age, this type of gossiping works! Your little child may not understand all your words, but she'll understand from your tone of voice that you value her!

- *Teach specific lessons.* Let's say two-year-old Helen is afraid of a dog. Rather than telling her, "Don't be afraid, it's a nice doggie," let her overhear you suggesting another approach to her teddy bear. "Yeah, Teddy, Helen was scared. She said, 'Home, Mommy!' But then I showed her how to be brave, and I said, 'Go away, you doggie, and don't be mean! You have to play nice with little girls!' Then I hugged Helen because I love her soooo much!!!"

- *Pretend you need help.* Three-year-old Isabella usually ignored her mother's pleas for help. She acted like she was deaf. But when Joyce went into the next room and whispered loudly, "Oh, I wish—I wish someone would help me pick up all these toys," Isabella came right over to pitch in!

Gossip and Imaginary Friends

Some toddlers develop imaginary friends—it's a great way to have a playmate anytime they want, while also practicing their social skills. You may hear your child reveal many thoughts during chats with her imaginary friends: "Mommy is mean! She says no more TV!". And in a similar way, you can send important messages via your child's side door—by talking to her phantom buddies: "Zookers, if you and Susie get your shoes on quickly, you can both come with me to the store." A warning: Some toddlers don't want you to talk to their imaginary buddies. They'll warn, "She's MY friend! Don't talk!"

One day Louise brought three-year-old, Turner, to see me for a sore throat. He wasn't crying, but he was ignoring me. Rather than get into a battle by asking

> him to open his mouth, I decided to use some gossip. I
> leaned forward and loudly whispered to Louise, "I
> really like it when Turner opens his mouth and shows
> me his big lion teeth."
>
> As I said it, I held my cupped hand close to my
> mouth, like I was telling a secret. I moved my cupped
> hand a little to allow him to see me opening my mouth
> and sticking out my tongue so he knew exactly what I
> was talking about. Although I never looked at him,
> like magic, when I turned on my light a few seconds
> later, Turner immediately opened wide!

You can also use a favorite toy as an "accomplice" in your side-door dialogue. Jack's dad, Keith, often calls Magic Bunny for advice. He says, "Wait, Jack, let me ask Magic Bunny." Then he turns away from his son and says in a loud whisper, "Hi, Magic Bunny, please, please, PLEASE help. Should Jack wash his hands before we eat?" Then Keith puts his ear near the bunny's pink felt lips, straining to hear the toy's "response." "WHAT??? What did you say? Oh, sure . . . Okay . . . He should wash his hands first?"

Jack watches, fascinated by the conversation, and Keith, nodding his head in agreement, continues, "But can he do it fast? He wants to eat NOW? Okay, okay, Magic Bunny, I'll tell him. Thanks!!! I love you!!" Then Keith turns to his son to relay the message. "Hey, Jack, I just spoke to Magic Bunny. He said he wants you to wash your hands SUPER fast and then give me five really hard!"

This routine takes an extra minute, but it helps keep things light and positive. Keith's little trick prevents struggles that used to last half an hour and ruin the whole day.

Try It: Fairy Tales ("Once upon a time there was a little boy . . .")

Classic stories like "Little Red Riding Hood" were first told around campfires in ancient times both to entertain children and to teach them important lessons, like not talking to "wolves" they don't know. The long-standing popularity of these fables testifies to their effectiveness! Like gossip, fairy tales are great for teaching toddlers over two through the secret side door of their minds.

These little stories exercise both halves of your child's developing brain at the same time. The left side learns language and an entertaining story while the right brain learns how she is supposed to behave.

Part of the elegant success of telling fairy tales is that your prehistoric friend won't even realize she's being taught. Like planted seeds, the lessons you weave into your stories will gently grow in her mind and help her begin to understand right and wrong.

Fairy tales typically have three parts:

- The Beginning. This part engages your child's mind by describing all the senses. Tell what the little froggie princess sees, smells, is wearing, is singing, ate for breakfast, how the sun feels on her face, what interesting things she sees on her walk to school, and so on. The beginning is important because it entrances your toddler. By the time you get to the next part, she'll feel so warm, snuggly, and safe that her mind's side door will swing *wide* open.
- The Middle. This is where you bring up the lesson you want to teach. For example, what happened when the little froggie didn't take turns or wouldn't wash her hair or hit her baby brother.
- The Happy Ending. Finishing your story with a happy ending is like wrapping your story up in a bow. It's very satisfying to your toddler's sense of order and security to know that the story always ends with the frog princess returning home to hugs, kisses, and her favorite game or food, and that she lives "happily ever after."

I encourage you to make up your own little fairy tales specifically tailored to the lessons you want your child to learn. Here are some more tips for doing that:

- Make the main characters happy little animals, like Steven the Mouse or Mimi the Moose.
- Avoid using little kids in your stories. They can make things seem a bit too real and scary.
- Use your voice dramatically: Raise it or whisper when you want to get your child's attention or to help her remember the story.
- Add little helper characters, such as angels, fairies, a talking toad, or a friendly tree that is always coming to the hero's rescue.
- Include a grumbly, bumbly, mean animal that always gets caught. (Your toddler's world is filled with things that are both joyous and scary.)

After a while you may find that your child wants to hear the exploits of the characters you're created over and over until they become sweet childhood memories!

> Three-year-old Gracie loves to hear her daddy tell her stories about Belle the Bear and her brother Bill who lived in a house far away in a place called Happyland. For Gracie, they're as "famous" as the Three Little Pigs or Sleeping Beauty!

Try It: Reverse Psychology ("Don't brush your teeth!")

> Nicola, a spirited little three-year-old, delighted in lifting up her dress. Of course, she loved doing it because it drove her parents crazy. At first they just said, "Please don't do that, sweetheart." But they had grins on their faces because she was so cute. Soon she was performing nonstop in front of Grandma, the old lady next door, and the grocery clerk. Those people laughed, too, which made her do it even more.
> Her parents tried everything to get her to stop, from reasoning with her to time-outs, but nothing

helped. Finally, they radically changed their approach. Instead of snapping "No!" they started saying in a serious voice, "Do it more! More! Higher! Keep it up! Don't lower your hands!" Within a week, Nicola's burlesque show closed down for good. She had only been lifting her skirt to show off her independence; once her parents made it into something they wanted her to do better, she lost interest in the game.

From 18 months on, our little Neanderthals love to defy us. It makes them feel powerful and allows them to show off their inde-

pendence. Making tendency to work in your favor is what's commonly called using "reverse psychology." (It used to be referred to as "child psychology.")

Of course, no technique works every time, but for strong-willed toddlers, reverse psychology is often fun and effective. It allows "macho" little boys (and girls) to cooperate while still feeling like they're saving face and retaining their self-respect.

I think of it as a side-door message because while kids are so busy rejecting the obvious request, the hidden request kind of sneaks in past their guard. The beauty of reverse psychology is that it allows toddlers to simultaneously assert their defiance *and* do the things we want them to do. Everybody wins!

Here are some fun reverse psychology techniques to try with your toddler:

- **Appeal to her feelings of "Mine!"** At the end of her two-year checkup, Mia wanted to take one of my toys home with her. I told her how sad I would be without my toy, but she was not budging. So I said, "Okay, no problem. You can take the toy." Then I scooped up all her clothes and said, "And I'll take your shoes, socks, shirt, and pants! Okay?" She immediately frowned and reached out for her clothes. I reached for my toy—and we made a simultaneous exchange like a spy swap at the Berlin Wall.
- **Don't do it!** Order your child not to eat something that's good for her. Plead, "No. NO! Don't eat your apple! Please. Pleeease!" while your child happily defies you. Or pretend you don't want her affection. Say, "Don't hug me! No, no! Don't do it!" and turn away, cringing in mock fear and saying, "Yucky!" as she plants hugs and kisses all over you.

Thirty-eight-month-old Mason was b-o-r-e-d sitting there while I was examining his sister. He suddenly decided he had had enough and said, "I'm gonna poke you in the eye." I replied in a begging tone of voice, "Well, just don't poke me in the leg. Please, please—not my leg! No, no—NO!!!" He gave a mischievous little grin and then, of course, proceeded to poke my leg like a pincushion as I strenuously "protested."

If your toddler respects your command and doesn't disobey you, toss her a little praise—"Good listening"—then switch tactics (like offering options or a reward, etc.).

■ **Gossip to stuffed animals and imaginary friends about what she won't do.** If your child refuses to put on her shoes, pretend one of her dolls is the Shoe Monster who wants to eat her shoes. The doll says, "Don't put them on—don't put them on—I want to eat them . . . give them to ME . . . NOOOOW!!!" When this trick works, she'll have her shoes on in one minute flat.

> *Jessica often refused to do what her mom, Tricia, asked her to do. But Tricia found that if she told Jessica's imaginary friend, Nana Mouse, that Jessica was too little to be able to do something—her daughter would hop right to it to prove her mom wrong!*

> *Arturo would pick up his toddler's precious lovey and say, "Mr. Puppy, will you please help me? Do you know how to eat carrots? My son Jason doesn't know how, he's still a baby."*

■ **Opposite Day.** Announce to your three-year-old that it's Opposite Day! Tell her that for an hour she has to do everything opposite of what you say. Of course, you can set a timer, so it's really only ten minutes. This is fun and gives your child an acceptable way to be defiant, and it teaches her to really listen to you. Make up a little song or give a small treat to mark the end of it.

"Nothing can be done without hope and confidence."

—Helen Keller

Let's face it, toddlers have it rough. They're small, clumsy, and slow. No wonder they fight us so hard—they just want to win occasionally! However, you can give your tyke little confidence boosters to help her feel strong without having to resist you.

> *Twenty-two-month-old Alice has a little game with her dad, Pat. Whenever she blows on him, he falls over like a feather—and she howls with laughter.*

> *Milo loves to tickle Grandpa, who hoots and wriggles while his grandson merrily tickles away. Grandpa had an off switch, so Milo couldn't keep tickling him for hours. (He turned off his tickle spot by twisting his nose.)*

My favorite confidence-building tactics harness both seriousness and silliness. I call the serious ones "Strength-Builders," the silly ones "Playing the Boob."

Try It: Strength-Builders

Here are some great ways to pump up your little one's self-confidence, so she'll feel stronger and less in need of acting defiant.

- **Ask for her help.** Requesting help really boosts your toddler's self-respect! Make her feel strong by saying, "This is kind of heavy. Can you help Mommy?" Or say, "This *may* be too hard, but can you help me . . ." (Use this one about something you know that she can do, and she will beam with pride when she shows you her ability!!)

- **Offer consistent, speedy responses.** Paying attention to your toddler's needs and promptly responding to them gives her the sense that you understand her and respect her opinions. She will love having you guys (the "king and queen" of the house) giving her the royal treatment!
- **Hand over a little decision-making power.** "Do you want to drink from the blue cup or the red one?" There are so many decisions to make every day; it's only fair to let your child make some of them. If you respect her choice on a handful of less important issues, she'll be more likely to give in when it comes to an issue that really matters to you. Simple choices limited to just two or three options are better than wide-open ones, which can overwhelm a toddler.

Giving Your Toddler Her Choice

You can try offering your one-year-old options, but children at this age aren't known for being great decision-makers.

Your two-year-old will love being given a choice. Offer her either/or options in a clear and enthusiastic voice. (More than two options may make her confused or frustrated.)

When offering choices to your three-year-old, act like you are slightly confused and need her opinion. "Hey, what do you think would be best: the red plate or the blue one?" To make it really fun, act like an absentminded professor. A few seconds after she says, "The blue one," ask, "Huh? What? I'm so sorry. Did you say the red one?" (This also gives your toddler a chance to review her decisions and learn to be a little less impulsive.)

Note: Never give your child a choice if you really don't want to live with her answer. For example, at the doctor's office, don't ask, "Is it okay for the nurse to take your temperature?" If she says no, the nurse will be forced to either not do her job, disregard your child's wishes, or waste a lot of time trying to get her to change her mind.

Try It: Playing the Boob,
or How Wacky Bloopers Work Wonders

Even the most defiant toddler usually has pity on us if we seem like total incompetents. Playing the Boob will convince your child that you're so lame, you should be helped, not resisted. Of course, older toddlers are in on the joke—they know you're not usually this ridiculously inept, but they still have fun. They just love the silliness. Use this fantastic technique to turn power struggles with your toddler into laughs and cooperation!

Here's a gaggle of fun ways to boost any toddler's confidence:

- **Be incompetent.** Wear your shirt backward, put your hat on upside down, make mistakes counting to five, place a toy down right on the edge of a table or chair, and when it falls, loudly say, "Uh-oh . . . UH-OH! No, no, NO! Don't fall!!" Repeat this scene three or four times, each time pretending to be more careful. (As I let go, I say to the toy in a commanding voice, "Now, you stay there!! Okay?")
- **Be clumsy.** Keep falling off your chair or bobbling the ball when you play catch.
- **Be blind.** Ask, "Where is the . . . ?" when the thing is right in front of you. When the child gleefully points it out, keep playing the boob. Look around, saying, "Where? Where? I don't see it."
- **Be weak.** Try hard to catch her, but let her wriggle away every time. Try to yank a toy from her but let her win the tug-of-war.
- **Be easily hurt.** Two-year-olds love to "give you five" and then watch you hop and howl in mock-pain, "Ow! Ow!" while blowing on your hand to take away the sting! With a three-year-old, say, "Gimme five," but then pull your hand away, saying, "I'm afraid. Are you gonna do it hard?" If she then gives you a gentle high-five, thank her for being so nice. If she whacks you anyway, hop and yelp, protesting, "You tricked me! You *tricked* me!"

- **Be a baby.** Reach for something your young toddler has, whine like a baby, and say, "Mine, mine!" Let her easily evade your grasp and defy your pitiful request.
- **Be wrong.** Say, "Hey, wait a second! Your name isn't Kris. You're Daddy! You're Daddy!" Your child will laugh, saying, "No, I'm Kris! You're silly!"
- **Be easily outwitted.** Tell your child you need to see if her hands are clean, but inspect her foot instead. Then say, "HEY! You're tricking me!! That's not your hand!" Now demand, "Give me your HAND!" But start looking in her pockets.
- **Be arrogantly incorrect.** Proudly sing the wrong lyrics to a song. "Happy *elephant* to you!" Your toddler will love to correct you, but act like she's wrong and say, "I did not say *elephant*." Then sing the song with the wrong words again and say defensively, "I didn't make a mistake. I am the best singer—IN THE WORLD!!!"
- **Be a pushover.** When she's upset, suggest several dumb choices that she can say "No!" to, such as "Would you like some delicious mud?" Spend a few seconds "begging" her to change her mind. Then say, "Okay, you win! You never do what *I* want!" Allowing your child to reject you is an old ambassador's trick to help her save face. After she turns down a bunch of your offers, your tot will feel more respected, and she'll have an easier time giving in to you on other issues.
- **Be absurd.** Say in a goofy voice, "Please eat your shoe!! Please—PLEASE!! I command you to eat it!! Okay, you win, but it's not *FAIR!* You always win. I NEVER get to win!!!" (I wouldn't use this approach if you have a soft-hearted child, but if you have a competitive little Stone Ager, you'll get a grin a mile long!)
- **Be forgetful.** Take your child's shoe, reach out for her foot, and say, "Give me your . . . ummm, uh," as if you can't remember the word *foot*. Repeat your unfinished statement over and over. In a few seconds, your toddler will lift up her foot or even finish your sentence for you! It will make her feel smart!

Is It a Bad Idea to Make Your Toddler Think You Are a Boob?

Of course, your child doesn't really think you're a boob. After all, most of the time you're smart and strong. This is just a fun tactic—not a full-time style of parenting! Playing the Boob is exactly like wrestling and letting your child win or playing hide-and-seek and pretending you can't find her. It's merely a form of flattery—one of the most basic and ancient tools of diplomacy!

One of the bittersweet realizations of parenting is that much of what you do every day is geared toward preparing your small child to leave you. You're readying her for that day by helping her become a strong, confident, independent person. That's why one of your most important jobs is to nurture her feelings of self-esteem.

So don't worry about losing her respect. You won't! In fact, acting a bit like a boob will actually teach her the valuable life lesson that even the most perfect people (her parents) sometimes make mistakes!

Encouraging Patience: Moving Your Toddler Toward Civilization an Inch at a Time

"A journey of a thousand miles begins with a single baby step."

—Adapted from a Chinese proverb

In the 1920s Andrew Carnegie was one of the richest men in the world. When asked how he got so wealthy, he said that success was like going into a gold mine. "At first when you go in, all you see is dirt. Then if you're lucky, you find a tiny piece of gold." He said that if a person could simply look past the dirt and stay focused on the flecks of gold, he'd eventually end up with pockets stuffed with treasure!

Teaching your toddler patience is a lot like prospecting for gold. Treasure every gleaming little nugget of patience you find. Encourage your toddler's baby steps of progress with many bits of attention and praise, and soon she will learn to share, take turns—and wait patiently for you to leave the bathroom or get off the phone!

Try It: Baby Steps, a Way to Teach Patience

Patience is like a muscle—it gets stronger with exercise. There are many ways to build up the power of your toddler's patience muscle. Here's one approach:

When your one-year-old whines for your attention, look at her, clap your hands three times to get *her* attention, and then say, "Wait!!" Then briefly look away, as though you're ignoring her. While looking away, hold up one hand and indicate with your fingers as you count out loud: "One . . . two . . . three . . ." Then immediately look back and pay attention to her for a minute. When you promptly reward her with attention for her patience, she'll grow up knowing, "My mommy always keeps her word!"

With children over age two, you can use a timer instead of counting. First explain what you're doing: "You're so good at waiting. When Mommy says, 'Wait!' I want you to wait until Mr. Dinger [show her the timer] says 'Ding!'" Let her hear what the timer sounds like. "Then we can play! Okay?"

Initially, just set the timer for ten seconds. When it rings, go to her and play for a few minutes. Later that day do the exercise again, but this time set it for thirty seconds. Suggest that your child play with a toy or look at a book. Ignore her even if she tries to interrupt you before the dinger sounds. Then immediately reward her with some play time to show her you appreciate her efforts.

Over the next few weeks practice this every day. (Sometimes surprise her by giving the reward even before the dinger goes off.) Your toddler will learn, "Wow, that minute goes by pretty fast. It's not so hard to wait." Within a month or two a toddler can learn to quietly entertain herself for three to five minutes. At bedtime remind her of what a good job she did waiting for you that day.

If your child has trouble waiting, talk to her about how hard waiting is. Say, "I wish we could do that right NOW!!" or "Wait, wait—yuck! I wish we just could play *all* day and NEVER have to wait!!" Then suggest some things for her to do while she waits: play with toys, draw a picture, give her dolls a pretend meal or bath, and so on.

If all else fails, try this: "Here's half a treat. I'll give you the other half when Mr. Dinger rings."

Parents Need Patience Too . . .

Even though it may take your toddler five minutes to do something that takes you five seconds—wait! Let her struggle a little. Before you know it, toddlerhood will be gone, and you will wish you could see her little like this just once more!

Put your hands in your pockets, seal your lips, take some slow deep breaths, and wait. Watch her lovingly, but don't hover. If she gets frustrated, of course offer help. If she does it on her own, even a little one-year-old will beam with pride as if to say, "YEA! I did it!"

Patience in Action: Baby Steps for Baby Teeth

You can use baby steps to sidestep struggles with your child over diaper changes, ear cleaning, nail clipping, and tooth brushing.

At first your primitive little toddler may let you put a toothbrush in her mouth for only a few seconds. That's okay—it's a good baby step of progress. Say, "Yea! All done. Gimme five! Let's go play!"

I know you can't do a great cleaning job in a few seconds, but gradually she'll let you do more. Why? Because you're not making a big deal out of it, and you're rewarding her cooperation with a dollop of fun afterward.

If she won't let you even put the toothbrush in her mouth, don't fight. This is a battle you can't win. Instead, try using a playful system of distraction. Say, "Okay, let's brush your knee. Okay, now the other knee. Okay, let's brush this arm and that arm and those fingers and these fingers, thumb, other thumb, hair, ear, other ear!" Momentarily touch the brush to each place named. Then shout, "Yea! All done! Good job! Go play!" Do this a few times a day to help your child to relax and start lowering her defenses. Eventually, you'll work up to brushing her teeth for a few seconds—and then gradually a bit longer.

Offering Rewards: Greasing the Wheels of Cooperation

"A spoonful of sugar helps the medicine go down."

—Julie Andrews in *Mary Poppins*

Many people don't like the idea of giving toddlers rewards. They feel children ought to do the right thing because it's *the right thing* to do or because "I said so!" But expecting your toddler to cooperate out of respect is like teaching table manners to a six-month-old—it's the right idea at the wrong time!

Think about it: Even adults are more cooperative when we're given an incentive. Why shouldn't we expect the same from our primitive little kids? Tangible rewards often help toddlers behave. That's why experienced parental "ambassadors" often grease the wheels of cooperation with little bonuses to get the family diplomacy moving.

By reward, I don't mean a shopping spree at the local Toys "R" Us! The number-one reward your child will love—is *you!* She'll love an extra five minutes of roughhousing, a tea party, insect hunting, a massage, storytelling, or a walk to the store with you. Of course, she'll also enjoy small material rewards, such as tattoos, stickers, cookies, and candy.

Wait! Did he just say cookies and candy? Many parents worry that using animal crackers or jelly beans as treats will make their toddler obese or crave candy. They won't—not if they're used in the right way. Sweets are a powerful reward for many toddlers (there are many healthy sweets). Save sweets for when you need to be really persuasive. Then plan on phasing them out after a few weeks. For example, if diaper changes are a problem because your toddler no longer lies still, let her stand and eat a special "diaper cookie"—a cookie she gets to eat only while you're changing her. (If she wolfs down the cookie and then starts to fight again, you may have to give her half the cookie during the change and hold on to the other half until after the fresh diaper is on.)

Aside from sweets, the more tangible and interesting-looking the reward, the more your toddler will value it. That's why colorful stickers, tattoos, and even Band-Aids are perennial favorites for toddlers of all ages.

Here are two other great methods you can try:

Try It: The Hand Check

Child development specialist Dr. Barbara Howard suggests parents reward a toddler by giving her a little check on the back of her hand every time they catch her doing a good thing during the day. What could be easier? Remember, just like ancient cavemen, toddlers love body decoration!

At bedtime, your child will love it if you take a few minutes to look at each pen mark with her and remind her what each one was for.

Try It: Star Charts

A Star Chart is a more formal way of rewarding good behavior in an older toddler (around age three). Pick three behaviors you would like to encourage. Choose two that are pretty easy for your child to accomplish (like washing hands, putting on socks) and one that's a challenge for her (like eating a tiny piece of broccoli, picking up her toys in five minutes, or brushing her teeth). *Note:* Avoid vague, hard-to-measure goals like "less fighting."

Next, make the chart together. Take your child on a trip to the store to pick out the stars or stickers you're going to use. Look through magazines together, and choose some interesting pictures you can cut out and use to decorate the chart. All this makes your child more invested in the process—it's *her* chart.

Every time your child succeeds at one of the goals, let her place a star on the chart.

Star Charts are fun for toddlers because they are such visual people. Your child will get a dose of "visual praise" every time she walks by and sees the stars of her success prominently displayed in the kitchen or her bedroom. Reinforce your appreciation for her hard work by letting her overhear you gossiping about it to her dolls.

(Most parents who use Star Charts keep them up for several weeks and then either redesign them to reward new behaviors or phase them out once the behaviors have improved.)

10

Time-in

How Routine and Play
Can Soothe Your
Prehistoric Pal

"Nothing is stronger than habit."

—Ovid, *The Art of Love*, 1 B.C.

Main Points:

- Time-in is the pleasurable time that you spend each day with your toddler.

- Daily routines and play are proof to your child of your love and make him want to cooperate.

- Toddlers love soothing routines: massage, loveys, Special Time, affirmations, and breathing exercises.

- Build fun into every single day, especially outdoor play, creative play, and reading.

You've probably heard of time-outs even if you've never yet used one. Time-out is a discipline technique where your child is put in isolation for a minute or two to deprive him of your attention and smiling face. It works because time with you is one of your toddler's favorite things. That's why many people call the happy time we spend with our little ones *"time-in."*

Time-in is any time you spend paying loving attention to your toddler, whether you're helping him get dressed each morning, playing with him in the afternoon, talking to him at mealtimes, or giving him a quick after-bath before-bedtime massage. Time-ins teach your toddler love, confidence, and trust in himself—and you.

Time-ins are also a great way to increase cooperation. Giving your tot lots of short time-ins throughout the day prevents conflicts the same way dropping coins into a parking meter throughout the day assures you'll never get a ticket.

Wow! you may be wondering. *Can playing catch and a quick little nightly massage really head off conflicts?*

Yes! Even your young toddler understands that the more you play with him and give him attention, the more cooperation he owes you. In essence, routines and recreation build up a wealth of goodwill with your child. (Tough little 18-month-olds often take—and take—and still pressure you for more, but even these pint-sized Neanderthals

become agreeable if you dole out little tidbits of time-in to them all day long.)

We've all seen little kids who whine, hit, and totally disregard their parents' words. Some act this way because their parents lack good parenting techniques. Others, however, are just spirited little Stone Agers who hate being cooped up all day! In the final analysis, regardless of the reason your child is misbehaving, there are only two forces that have the power to turn their challenges into cooperation: intimidation or love.

Many parents mistakenly believe that intimidation is the only remedy for bad behavior. Sure, we all need to be strict from time to time. (I'll discuss that in the next chapter.) But the best, most lasting way to convert a wild child into the happiest toddler on the block is to nurture him with love, respect, consistency, and play! That's why time-ins are so important.

Routines—Predictable Time-ins That Make Kids Feel Safe

Sometimes parents worry about becoming slaves to routine. Doing the same thing over and over may be boring to us, but to toddlers, predictable routines are as satisfying as milk and sunshine. Here's why:

■ *Routines are refreshing little pauses during your child's busy day.* Your child may love new toys and places to explore, but after a while too many changes may make him unravel. Stimulation is exciting, but familiarity is cozy and comforting. In a day filled with novelty, routines provide your tiny adventurer with a little dose of predictability to give him a chance to catch his breath.

■ *Routines boost your child's feeling of understanding and belonging.* Your toddler often feels surrounded by things beyond his control and words that everyone seems to understand but him. No wonder he sometimes feels frustrated and left out. (If you've ever visited a country where you didn't speak the language, you pretty much know what that's like.) Routines, however, are a breeze to understand because they are so familiar. They give your child the same chance to know what's going on and what's coming up as anyone else in the family! They level the playing field.

■ *Routines help your toddler tell "time."* Imagine you worked in an office that had no clocks or windows. It would be disorienting. (This is exactly what Las Vegas casinos do to keep you from realizing how much time you've spent gambling.) Routines help your toddler keep track of time and bring some predictability to the daily chaos: "After I wake up, I get dressed and eat breakfast. After lunch, I take a nap," and so forth. They're like your toddler's wristwatch.

The Same—But Different: How Routines Change Over Time

The routines you establish help both you and your toddler get through the day as smoothly as possible. And they often become part of the sweet memories of growing up.

Charming Chimp-Child and Knee-High Neanderthal (12 to 24 months)

By his first birthday, your toddler will be an expert in figuring out the patterns of the day (getting a new diaper when he wakes up, having a bath before bedtime, and so on). Your consistent pattern of love and availability helps him feel secure enough to leave the safety of your lap and begin exploring the world.

Routines are valuable to young toddlers because they are little islands of predictability in a sea of constant change. When you're one, life is a kaleidoscope of new sights, sounds, and sensations. Familiar routines help you regroup and prepare for the next round of excitement. Even routines that don't involve sleep (such as lunching every day at noon or reading stories after a bath) are like little "rest stops" in a busy day. Without the calming effect provided by regular routines, new experiences often wind up being stressful and overwhelming. (Some toddlers can handle this stimulation much better than others. See Chapter 6 on temperament.)

Clever Cave-Kid (24 to 36 months)

Daily routines may become a bit boring to you as the months wear on, but their consistency is exactly what makes them so cherished by your child. While routines are helpful for one-year-olds, they're a *huge* bonus for two-year-olds. In addition to the usual benefits (security, relaxation, marking time), they fill the deep craving for predictability that young toddlers have.

Cave-Kids tend to like everything "just so." After working so hard to figure something out, they don't want it to change so they can start focusing their attention on something else. In fact, they sometimes explode when there are even tiny deviations from their expectations. The trigger may be as minor—to us—as a broken cracker or a guest who unwittingly sits in *Daddy's* chair.

Remember that cavemen also were not into "new and different." They kept the same design of stone tools for 100,000 years! Phillip's mom, Joan, groaned to herself every day when Phillip, 22 months old, awoke at six A.M. and begged to watch his tractor video—over and over. But to her toddler the repetition was bliss. The familiarity made him feel like a genius. "I *knew* that was gonna happen!" you can almost hear him telling himself as he watched with glee.

So when your Cave-Kid insists on the same book, same CD, same food, same dish, same cup, same spoon, and same seat, he's not being difficult. It's what he *needs*. Keep things as similar as you can from day to day. If you get interrupted while reading *Goodnight Moon* don't be surprised when your primitive little friend wants you to begin again—from page one.

Versatile Villager (36 to 48 months)

Your three-year-old's growing awareness of the world may lead her to new fears and worries. Routines offer comfort and security that let her know that everything's going to be fine. Mina, age three, wore a princess outfit complete with crown and ballet slippers to playgroup every single day. Arnie loved his fireman shirt and hat so much that he wanted to sleep in them every night!

But where two-year-olds *demand* sameness in most aspects of their lives, Villagers are more flexible. They sometimes now enjoy little variations in their routines to make them more unpredictable and therefore more fun. For example, they may insist on wearing the same clothes day after day, but then switch their fervent allegiance to a different outfit. Variety becomes more important. Three-year-olds begin to prefer reading a different book each night at bedtime, instead of repeating the same one. And the song you use to announce bath time every night will now be more appealing if you occasionally throw silly, unexpected words into it!

What Are *Your* Routines?

In the distant past, life for toddlers was probably pretty much the same day after day . . . after day. They'd hang around with their moms and the other women; watch the older kids play; and pick up rocks, branches, or whatever caught their eye.

Today our lives are far more revved up. A typical day for a modern toddler may be jammed with outings—to nursery school, babysitters, playgroups, shopping centers, playgrounds—all resulting in a variety of new sights and sounds, not to mention the many different people and places glimpsed through car windows on the way to and from these destinations. These everyday experiences may seem humdrum to us, but they can easily overstimulate your young child's mind. That's why children benefit from routines that punctuate fast-paced days with serenity, just as commas let the mind briefly pause when it scans a sentence.

How hectic is your day? What are the best times for you to intro-
duce routines to give your tot a little more peace and predictability?

To start answering that question I suggest you carry around a little notebook for a few days. Write down everything you do with
your toddler. Use this chart to help you keep track:

Day One:

6 A.M.–9 A.M.: _____

9 A.M.–noon: _____

noon–3 P.M.: _____

3 P.M.–6 P.M.: _____

6 P.M.–9 P.M.: _____

Day Two:

6 A.M.–9 A.M.: _____

9 A.M.–noon: _____

noon–3 P.M.: _____

3 P.M.–6 P.M.: _____

6 P.M.–9 P.M.: _____

Day Three:

6 A.M.–9 A.M.: _____

9 A.M.–noon: _____

noon–3 P.M.: _____

3 P.M.–6 P.M.: _____

6 P.M.–9 P.M.: _____

The idea isn't to schedule your toddler's entire day so that there's
not a spontaneous minute to spare. All I'm suggesting is that you de-

velop an outline for the day, and then sprinkle it with some routines your toddler can count on.

Chances are, you're already doing many things with your toddler at the same time and in the same order every day. Now look for ways you can make these routines (like tooth brushing, dressing, eating, and bedtime) even more regular and predictable. For example, do you always perform bedtime activities in the same order? What happens right before and right after meals? Can you do the things you're already doing even more reliably every day? Can you add short songs, dances, or quirky little habits (jump twice and spin after you brush your teeth) to balance your toddler's day with more order and consistency?

Little Rituals That Make Routines More Fun

Rituals are special, elaborate mini-routines. They are fun to invent and to practice. Here are some rituals that many parents and toddlers really enjoy:

- Sing a special song every morning and night at tooth-brushing time.
- March around the table three times beating a little drum before starting a meal.
- Play the same music every time you go for a ride in the car. (At least make it the first tape you hear, to begin the trip with a little familiarity.)
- Have your child say a "magic word" before you press the remote button to open the garage or car door.
- Let your child lay out tomorrow's clothes flat on the floor to look like a person, right down to the shoes and socks.

Extra! Extra! Special Routines Your Toddler Will Love

You probably have little rituals that add extra comfort to your day, whether it's a late-morning tea break or a Sunday-morning call to your sister. Special little additions to the day can serve a similarly soothing function for small children. Among my favorites for toddlers are: massage, loveys, Special Time, affirmations, and Opening and Closing Ceremonies, all of which I describe later in this chapter. One or more of these may well become your toddler's favorite special routines.

Toddler Massage: The Miracle of Touch

> *"Massage is love which is one unique breath, breathing in two."*
>
> —Frederick Leboyer, French obstetrician
> and infant-massage pioneer

As I mentioned in the last chapter, there's an old saying that "a child is fed with milk and praise." But it would be just as true to say that he is fed with milk and caresses. Touch, like milk, is a rich "food" for growth. Your toddler could easily live without milk, but deprived of your loving touch, he would probably be scarred for life.

A routine of a nightly massage is a wonderful gift. It soothes growing muscles; teaches gentleness and intimacy; strengthens the immune system; and calms and prepares him for sleep. As an extra bonus, giving a massage also lowers *your* stress, anxiety, and depression and boosts *your* feelings of self-esteem!

Why don't more of us "stay in touch" by massaging our children? Children in other cultures are touched, stroked, and caressed by their mothers for many, many hours day and night. By comparison, children in the United States may only be cuddled for a few minutes each day. And when they are touched, it's usually through layers of clothing.

Please, fight this trend. Lavish your toddler with lots of your loving touch! Evidence continues to pile up proving how wonderful skin-to-skin touch is for children and parents alike. Noted psychologist Virginia Satir said that four hugs a day are the minimum needed for survival, eight for staying calm, and twelve to grow stronger.

A recent study from McGill University in Montreal bears this out. It asked the question "Does extra cuddling make animals smarter?" The researchers looked at two groups of rat pups. The first group had very "loving" mothers who licked and stroked their babies a lot. The second group got a much smaller amount of this type of affection.

When the rats became old enough to be taught mazes and puzzles, scientists noticed that the cuddled animals were extra-smart. They had developed lots of connections in the part of the brain crucially important in rats (and people) for learning.

The moral of the story is clear: Cuddling your child not only feels good—it may even boost his IQ!

> *"When Abigail was one month old, we began using massage because she was so sensitive. It calmed her down. Before long she began to get happy as soon as she heard me rubbing the massage oil into my hands!*
>
> *"We've continued massaging her every day since infancy. Now at 18 months, she'll ask for, 'Rub, rub' after her bath. It's our special bonding time. Best of all, massage helps her find her inner peace so that even the wildest days end on a calm and cozy note."*

Here are five steps for giving your toddler a perfect massage:

1. *Prepare for pleasure.* Right after your child's bath, dim the lights and turn up the heat a little to signal her nervous system to start winding down. Then remove your jewelry, turn on some soft music or nature noises, and take the phone off the hook. Have vegetable oil (almond oil is great) within easy reach, a couple of soft towels, and some wipes and diapers, too, just in case.

2. *Bring yourself to the moment.* Wearing comfortable cotton clothes, sit beside your undressed child on your bed or on a soft mat on the floor. (If he resists lying down, you can start massaging him sitting up.) Place a towel over his body to keep him warm. Take two deep breaths to allow yourself to be fully present for this wonderful experience; massage is not a mechanical routine, it's an exchange of love. You will

naturally begin to focus on your fingertips, your child's soft skin, and your giving heart.

The first few massages may last only a minute or two if your toddler seems resistant. But don't worry—once you both become more familiar with the routine, chances are he will begin to relax and enjoy the gift you are giving him.

3. *Speak to your child with your hands.* Warm up some oil by vigorously rubbing it between your hands. Then start deeply stroking your child's forearms and hands. Uncover one limb at a time and massage it with a touch that is fluid but *firm* (the touch used when kneading dough). Gradually let your strokes become long and slow . . . like calm breathing. Try to always keep one hand in contact with his skin.

Use smooth, repetitious strokes, over his hands, arms, back, legs, feet, ears, face, chest, and finally his stomach. Gently rotate, pull, stretch, and squeeze his body. Learn what he likes. Twist his arms and legs as if you were lightly wringing out a wet sponge.

4. *Speak to your child with words of love.* As you massage him, softly talk about what he did that day that pleased you, how strong and healthy his muscles feel to you, the importance of good food, how much you love him. Enjoy this time together.

5. *Follow your toddler's signals.* If your toddler begins to get restless, it's a sign to change your pace or end the massage. Wipe the excess oil from his body, letting a bit remain to nourish his skin.

The Portable Routine: Blankies and Loveys

Natalie, age three, loves her blankie (now in tatters). She likes to stuff little bits of fabric into her

mouth while she strokes her right ear with another little piece.

Linus of the classic comic strip *Peanuts* has his famous security blanket. The mischievous cartoon rascal Calvin goes everywhere with Hobbes, a stuffed tiger. For Christopher Robin, it's Pooh. By early toddlerhood, many little ones have developed a special love for a particular blanket, bear, or dolly. If that's the case with your toddler, count your lucky stars!

These cuddlies sometimes annoy parents. Some worry about them getting dirty, germy, or worse . . . *lost.* Others avoid them because they worry their child will seem too "babyish." But let's face it, your toddler still *is* a baby in many ways. Besides, what if I told you that loveys actually make bedtime easier and boo-boos feel better? Now they're really looking like a good invention!

I encourage you to give your toddler a chance to develop a "relationship" with a satiny blanket. Keep one around him all day long and with him at night. Touch it a lot yourself. That will give it your scent and invest it with magic Mommy power.

These calming toys are basically Mommy substitutes. They're a step between you and your child's first real friend. (That's why they're also called "transitional objects.") They provide a quick hit of love and security when you're not nearby. These security blankets help toddlers deal with illness, parental absences, trips, new siblings, frightening situations, and just about any stress that you could imagine (like a trip to the doctor's office, where I see them all the time). At bedtime these "first friends" play a huge role in helping our tots separate from us and relax.

In fact, far from keeping your toddler immature, a lovey represents a big step toward maturity and self-reliance. I've seen kids attracted to cotton diapers, old scarves, wooden tools, wigs, and toy cars. For years, one little boy, Alex, was hooked on sleeping with a plastic Captain Hook's hook. Some sensual kids embrace *anything* soft and silky, but most are loyally attached to just one object.

If your toddler has bonded to a particular lovey, try to find another just like it (or if it's a blanket, cut it in half and hem the edge.)

It's wise to do this just in case something happens to the original. Alternate between the two, rotating them every week or two, so they'll both have the same comforting worn-in feel and smell.

Never take away a lovey as punishment (or even threaten to). Far from making your toddler pay greater attention to you, you'll make him feel insecure. And you'll weaken the soothing power of this trusted and important friend.

Pacifiers, Thumbs, and Bottles

Sucking is a very comforting ritual for toddlers, and it's totally normal. For millions of years, every cave-toddler suckled at the breast till the age of three or four. (That's what young kids still do in many societies around the world.)

Few moms in *our* culture are encouraged to continue giving their little ones the pleasure of nursing past one or two years of age. However, many still give their toddlers bottles or pacifiers, and some children take matters into their own hands, literally, and suck their thumbs. These kids rely on sucking the same way others rely on blankies or teddy bears. For the most part sucking is a smart thing to do! It's a sign of increasing self-reliance. And while there are a few potential problems associated with sucking, these usually can be avoided without depriving your toddler of this wonderful self-soothing mechanism.

A Slurp Off the Old Block

Did you know that sucking on fingers or pacifiers is a genetic trait? It's every bit as hereditary as hair color or having freckles. Only in very rare situations is sucking a sign of insecurity or emotional immaturity.

Sidestepping the pitfalls of bottles:

- Don't give your child a bottle when he is lying flat on his back. It may increase the risk of ear infections. (Just elevate the head of his bed a couple of inches by putting a thickly folded blanket under the mattress at the head of the bed.)
- Don't let him suck on a bottle for a prolonged period when he's asleep. Sucking bottles of milk or juice more than thirty to sixty minutes at a time can begin to rot a child's teeth.
- Don't let your toddler carry a bottle around in his mouth. Bottles are to be drunk (usually within twenty minutes) and then discarded.
- Don't offer a bottle for every little frustration. Although they're useful when your child is really under stress—such as a new sibling, or an illness—I normally limit toddlers to two to three bottles a day. That provides them with comfort and still encourages them to find other ways of self-soothing.

Sidestepping the pitfalls of pacifiers and thumbs:

- Avoid pacifiers if your child gets frequent ear infections. Try offering a lovey instead. Fortunately, toddlers who love to suck usually also love silky, satiny fabric.
- Wean your child from the pacifier by age three or four to avoid buck teeth. (I actually prefer pacifiers to thumbs because weaning a child off "pacies" is much easier than banishing a thumb from the mouth.)

Special Time: A Great Way to Pack a Lot of Fun into a Very Short Amount of Time

> *"I Only Have Eyes For You"*
> —Song by Harry Warren and Al Dubin,
> from the movie *Dames,* 1934

You give your toddler *hours and hours* of playtime. So why does he get so demanding the minute you ignore him to talk on the phone or balance your checkbook? It's because:

- *Your toddler's perception of time is fuzzy!* When he's having fun with you, time just flies by. Left alone, it can drag like molasses.
- *Your toddler wasn't expecting to live in the modern world.* Ancient times were nonstop fun for toddlers! There were animals and kids running around, nature to explore, and a constant supply of interesting adults. Sitting alone, waiting for you is boring.
- *Your toddler craves you.* You have lots of important things to do each day, but your toddler has only two: to explore and to spend time with you. The time with you is more than just fun—it nourishes his self-esteem. He thinks, *If the wonderful king and queen of my house spend time with me, I must be really special.*

The reality is that it's hard for one parent (even for one couple) to juggle all the responsibilites of work and family (not to mention replacing all the excitement of a village).

Fortunately, there's an amazingly simple way to get your work done and give your toddler more of the "you-you-you" he's so hungry for. It's something I call "Special Time." Special Time uses some tricks borrowed from the advertising wizards of Madison Avenue to make sure that your toddler gets all the enjoyment possible from the nuggets of high-quality time you give him.

What you do is set aside two or three times a day to spend five to ten minutes doing any activity your toddler wants. Announce his

Special Time with a peppy little song: "It's Tony's *Special* Time." Then set the timer, and give him your undivided attention. When the timer rings, say, "Aww . . . I'm so sorry, honey, Special Time is over . . . it was really fun . . . we'll have another Special Time in a little bit (or tomorrow)."

Now, I know this seems like such a tiny amount of time. You're already spending far more time than that playing with him. But this is different. This is a gift, a bonus. Your toddler will love this little bite-size treat. The way you promote it and announce it and the undivided attention you give him will truly make this routine feel like *special* time.

Some Rules for Special Time

- Try to do it approximately the same time every day (separate from naptime or bedtime). Two short periods a day are better than one long one.
- Use a timer, so there is a clear beginning and end.
- Avoid interruptions. Put cell phones, pagers, and beepers away!
- Promote Special Time. Talk it up during the day to help build anticipation and make it more special. ("Pretty soon it's going to be your Special Time. I wonder what fun things we'll do today?")
- Make up a silly ditty announcing Special Time. Have a special ending, too, like a Special Time hug or dance. These help bracket the time, so that it's set apart from the rest of the day.
- Let your toddler pick the play. (Give suggestions if you need to.) Interactive activities, such as reading, drawing together, building, roughhousing, dancing, or hunting insects are best. If he insists on watching TV—which I'd discourage—make it something like a gentle nature video and discuss it as you watch together.
- Never threaten to take Special Time away. It's particularly helpful when you and your child are having a rough day. It can help you get back on the road to being friends again.

- Special Time is *not* a replacement for the longer periods you currently give your child. It's a bonus.

If your toddler pushes you to extend Special Time when it's over, be understanding but firm. Tell him you know how much he likes it. Remind him when his next Special Time will be, and then get busy doing something else.

If your two-year-old is having a particularly tough day, be flexible with Special Time. Adding an extra one may help him stay cooperative: "Sweetheart, Mommy's on the phone, but when the timer rings, I'll get off, and it will be time for our Special Time. Yea!" Try getting off the phone even sooner than you promised. This builds your child's trust and it helps him learn that waiting is not so hard.

Special Time is the perfect marriage of routine (knowing what is going to be done), recreation (keep it fun, fun, fun), and respect. He feels respected because you've let him choose the activity, and he gets your undivided attention. It is for a brief period, but the fact that it belongs *only* to him makes him eagerly anticipate it.

Affirmations: Sharing With Your Child the Power of Positive Thinking

> *"There is nothing either good or bad, but thinking makes it so."*
>
> —William Shakespeare, *Hamlet*

In Chapter 9 I said that you can boost your toddler's confidence by dishing out bits of attention and praise to him all day long. An especially powerful way to do this is by adding a simple approach called "affirmations" to his nightly routine.

Affirmations are statements that describe your child's strengths, acts of kindness, and basic goodness. They're a loving treat you can whisper to him at bedtime. Right before sleep is the perfect moment to give praise, because it's a time when a child's mind is highly receptive to gentle persuasion.

Affirmations come in many different "flavors."

- Gently praise some small things he did that day, such as sharing, good listening, finishing his food, or coming to brush his teeth the first time you called him.
- Softly recite qualities he has that you value; tell him he's thoughtful or a big helper or that he cares about how others feel or is a good turn-taker.
- Talk about the good, happy feeling you have when you watch him and how deep your love is for him.
- Review the next day and all the interesting things that are scheduled.
- Suggest what wonderful things might soon happen in his life. Say, "You know, I wouldn't be surprised if . . . !"

Tips on Being the Best Affirmation-Giver on the Block

1. Don't worry if your child doesn't understand all the words you say—even if he doesn't, he *will* understand the *feelings* behind your words.

2. Do it during or after a sweet cuddly time or a massage.

3. Don't overstate it. By three years of age toddlers begin to get a little skeptical of excessive praise. Affirmations should be understated—more like a beautiful, quiet candle than a fireworks display.

4. Be specific. For example, it's better to say, "I like all the red you used in your drawing," than to offer a broad generalization like, "You made a beautiful picture!"

Opening and Closing Ceremonies: The Routine of Calm Breathing

Have you ever been so upset that you told yourself, "Okay—take a deep breath"? When we are stressed, frightened, or in pain, we automatically tighten up and hold our breath. Over time that tension can lead to headaches, anxiety, high blood pressure, and other illnesses. That's why being able to handle stress is a great talent. People in our culture usually pick one of two ways to release stress—relaxing (like sleeping) or distractions (like watching TV). Yet our bodies have a third, natural, built-in ability to drop stress levels—simple breathing! Slow, deep breathing can produce rapid calming, even for toddlers.

Of course, you're probably not going to be able to just sit your rambunctious little primitive down for ten minutes of meditation and prayer. But a great way to teach him deep breathing is with a game I call "Opening and Closing Ceremonies" (a name taken from part of the festivities at the Olympics).

The Olympic Games always start and end with the slow march of athletes and flags. This is the quiet order that comes immediately before and immediately after all the exciting play. I recommend you practice deep breathing in the same way. Begin a calming breathing routine immediately before and after some dynamic play. That way your prehistoric pal will learn how to quickly go from wild to peaceful. As with any exercise, the more he practices self-calming, the better he'll get at it. Soon you'll notice him becoming more civilized, confident, self-reliant, and emotionally resilient.

A little confused? Let me explain exactly what to do. (Stick with me on this, because it's a great routine!)

How to Do Opening and Closing Ceremonies

First, teach your child how to take a deep breath (works best with kids 30 months or older):

- Form a small, tight O with your lips, and breathe in and out—noisily. (Each breath should make a whooshing sound and take about six seconds.)
- As you inhale and exhale, mirror your breathing with your hands. Slowly raise and lower them with each breath. (See illustrations.)

Don't be pushy about teaching him all this. For the first week, just do the breathing a few times a day when he is sitting with you. He may be curious and want to imitate you.

The noise of your breathing and your hand movements help him see what you're doing. Some parents even have their older toddlers put their hands together in a position of prayer and slowly lift them as they inhale and lower them when they exhale. If your child has trouble getting the hang of slow breathing, wait a month and try again.

Next, help him practice taking breaths:

- Sit in front of him and use your hand to guide him through a breath. Lead him through two to three breaths, and reward him with lots of tidbits of praise: "Hmm . . . good breathing!" "Good following my hand." Later in the day use the gossip technique to praise his good breathing to your spouse or your toddler's teddy bear.
- Once he gets the hang of taking deep breaths, do it right before and right after a fun, vigorous activity such as playing catch, wrestling, having a pillow fight, or having a "battle" with crumpled-up newspaper balls. His reward for doing a few breaths with you is the exciting play.
- Use a timer to limit the play to about five minutes. If your child protests tell him, "Sweetheart, Mommy knows you want more . . . this is really fun . . . but Mr. Dinger said, 'No more for now.' Let's do our happy breaths, and then we can do more wrestling later."
- Start out by doing just one or two deep breaths. (Over a few weeks you may build up to four or five at a sitting.)

A secret for getting the most out of deep breathing is to make the out-breath longer than the in-breath. Take a couple of deep breaths right now. Notice that breathing in lasts longer than breathing out. Yet the trick to calming breathing is to learn to *exhale more and more slowly.*

Most toddlers get confused when asked to breathe out slowly.

That's why it's helpful to guide your child by using your hands like a conductor. Another way to teach three-year-olds to breathe out slowly, used by child psychologist Dr. Edward Christophersen, is by having them blow bubbles. As you've probably noticed, if you exhale quickly into a bubble wand, only a few bubbles will come out, but if you make your exhalation long and slow, a whole string of little bubbles will be born. Once your child has learned this trick, he can practice his breathing anywhere, anytime, by just pretending to blow bubbles!

Another way I help older toddlers learn to exhale slowly is by using a three-inch strip of single-ply toilet paper. As I exhale, I hold one end of the strip against my mouth (just above my upper lip). Children can easily see that the longer I breathe out the longer the paper flies. Then, while I slowly count, I have them see how long they can keep it aflutter with one breath.

Once deep breathing becomes easy for your toddler, put it to work to help calm him when he's upset. First use a little Fast-Food Toddler-ese. For example, say, "That big dog was SCARY!! You say, 'No, no, NO! Go 'way, doggie! Go 'way!'" Once he starts settling down, do some breathing with him to complete his calming.

Opening and closing breaths help your toddler gain self-control. He already knows how to turn a light on and off. Now he can learn how to turn his own little "activity motor" on and off.

Deep breathing is a powerful and positive health habit. Once your child has mastered it this valuable life skill will always be there for him whenever he's scared, in pain, upset, or worried.

Extra Tips for Opening and Closing Ceremonies

- Try to do them in the same place every time; your toddler will begin to associate that particular seat or place with a feeling of calmness, which will help him get into the relaxed frame of mind faster. Once he gets really good at it, you can do the breathing wherever you want.
- Practice several times a week. The more you practice, the better your toddler will get at it. (Eventually he'll be able to do it even when he's under stress.)

- When your toddler is first learning the technique, it may be easier for him to do it before a nap or in the early evening, when he's already a bit relaxed.
- Never pressure him into breathing. If he refuses, casually remind him that he has to do "magic breaths" if he wants to play the game. If he still refuses, just say something like "It's okay, maybe we'll wrestle later! I wonder who'll win?" Then ignore him for a minute or two.
- Don't get frustrated if your child doesn't get the hang of this right away. It often takes five to fifteen tries to figure it out.

Play: One of Life's *Fun*damentals!

"The play's the thing."

—William Shakespeare, *Hamlet*

Play Stimulates the Immune System

Laughter stimulates the immune system and erases the damaging effects of stress. Adults have even reported using laughter to help fight serious diseases like arthritis and cancer. And while those ailments are blessedly rare in young children, stress is not. We all experience it. For a toddler, stress can be the moment of separation from Mom or Dad at day care, a tantrum because he doesn't want to stay in a shopping cart seat, or the sight of the big dog on the corner.

Play is an instant stress-reliever. Who knew helping your child be happier and healthier could be so much *fun?*

Recreation literally "re-creates" within your toddler the joy, health, and completeness that he was naturally born with. Because of its overwhelming benefits, I think of play as a toddler's number-one essential vitamin. He needs large doses of it every single day.

Play . . .

—thrills the senses
—helps toddlers master movement
—stretches the mind
—stimulates language use
—boosts friend-making skills
—stimulates the immune system
—builds self-confidence
—improves nighttime sleeping

What Kinds of Play Do Toddlers Love Best?

Of course, ancient Neanderthals didn't have to set up play dates for their toddlers. For them, life was one continuous fiesta—the wind, the weather, the trees, the birds, and the children and animals of their tribe. That's the same kind of world our children expect to be born into! Little do they know that in the past hundred years (a relative blink of time), we've moved into airtight homes with monotonous carpeted floors and few if any other humans or pets. No wonder your toddler's face lights up and he shrieks with delight whenever a baby or a puppy passes by.

Variety really is the spice of life. Your toddler needs a balanced diet of play experiences, including physical games; music and songs; art play (including clay, collage materials, crayons, and fingerpaint); pretend play (including dolls, toy dinosaurs, and dress-up clothes); imitative play (including household items such as pots, pans, and a miniature broom); and sensory play (with sand, water, clay).

The whole subject of play could take up another entire book. (Two fun books filled with play ideas for you and your toddler are *Playful Parenting* by Lawrence Cohen and *Gymboree Toddler Play* by Wendy Masi.) There are a few types of recreation, however, that I consider absolutely essential for every toddler—every day: outside activity, creative play, and reading!

Outside Play: Why Toddlers "Go Crazy" When They're Cooped Up Indoors All Day

Can you remember rolling down a grassy hill as a child? Stomping through puddles? Jumping into a big pile of fallen leaves? (Maybe you're the rare grown-up who still takes time to do these things.) The great outdoors is a wonderland for toddlers. There's an endlessly changing display of lights, sights, sounds, and textures—and other kids!

You know what it's like when you want to step outside for a breath of fresh air. Well, toddlers don't merely want fresh air—they c-r-a-v-e it! A two-year-old cooped up in a house all day is like Tarzan stuck in a straitjacket.

Make every effort to include outdoor time in your toddler's schedule every day. Don't worry that it's too cold, too hot, too wet, or too snowy. We're lucky to have warm clothes, waterproof boots, and even fabrics that keep out harmful UV rays. Except for the most extreme conditions, it's never a "bad day" to take a toddler out. In fact, the rain, wind, and other weather changes add to the fun!

Creative Play: The "Creation Recreation" Called Imagination

Cave paintings aren't the only evidence we've found of early man's artistic side. Archaeologists have dug up carved beads and little carved statues that date back more than 40,000 years. Something had "clicked" in these prehistoric Picassos that made them want to, and be able to, make these works of art. It was imagination!

My mouse pad bears a picture of Albert Einstein and the quote "Imagination is more important than knowledge." Imagination is the creative spark. It's the key to mankind's extraordinary progress in the arts and sciences. (And for this reason I am deeply saddened by the loss of art classes in schools across our nation. Science and math are very important subjects, but to paraphrase Thomas Edison, the inventor of the lightbulb, creativity is at the very core of genius.)

Make a variety of art materials available to your little *artiste*. Don't bother showing him "how" to draw a person or a cat. Let his own amazing creative spirit run free. Even when his art looks like a blob to you, stretch your mind to find something positive to say about it like "Wow, you used a lot of circles. I *really* like circles!"

Does Your Toddler Prefer Dollies or Dump Trucks?

Why do two-year-old cave-boys love trucks? For the same reason 18-month-old Neanderthal girls love stuffed bears: evolution!

Boys prefer action toys because they hail from a long line of movement experts. Stone Age men had to run and capture food. They were built to chase and capture moving things. Girls tend to prefer toys they can take care of, because they are the descendants of Stone Age women who kept the homes and cared for the children. (I think this makes scientific sense, but please don't ask me for the location of the gene that makes little girls so partial to pink!)

Does this mean that you should provide only cars for sons and dollies for daughters? Of course not. But you can't ignore the influence of millions of years of genetics. So if you find that "typical" girl toys are what your little princess veers toward, that's what you should give her!

Give a bit of encouragement to every flicker of inventiveness and creativity your toddler exhibits. It will help his imagination blossom into an extraordinary tool that he will rely upon for his entire life.

(By the way, Einstein's full quote on my mouse pad reads: "Imagination is more important than knowledge. *For while knowledge defines what we currently know and understand, imagination points to all we might yet discover and create.*")

Book Play: Reading Is Feeding

If you want your child to have a smart, healthy brain, feed it! A great way to nourish the brain is through reading. The key to reading with a toddler is to do it *with* him, not *at* him.

Your active little 18-month-old may be too busy most of the day to sit still with a book. So pick a time when he's getting tired and has more patience for focusing on pictures and flipping through the pages. Give a running commentary on everything you see. "Look at the doggie! What does a doggie say?" (Books with tough cardboard pages are best suited to a one-year-old's imprecise grasp. What's more, you won't have to warn him every two minutes not to tear them.) With a really active toddler, turn the book into a game: "Okay, you be a doggie like the one in the book. Bring me your bone. Okay, now let's see what other animals we can find."

By the age of two, your rule-loving toddler may howl in protest if you stray even one single syllable from the story line he's learned by heart. "No, no—do it right!" he'll say. Not only does he respect rules, he wants *you* to follow them too!

Your three-year-old Villager will love stories about other places and people. He will probably have questions about what's going on in the book and even want to discuss it later. Your Villager is also a brilliant storyteller in his own right. You'll often overhear him repeating lines from books you've read together to his dolls and stuffed animals.

Reading to your child feeds his brain and kindles his imagination. But don't do it just because it'll make him smarter. Do it because it's a wonderful chance to snuggle together and intertwine your hearts and souls.

11

Gentle Diplomacy: Ways to Set Up and Enforce Limits

"Spare the discipline, spoil the child."

—Dr. T. Berry Brazelton

Main Points:

- Your toddler's job is to push the limits. Your job is to respectfully enforce them.

- Why good toddlers sometimes act "bad."

- How to set limits your toddler will respect.

- Detours, not roadblocks: How to use distraction and bartering to get cooperation.

- Perfect punishments for little primitives: When to resort to ignoring, loss of privileges, or time-outs.

Setting Limits:
How to Guide Your Child Down the Path of Life

Every parent's first job is to give their child love, food, and shelter. But once your toddler begins to toddle, a new task is suddenly thrust upon you: limit setting. Now your little cave-ling needs to learn that you'll put the big kibosh on her if she hammers on the window, runs into the street, or eats the dog food.

Your loving limits are like walls that guide your child down the path of life. You may build those walls close together (strict limits with lots of rules) or far apart (permissive limits with lots of flexibility). But I know you'll set up some kind of boundaries, because her new mobility and growing curiosity will force you to!

Your limits will help your toddler learn right from wrong, what is dangerous, and so on. But no toddler simply skips down the path

When you decide to set a limit, make it firm !

you set for her. She'll toddle straight to the wall and test it out with pushes and shoves. If the wall (your limit) is firm, she'll soon give up and continue down the path, but if the wall is "mushy," she'll push and push until she breaks through or you decide to harden your message.

Your toddler may resist your limits now, but in the long run they will make her happier. Children without limits feel out of control, insecure, and even unloved. No wonder they keep pushing until we take a stand. And that's only one of the reasons your sweet child may suddenly try to steamroll you!

Pushing the Limits: Why Good Toddlers Act "Bad"

Let's take a minute to talk about the six reasons why even the best toddlers sometimes rebel against their parents' rules and limits:

1. **Toddlers can't explore without pushing some rules.** Your toddler is an ace explorer—persistent, gutsy, and a little rough around the edges. Her job is to explore, touch, jump on, and pull everything. No wonder it feels like she's pushing the limits *all* the time. From her point of view, however, you're annoying her on a regular basis because you're blocking her greatest joy—discovery.

2. **Toddlers are impulsive, self-centered, and short-sighted.** Adventurous as she is, your little friend is no Indiana Jones. She is run by her impulses and doesn't worry much about the consequences. You can't expect an 18-month-old, or even a three-year-old, to use good judgment about not eating medicine, for example, or to stay by your side in a parking lot.

3. **Our rules are often confusing.** Having limits must seem strange to your toddler. *Let me get this straight,* she thinks. *I love jumping on the sofa more than anything in the world—and you want to stop me? Don't you love me anymore?*

4. **Our rules are often unrealistic.** Sometimes our toddlers act "bad" because our expectations are too high. Usually this happens when parents don't know what normal kid behavior is. You shouldn't expect your 18-month-old to share, your two-year-old never to lie, and your three-year-old to sit still in church. *Warning:* If your standards are too high, your child may rebel, as if to say, "Why bother! It's just too darn hard!"

5. **We accidentally encourage bad behavior.** Your toddler has carefully observed you since birth. She's learned to whine and nag because those techniques work. In fact, even one-year-olds soon learn the exact level of shrillness to cry at that gets our attention the fastest.

6. **Sometimes your toddler is just having a bad day.** We all have good days and bad days. And our mood sometimes totally flips if we find a twenty-dollar bill in the street or get pulled over by a traffic cop. And our emotional little Neanderthals are even easier to knock off balance.

   The things that may make our little primitives even more primitive than usual include fatigue; hunger; teething; illness; boredom; jealousy; stuffy rooms; watching parents fight; TV; changes in routines; caffeine (in soda, iced tea, chocolate, or cold medicine); and sugar. These problems are like speed bumps—you just have to slow down and deal with them.

The Art of Prehistoric Diplomacy

"Pay attention to what you like and ignore or discourage the rest."

—Karp's law of diplomacy

Your misbehaving toddler can drive you bonkers. But please resist rolling up your sleeves and fighting your little tot *mano a mano.* Re-

The Law of the Soggy Potato Chip

In Thomas Gordon's excellent book, *Parent Effectiveness Training*, he says that kids love potato chips so much they'll even eat soggy chips rather than go without them. Similarly, toddlers love our attention so much that they'd rather we get upset and yell than ignore them. That's why toddlers whose parents only notice them when they're misbehaving start breaking the rules like crazy!

Of course, we never *intend* to teach our kids to have fits. We're just . . . busy. But the accidental message is clear even to toddlers: Play nicely, and you'll be ignored. Be a nuisance, and you'll get attention. In her primitive little mind, when your tot is breaking your rules, she may actually be saying, "Hey! Look at me!!" Of course, she doesn't *want* to be yelled at. But she's craving the "potato chip" (your attention) so much that if all she can get is a "soggy one" (you being mad), it's better than "going hungry" (being ignored).

The solution? Lots of little time-ins—to keep her appetite for you satisfied—and a bit of limit setting when necessary.

member, you're an ambassador, and you must always try to show dignity, restraint, and diplomacy.

You are like the representative of a superpower. If you wanted to, you could crush your toddler's every act of defiance. But force always backfires. It can stunt a child's confidence or fuel her resentment or, even worse, inspire her attempts at *revenge*. That's why the best statesmen try to avoid confrontations and instead use their charm, persuasion, and bargaining ability, to build long-term bonds based on respect. So put away your boxing gloves, and start sharpening up your diplomatic skills.

In Chapters 8, 9, and 10 I discussed how to reward your toddler's good behavior with respectful listening (the Fast-Food Rule), praise, attention, and play. In this chapter, I'll review the second half of Karp's law of diplomacy: how to put the brakes on unwanted behavior.

How to Set Limits Your Toddler Will Respect

*"Lord, give me the serenity to accept the things I
cannot change, the courage to change the things I can,
and the wisdom to know the difference."*

—Serenity prayer

Parents often have trouble setting limits. We alternate between thinking of our toddlers as babies and seeing them as rational little people. That's why, in place of discipline, we too often try using logic, reason, and conflict avoidance. That's fine for dealing with calm young children but rather unhelpful for controlling raging little Neanderthals. I strongly believe in treating toddlers with respect. But parenting is not a job for those who are rigidly politically correct. Your family is *not* a democracy! It's a benevolent dictatorship in which you serve both as ambassador *and* ruler.

Gentleness, fairness, and patience are essential, but so are courage and resolve. Setting firm limits with kindness and humility is not an option: it's your responsibility. That's why for the next few years your family's theme songs will be "Respect," "You Are My Sunshine," and "My Momma Done Told Me," and your family crest will be the Carrot and Stick.

Of course, your goal will be to use as many carrots and as few sticks as possible. Plan to start every new day with joy, prepared to forgive and forget. But when push comes to shove (and shove to bite), you must not hesitate to respectfully wield your parental power to do what needs to be done.

As you have learned by now, however, it's one thing to decide on your rules but quite another to make them stick. Here are my lucky seven secrets to successful limit setting:

1. **Start with appropriate expectations.**

    Of course, you'll have rules about violence, risky behavior, meanness, and a few things that really matter to you (like not jumping on your white sofa). But if your expectations are unreasonably high, you'll only be setting your child up for frustration. (Review Chapters 2 through 6 to learn more about your toddler's physical, mental, verbal, and emotional abilities.) Better to move fragile things away and change your home to fit your kid (like using stain-resistant slipcovers on that sofa) instead of trying to change her to fit your home.

2. Pick limits that you know you can enforce.

I know you're the parent, but even a parent can't win every fight. For example, you can't *make* your child eat broccoli, apologize, share, brush teeth, poop on the potty, not be afraid, climb up the slide, etc., etc., etc. This point is critical for you to understand, because if you keep picking battles you can't win, you'll start losing your authority—and chaos and defiance will inevitably follow. (Your cautious child may become more fearful, and your spirited child more rebellious.)

When you sense you're entering a struggle with your toddler that you can't win, be prepared to switch tactics and use the old diplomatic tools of charm, compromise, and ingenuity.

One of the things that really bothered Jessica was when her three-year-old daughter, Lucy, refused to say she was sorry to her 9-month-old sister, Camille, after hitting her. Finally Jessica gave up trying to force Lucy to say it. Instead, she would immediately get between the two of them; turning her back to the older Lucy, while sweetly talking to Camille so that Lucy could hear. "It really makes you sad when Lucy hits you," Jessica said. "Tell her, 'Hitting hurts me, and I don't like it!' But if Lucy says she's sorry, it will make Mommy very happy!"

Usually a moment later, Lucy would say she was sorry, and Jessica would immediately turn to her, saying, "Thanks, Lucy." Then she would turn back to Camille and say in a loud whisper, "Did you hear,

Camille? Lucy said she's sorry. She did a good job using her words to apologize. I really like it when she uses her words like that. Yea, Lucy!" Then to both of them she would exclaim, "Hey, come on, everybody, let's go get some lemonade!"

3. **Keep statements brief and positive. Too many words work against you.**

If your toddler isn't listening to you, it might be because of "bad listening," but it also might be because of *"bad telling."* You can try saying, "Debbie, come here please and sit down. It's time to put on your shoes, etc., etc.," but if she ignores you, it may be because you're being too wordy.

Make your comments short and sweet and express them in a confident, nonjudgmental voice. Say, "Toys go in the box!" or "Toys are happy in the box!" or "Shirt! Shoes! Now!" or "Crayons stay in the den." (Drew's mom said that when talking to her son she used the same kindly, no-nonsense tone of voice that she perfected when she trained her dogs.)

Reminding your child of a rule is more effective and causes less defiance than commanding her to do (or stop doing) something. Say "This is a walking place" or "Chairs are for sitting" as opposed to "Don't run" or "Sit down now."

4. **Be consistent. Be consistent. Be consistent.**

Think about it. If you got a ticket every time you drove fast, you'd soon stop speeding. On the other hand, if you only got a ticket one out of every two hundred times you sped, you'd probably push the limit every time.

The basis of effective discipline is consistency and predictablity. The more your child discovers she can get away with rule-breaking, the more she'll do it. But by consistently enforcing your rules, you'll help her develop a clear sense of right and wrong.

5.   Use *her* language—Toddler-ese—for maximum success.

Use all four parts of Toddler-ese to get your message across: short phrases, repetition, an expressive voice, and dramatic facial and body gestures. For example, when I see toddlers doing something hazardous such as running in a parking lot, I scare them a little. I look very alarmed and frown as I say, "No, no, no, no, no! Look! CAR! Danger . . . ow! Ow! OW!!!!!!!" (Save the lecture about getting squashed under the tires and looking both ways for a quiet time later on in the day.)

When you're not pushed to immediate action by dangerous or aggressive behavior, it's best to first try the Fast-Food Rule (see Chapter 8). Narrating *her* actions and feelings back to her will make her more receptive to *your* feelings.

For example, if you see that your son Aaron is about to whack his best friend over a dispute, first let your little Neanderthal know you understand exactly how he feels. Stomp your feet, shake your head, make a big frown, and flail your arms like a person vigorously gesturing "the deal's off!" At the same time passionately say, "Mad! Mad! MAD!! Aaron mad!! You say, 'No, Tommy! No, no, NO! No truck!!' Mad! Mad! Mad!"

In the heat of the moment, you'll be a much more successful ambassador if you start by mirroring his feelings in your best Toddler-ese. Then, after thirty to sixty seconds, *briefly* state your rule. "No hit. No hit!! No, no, no!! No hit, Aaron!!" Later in the day, when tempers have cooled, gossip about the incident to Aaron's teddy or talk to Aaron directly. That's when you should teach him all the reasons it's wrong to hit.

> *"Benjamin understands that I am serious when I make a rumbling growl," says Claudia. "It works better for me than saying, 'Gentle, gentle' or 'Use your words.' He immediately stops biting, and though he gets kind of sad, he wants to curl up next to me and be friends. I've*

even taught him to growl instead of bite when he is mad. Growling gives him an outlet for his aggression and still gets the message across that biting is not acceptable.

"Now when Benjamin and I play bears on the bed we move our legs and growl! It is fun for both of us and it seems to release some of his pent-up energy. I feel like a mama bear teaching her cub!"

Don't be surprised if your toddler acts a little confused the first time you try growling. She may smile or even growl back. If so, add a "double take" to the growl. Here's how to do it: Simply growl again; this time make an even lower menacing rumble, and turn away for a few seconds. Then turn back to your child, growl again a bit louder, frown, shake your head, and say, "No. No touch." If *you* accidentally smile, bite your lip and look away for a second to regain your composure, then look back and say, "I know my face was smiling, but I am *not* smiling inside—I say 'No, no!! No hitting!!'" (If she continues to defy you, consider using a time-out, a technique I'll discuss later in this chapter.)

A Grrrrrrrreat Nonverbal Message!

Another great nonverbal way to show your toddler you really mean business is . . . *growling!* All furry animals (and prehistoric kids) understand this sound. A serious look and a low rumbling grrrrrrrrr warns other creatures to stop—*now!* One- and two-year-olds especially understand this message, though it works with all toddlers.

When you growl, clap your hands hard and fast a few times, put on a stern face, and say with a serious voice, "No, no NO!!!" Then frown, narrow your eyes, shake your head slowly, and give a low dog-like growl. (See example of growling in cartoon on page 130.)

Practice growling in front of a mirror until you can do it with a straight face. I know it feels like acting, but give it a little time. With time, growling may become one of your favorite discipline tools!

---

6. **Avoid mixed messages: Don't smile or use a sweet voice when you're serious.**

Your toddler may smile at you while he's misbehaving. He's not being disrespectful; nor does he think what he's doing is funny. Instinctually, he knows that if he smiles at you, you usually smile back, and your smile means that everything is okay. (Remember the power of the nonverbal message!) So lower your voice and put on a serious face to ensure that you're not accidentally sending a mixed message.

7. **Be creative.**

Spirited kids really hate being ordered about. So with these challenging toddlers, look for ways to announce limits and rules that are less confrontational and more fun! How? Some examples include whispering, making a trumpet sound to announce what's coming next, putting on a funny hat, using a funny voice, or showing her how to make her dirty socks "march themselves" to the hamper. I bet that once you start thinking about how to get your message across without barking orders, you'll probably come up with dozens more fun ways.

Rick likes to adopt an enthusiastic "camp counselor" voice with his twins Bethany and Brittany: "Okay, all you rugrats, it's time for the thrillin', chillin' race to get pajamas on! Racers, start your engines! Rrrrrrrrrrrrr! On your marks, get set, GO!"

A Way to Keep It Positive: Sandwiching

Try to sandwich your demands and requirements between fun activities you know your child will enjoy. For example, say, "Let's read this book. Then we can have a race and see who can pick up more toys. Then it'll be time for a snack!"

Detours, Not Roadblocks: Using Distraction and Bartering to Make Limits Work

"Never say 'no' to a hostage taker, it's in the manual."
—Samuel L. Jackson in *The Negotiator*

When your toddler breaks a serious rule, you may need to discourage her with a big, fat roadblock like punishment. But if she's only *mildly* pushing a limit, don't frustrate her with a big, unpleasant "No." Instead, show your child you're interested in her feelings by repeating them: "Yes! You really want THAT!" Then, once she knows you truly care, just give her a little "detour" to get her back on track.

Detours (distraction and bartering) work better than roadblocks (saying no and punishing), especially for challenging toddlers. Try a distraction like giving her what she wants in fantasy. Say, "Cool! I wish I could give you a million of those." Or offer some compromise where you both can win. This approach recognizes what top ambassadors have known for years: Being told "No!" makes most self-respecting people dig in their heels—especially when that person is a Neanderthal!

Being told "No!" is like having a door slam in your face. Try to avoid saying "No" right away, even if that's what you're thinking. Instead, reflect her feelings: "You're mad, mad, MAD! You want those cookies . . . NOW!! But nooooo . . . no cookies till after dinner . . . but I can give you some raisins, or we can play catch!"

Don't get me wrong, As a parent, there are plenty of times when you have to say "No," and you should never hesitate to do so when you have to set a firm limit. For example, if your child is about to touch a hot stove, you should say "NO" loudly and quickly! But in general, when "No" is the first word you say to your child, you're provoking a power struggle.

A better first step would be to acknowledge her point of view. Once you both agree about how much she "really, really, really" wants to do something, then you can respectfully distract her, offer a compromise, or if necessary, enforce a strict limit.

Distraction: A Detour for All Seasons

> Maisy, 13 months, toddled over to the bookcase and
> began flinging books off the shelf. Her dad, Bryan, tried
> picking her up and setting her down in front of some
> blocks, but a minute later she was clearing the
> bookshelf again. Instead of yelling, "No! No!" Bryan
> decided to try to detour her away from her desire to
> demolish the library. "You want book! You want book!
> BOOKS!!! Books!" he bubbled in excited Toddler-ese.
> Maisy paused. "But no throw! No throw books! Books
> are friends." Bryan then offered her a detour. "Hey!" he
> whispered. "I know a special, special book we can read
> together!"

What it is: The simplest response to misbehavior is to change the subject. If the road your toddler is on has gotten bumpy, reroute traffic with a detour to a different activity or place to play.

Best used for: The youngest toddlers, who are more easily distracted and therefore more willing to go along. But all toddlers will respond to being distracted if the circumstances are right.

How to do it: Start by narrating back your child's feelings (the Fast-Food Rule), using your best Toddler-ese. Then try a simple distraction. For example, ask for her help with something: "It's too hard for me." Or change the venue: "I know, let's go outside now!"

Offer alternatives to help detour behaviors you don't like. For example, if your child is chasing the cat, rather than saying "No!" bring out a big book of cat pictures or initiate a game with a ball of yarn where your toddler is the cat. Options make your toddler feel respected.

If those efforts don't work, then you can get a little tougher with your limit setting.

Let It Out!

Help your child blow off steam before it builds up to a full-scale explosion. Narrate everything you see going on in her by using Toddler-ese. Mirroring back what your child is feeling shows her a better way to express pent-up feelings. For example:

- *Charming Chimp-Children (12 to 18 months):* Model for her how she can vent frustration. Stomp your feet, clap your hands, shake your head vigorously, and teach her how she can go "Grrrrrr!" when she's upset!
- *Neanderthals (18 to 24 months):* Do all of the above and teach her how to further vent her feelings by repeating words over and over again, like "No!" or "Mine!" or "Stop!"
- *Cave-Kids (24 to 36 months):* On a calm day, have your toddler practice different facial expressions: "Show me your happy face . . . your sad face . . . your mad face." Show her yours, so she can see what you mean. Point to pictures of emotional kids in books and say "Look at that sad baby." Make your own photo book with pictures of different expressions cut from magazines.
- *Villagers (36 to 48 months):* Teach her words to use when she's upset. Use pictures in books as a starting point when you're reading. Ask "How does that boy feel? Why is that girl sad?" Or say, "When I get mad my blood boils, and I feel like this [make face]."

Bartering and Compromise: How Diplomats Turn a *Won't-Won't* into a *Win-Win*

When James, three, threw raisins on the floor, his mom, Tess, angrily said, "Pick them up." When he asked for help, she replied, "You threw them. You have to pick them up by yourself." James refused, pleading, "No! I need help!"

Now Tess had an escalating battle on her hands, and it was not a battle that she could easily win. The way out? Offer James a compromise: "You threw them, but you want me to help you. Hmmm, okay, if you pick up the first one, I'll pick up . . . how many? Two? Three? How many do you think I should pick up?"

What it is: Exchanging goods and trying to find win-win compromises is an ancient part of being a diplomat. Cavemen began bartering more than 100,000 years ago. Haggling is still expected in many cultures. It's a custom that builds mutual respect and lasting friendships.

This kind of bargaining, however, is foreign to many Americans. We prefer straight talk and putting our cards on the table. *But that's not the way your prehistoric little child sees the world.*

Hashing out compromises is one of the most basic give-and-takes of social life. Most older toddlers feel at home with the drama, hard bargaining, warm social embraces, and compromise that make up the art of bartering. It combines your tot's ability to read your feelings (which began around the first birthday) with her growing ability to compare several ideas in her head at one time (beginning between the second and third birthdays).

Some parents get confused when I tell them about compromising with their toddlers. "Doesn't it mean giving in?" they ask. "Won't it spoil them?" Of course, setting up a pattern where you *always* give in *would* spoil your child. Compromise, on the other hand, teaches her that loving people can give in to each other and still be strong.

And when you let your toddler win many small struggles, she'll be more likely to graciously give in to you when you insist on winning.

Best used for: Older toddlers, ages two and up, respond better to bartering than to distraction or redirection. Bartering helps build a relationship in which your child obeys you because she feels respected and respects you, not because she feels ashamed or intimidated.

But even the youngest toddlers have a simple desire to barter. If your 15-month-old takes your sunglasses and refuses to give them back, don't get into a tug-of-war. Simply ignore the glasses and start removing her clothes! With each piece you take off, proudly crow, "Mine! This is all mine!! Mine, mine, mine!!!" Usually, by the third or fourth piece you've "confiscated," she'll hand back the glasses in an attempt to "make a deal" with you to get her clothes back.

How to do it: Here's how negotiating works: Start by making a big demand. Pompously proclaim, "Eat all the peas. You must!!! I insist!" If your child rejects your offer, start to come down—a lot. Ham it up! Play the game! Lower your demands, then seem to regret your decision. Say, "Okay, just five peas. Wait a second! No, no, no! It has to be six peas. That's my final offer! Okay?" When your three-year-old shoots back, "No, just one!" keep pretending you're upset. Groan, "No!!! One is too little!" It is the vigor of your protest that will make her feel like she is victorious!

Finally, even if she only eats half a pea, say, "Okay, okay, you win. You're a good bargainer. You ate your half a pea, now you can have some more milk." That's a solid victory. Give your child extra attention to show her the benefits of cooperation. This is how you begin to build a relationship of mutual respect with your child. Next time you can push for a few more peas.

What if your child begs for a cookie right before dinner? You could choose to forbid it and offer a distraction: "No cookies! That's the rule, but let's go out and play catch!" Or you could try to find a compromise: "Eat this piece of fruit. Then you can have the cookie" or "Here's half the cookie. After dinner you can have the other half."

Jack, three, only liked wearing sandals. He hated
shoes and socks. In Los Angeles that's okay most of
the time, but this day it was raining badly. Still, he

All master negotiators know they sometimes have to pull out of the bargaining if they're not being treated fairly. If your toddler is not willing to compromise at all, you may have to turn your back and ignore her for a minute or two before trying again. (To learn more on ignoring, see next section.)

insisted on wearing sandals. He didn't give in even after his mom, Shaya, mirrored his strong feelings (the Fast-Food Rule), so she tried offering a compromise: He could wear one shoe and one sandal now and put the other shoe on at school, or he could wear sandals to the car and put shoes on when he got to school. He accepted the latter offer. Then, to reward him for being such a good sport, Shaya took a pen and made a little check on his hand, and everything was fine.

Three Common Discipline Traps: Comparing, Exaggerating, Using Hurtful Words

Avoid comparing. Don't say, "Your brother does it—why don't you?" Comparisons build resentment and teach the wrong lesson. You want your child to do something because she feels it's the right thing to do, not because someone else does it. In fact, before you know it, you'll be telling your child not to do things that other kids do! And goodness knows, you'll hate it when she starts comparing you to other parents.

Better technique: Focus only on your child's actions, no one else's.

Avoid exaggerating. Don't say, "You never . . ." or "You always . . ." Such sweeping statements are rarely accurate. Even when such comments hold a grain of truth, they're demoralizing and cause great resentment.

Better technique: Use "you-I" messages. For example, tell your child, "When you say I'm mean, I feel very sad inside." Or, you might give your child the benefit of the doubt by saying, "You usually keep your feet off the new sofa, but I guess today you forgot."

Avoid hurtful words. Can you imagine an ambassador calling the head of a country "stupid"? Hurtful words can be as damaging as slaps and spankings. They attack a child's very core. Most parents who say such things are unconsciously echoing what they were told when they were little. Calling your little Neanderthal names can break her spirit and create anger and resentment.

Better technique: When you are upset, criticize your child's *action,* not your *child.* Don't say, "You're bad because you hit Johnny." Instead say, "Hitting is bad."

Perfect Punishments for Little Primitives: Ignoring, Loss of Privileges, Time-out

Susan is at her wit's end. Her 18-month-old, Shane, used to be docile and agreeable. Now he gets madder than a thirty-pound hornet when he can't have his way. "I've tried to divert his attention, but that doesn't work anymore. Sometimes I can barter my way out of a bad situation," she says. "But lately he's taken to hitting when he's mad. I don't know what to do. I don't want to spank him, but what should I do when he looks me right in the eye and disobeys me?"

What if you've tried empathy, humor, distraction, and bartering, but your primitive little buddy is still determined to plow right through your limits? Well, as every seasoned ambassador knows, you should always be prepared to back up your words with actions. Now let's talk about how to punish your child when your detours and distractions fail to stop her bad behavior.

It's your responsibility to take control of your toddler's behavior when she is unable (too upset or too mischievous) to respect your fair and reasonable rules. Punishment is just a stronger way of telling her she has come to a limit that you will not compromise about. That's why I said earlier that, during the toddler years, your family coat of arms is the Carrot *and* Stick. To put it in more modern terms, perhaps I should say Carrot and *Timer*, which you will find very useful for time-outs.

Before I go any further, I want to reassure you that punishment is not a bad thing. It is not something mean or terrible that you should avoid. Although you should never use punishment out of anger, revenge, or meanness, it is an essential tool for putting the brakes on kids who don't have the ability or willpower to stop themselves. Experienced parents resort to punishments when their child's behavior leaves them no other reasonable choice.

Remember, your child is causing the punishment to happen because at that particular moment she is her own worst enemy. Like an ambassador, you are saying to her, "My dear opponent, I am so sorry I can't allow you to use markers on the wall. But since you didn't honor my requests to stop, I have no choice but to respectfully put you in time-out for three minutes."

Of course, before you turn to punishment, you should first consider the steps in Chapters 8 through 11 to try and avoid this situation, such as speaking Toddler-ese, giving lots of time-ins, setting clear limits, providing outdoor play, making offers for reasonable compromises, and so on. But if your child won't give in, she may indeed need a stronger reminder that *you* are the authority in the house.

Three types of punishment work best with toddlers: ignoring, loss of privileges, and time-outs.

The Classical Roots of Discipline

The word *discipline* comes from the Latin verb *discere,* which means "to learn." The word *punish* comes from an ancient Greek word meaning "payment" or "penalty."

Ignoring: Giving Your Toddler the Perfect Cold Shoulder

> *Sadie, 15 months old, found a fun new thing her*
> *voice could do: screech! She began to make this shrill*
> *sound whenever she wanted her parents' attention.*
> *"At first we went rushing over to see what was the*
> *matter," her father, Bill, explained. But they soon*
> *realized that Sadie was infatuated with screeching. So*
> *rather than reward the behavior by hurrying over, her*
> *parents decided to totally ignore her until she became*
> *quieter.*
>
> *Now, with all the passion of a 15-month-old, Bill*
> *vigorously points, saying, "You want! You want!! You*
> *want book!! No screech! OUCH!!! OUCH!! No like!!!"*
> *Next he makes a sour frown, vehemently wags his*
> *index finger, and shakes his head "No" then turns his*
> *back to her for 30 seconds. "It is amazing," Bill reports.*
> *"Now she just stops—in seconds!"*

What it is: Every actor needs an audience. Toddlers don't keep acting up if no one's listening. The expression "giving your child the cold shoulder" may sound harsh, but it's really not. All it involves is turning your back on her for thirty to sixty seconds. Think of it as a little mini–time-out.

Best used for: Ignoring should not be used for serious infractions like aggressive or dangerous actions. But it's perfect for nuisance behaviors like whining, clinging, begging, badgering, screeching, screaming, and rudeness. It's also a good response for mild defiance (such as when your child looks right at you and drops food on the floor) or a halfhearted bite or swat.

Remember, kids who are bored want to get a reaction from you any way they can. That's why not responding is often the best response of all.

How to do it: When giving your toddler the cold shoulder, use the three-step method:

1. First, reflect your child's message (boredom, frustration, etc.) using the Fast-Food Rule and Toddler-ese.

2. Then very briefly say how her misbehavior makes you feel. If you have a young toddler, a response like growling may be more effective than words. Remember how tuned in toddlers are to nonverbal communication. Be sincere but dramatic in your response. Make a big frown, knit your eyebrows, make a deep, rumbling growl, and shake your head as if to say, "You must be kidding."

3. Finally, if she refuses to give in, take yourself away. Make yourself seem busy so that she can't easily connect with you for one to two minutes. But pay attention to her sooner if her behavior suddenly improves!

One of the goals of ignoring is to let your toddler know that you won't just be an audience for her antics. A great way to make this clear to her is to put her "on hold."

Here's what you do: After a few seconds of frowning and growling in response to her misbehavior, suddenly raise your finger in the air (the way you would if you wanted someone to wait a second) and, while keeping the finger raised, look away for a few seconds. Like putting someone on hold on the telephone, it says to her, "I'm the boss. You wait for *me!*" Then take a quick look back at her, scowl a little, and say, "No, no!! Stop that NOW!!" Then look away again. As soon as she's acted properly for ten seconds, pay a little attention to her.

For an older toddler, raise your finger, and before you turn away, say something like, "That whiny sound hurts my ears. I'll be happy to listen to you when you remember how to talk in your normal voice." Or if your little Neanderthal is throwing a fit to get candy, say, "Wow! You are mad, mad, MAD!! You want to s-c-r-e-a-m!! But, no, no . . . no!! Mommy doesn't like yelling. It hurts my feelings and makes me sad. Mommy knows you are REALLY mad!!! You wanted that candy soooo much. But I don't like yelling. While you yell, I'm going to the other room where it isn't so loud."

The Blessing of a Skinned Knee

I hope by this point in your parenting adventure you have discovered one wonderful fact about children: They're resilient! Your toddler is not a hothouse flower who needs to be protected from all problems. Don't try to shield her from all conflicts or from the consequences of her actions. As Wendy Mogel discusses in her important book, *The Blessing of a Skinned Knee*, difficult situations have valuable silver linings—they strengthen a child's ability to deal with life's inevitable frustrations and struggles. You've heard the expression "survival of the fittest"? Challenges make your toddler more emotionally fit!

Loss of Privileges: A Punishment Older Toddlers "Get"

> Maura's twins, Jake and Pete, 32 months, both wanted the same red ball. "BALL!! BALL! BALL! BALL! BALL! You both want it!" she said vigorously. "You want it NOW! But no fighting, or Mommy takes ball away. I like it when you play nicely."
>
> She got them rolling it back and forth (a tiny time-in) and then left them alone. Not three minutes later, they started squabbling again. "BALL! BALL! BALL!" Maura said passionately. "You both want that ball, but remember Mommy said, 'No fight, no fight.' So the ball is going 'night-night' for right now. You can play with it later." She put it out of reach and brought out two identical trucks for them to play with instead.

What it is: Loss of a privilege is a simple punishment that makes sense to a toddler's sense of fairness. From the earliest months of your child's life, she has noticed that certain things always happen together, that there is some order in the world. For example, she probably realized that every time she heard your keys jingle, it was time to go out. Use your child's ability to figure out cause and effect to help her be more cooperative. Once she learns that a certain behavior will backfire on her and cause her to be punished, she'll start to think twice about doing it . . . no matter how much fun it is.

When punishing an older child, you can also deprive her of a privilege that's totally unrelated to the misbehavior, like not letting her go to a friend's house if she doesn't clean her room. But this approach is not very effective with our "live-in-the-moment" toddlers. A two-year-old won't understand that picking up toys has anything to do with being allowed to go out later. Young toddlers really don't plan that far ahead in time. For your Stone Ager to learn to be better behaved, she needs an immediate consequence that is directly related to her misbehavior. (It's sometimes called "logical consequences.")

Best used for: Toddlers of any age.

How it works: You immediately take away a privilege that is directly linked to the misbehavior. For example, if your toddler hits a friend with his toy bat, take the bat away.

Don't take away just anything. It should always have a direct link to the behavior you're correcting. (Never take away a lovey.)

If your toddler keeps tossing crackers over the side of her high chair, take the crackers away. If she's having a pokey morning and won't get dressed to go to the park, say, "Get dressed before the dinger rings or we just won't have time to play in the park." Then turn your back for a few moments. If she doesn't respond, you can warn her one or two more times, but don't beg or continue to issue warnings. If she doesn't listen, she will have to learn by experiencing the consequences of her ignoring you. When you take away a privilege tell your child in Toddler-ese that you know how much she wanted it, as Maura did in the example above.

Ideally, you should even try to catch your child's misbehavior as it is happening. That's the best time to teach her a lesson. Sometimes I have parents set up extra mirrors around the house so they can watch their toddler and stop her misbehavior even when it's going on silently in the next room.

The Prehistoric Time-out: Your Ace in the Hole

What it is: Time-outs are very effective for punishing toddlers who just can't stop themselves. In my experience, they work better for one- to four-year-olds than for any other age group. I teach the basics of time-outs to all parents in my practice at their toddler's one-year visit. I do this because the year between one and two is one of the most dangerous in childhood, and parents need to be able to teach their impulsive little tots a signal that means "stop this instant!!"

I encourage you to use time-outs repeatedly during your child's first year of toddlerhood to help her learn to take your words seriously. Please don't see time-outs as a sign of failure, either yours or your child's. Time-out is merely just another very valuable parenting tool. It is a routine that helps give structure and order to your child's chaotic life.

Time-outs work because they deprive your child (very, very temporarily) of something precious to her: the privilege of being with you.

When to use it: Your toddler is ready to start having time-outs around her first birthday. By then she's gotten really good at learning patterns. For example, even though she herself can't count, she can certainly learn that when you count to three (with a serious voice and stern face), it's a warning that a time-out is coming unless she immediately stops what she's doing. By age four, time-outs become less needed. Older kids respond better to less confrontative approaches like negotiation and loss of privileges.

On occasion, you will need to move your toddler right into a time-out—say, if she does something violent, dangerous, or blatantly disrespectful. But in general, you should always give a warning first (like counting to three).

How it's done: Unless you need to instantly stop your child's behavior, briefly use the Fast-Food Rule, one last time, to show that you have empathy and would like to avoid doing a punishment, if possible.

For example, if Jamie starts having a tantrum because her mom won't let her play with the sugar bowl, Mom might tell her, "Mad. Mad. Mad. Jamie's mad at Mommy. Mad! MAD!" When you have your child's attention, state your rule: "But no play with sugar! No, no, No!" Of course, if this works, go to one of the detours described earlier, like distraction. If not, however, warn her that a time-out is imminent: "You're having so much trouble with the rules right now, I think you may need a time-out." Then count to three to signal that the time-out is coming, unless she corrects her behavior.

Do not use a lot of words or emotion at this time! Once you start counting, the time for talking has passed. Now is the time to act with the courage of your convictions. Put on a stern face, use a serious tone of voice, shake your head no, growl a little, then put up fingers as you count to three.

Wait two seconds between each number. If your child hasn't complied by three, put her in your time-out place. Seats or open rooms are fine time-out places for compliant kids, but feisty ones usually need to be confined in playpens (under age two), or in their rooms (over age two). If you put your child in her room, make sure there are no breakables or sharp corners. Never put your child in a closet, bathroom, or basement.

Time-out Tips for Prehistoric Limit-Testers

Practicing a few fine points will make you a time-out expert:

Don't say much. The quickest way to undermine the effectiveness of your time-out is to talk too much or show too much emotion. *When you do a time-out, you want to be calm and almost a bit removed.* The time for explanations and being friends will come after it's over.

Always do time-outs the same way. This allows your child to learn what to expect. Usually, after five to ten time-outs, your toddler will recognize the time-out warning and back down the moment you start counting. Believe it or not, your consistency and predictability will eventually teach her to obey and respect your request even before you get to three! In fact, after just a few months of doing time-outs, most parents find they actually end up needing to do them less and less!

> Janie, the mother of 26-month-old Jim, said that
> when she was growing up, her mom's warning that a
> punishment was coming was just to raise one of her
> eyebrows a little. She knew she had better stop
> immediately, or she wouldn't like what happened next.

Don't wait too long. Lynn's 18-month-old, Stuart, became very demanding. "I never give him time-outs, but I occasionally get so furious that I give myself a time-out," she says. What Lynn really needs to do is give him a time-out *before* she gets so upset that she abandons him because of her anger.

The parent who waits until she's ready to scream, "That's it! You're getting a time-out!" has waited too long. Her emotional display may have one of two bad effects. It may scare her child, or it may teach him exactly how to yank her chain, something he may be tempted to do whenever he's bored or mad.

Time-out Doesn't Work Without *Time-in*

The success of time-outs is based on your giving your child many *time-ins*. In fact, the real incentive for her to avoid time-outs is not really their severity as a punishment (they're actually pretty mild). Rather they work because you are briefly withholding a very powerful reward: your loving attention. Your toddler loves to be with you so very, very much!

Time-outs for Beginners

The first few times you do a time-out, you don't have to put your toddler in isolation. If she doesn't comply with your request ("Give me the fork—*now!* One . . . two . . . three . . ."), simply pick her up, deposit her in another room, leave the door open, and walk away (don't forget to take the fork!). It's little more than a stronger type of ignoring.

After doing this mild version on two or three separate occasions, you can then begin putting her in a real time-out for a minute. Count to three, remove your child to your chosen time-out place and ignore her for thirty to sixty seconds. (If she is over two and you have chosen to put her in her room, you may have to close the door if she refuses to stay inside when it's open.)

Even if she cries, leave her alone. Try not to look at her (some parents set up a mirror so they can secretly watch what their child is doing). The whole point of a time-out is to deprive your toddler of your smiling face for a short time. Don't worry about her feeling abandoned. All the love and attention you give her the other 23 hours and 59 minutes of the day more than make up for this small, momentary indignity!

Once the time is up (even if she is still upset), join her and play with her quietly, or lovingly pay attention to what she is doing. If she's still really out of control, however, try taking her out of the time-out place but ignoring her for another thirty to sixty seconds.

After the time-out, don't immediately start teaching her your behavior lesson. For the next half an hour, don't even talk about the time-out, what she did, what you did, or how she reacted to it. Later, you can go over what you want her to learn from the experience. Better yet, let her overhear you gossiping to her toys about it! That way she won't feel as though she's been given a lecture.

I actually encourage you to look for reasons to do time-outs once your toddler reaches twelve to fifteen months! Soon she will be capable of getting into very dangerous accidents, like running away in a parking lot, pulling down a lamp, or playing with wall sockets. And when you run toward her if she gets too close to the street, there's a chance she might think it's a game and run away! She needs to learn that when you say "No!!" with a stern face and voice, she must stop immediately. It's not a game!

Once your toddler gets used to the idea of time-outs, the isolation should last a minute for each year of her age. Use a timer that dings when the time is up. Some experts recommend that a child should then be brought back to finish what she was refusing to do before the time-out, but I disagree. For toddlers, the time-out is total payment for breaking a rule. Going back to what happened before only reignites the cycle of power struggles.

Time-outs: Real-Life Questions

What if she keeps getting out of her room?
For toddlers under two, I recommend playpens. (I think of them as play-penitentiaries.) For toddlers over two who won't stay in time-out I recommend putting a hook-and-eye latch on the bedroom door. Take a minute when she's calm and happy to show her what you've done and how that will keep the door shut the next time she has a time-out. Let her see you lock it and tell her to try to open the door as you stand there watching. Say, "See, honey, no open, no open!" This lets her know that when it's latched, she won't be able to open the door.

Using the latch to keep her in means you won't have to be on the other side of the door holding on to the doorknob! The penalty of a time-out is for her to lose your attention and be alone for a minute. That effect is totally lost if she has you caught in a game of tug-of-war with the doorknob.

Will she think a time-out is coming if I count "one, two, three" when I am just playing with her?
No. It isn't the counting that she associates with the time-out; it's the seriousness of your face and voice.

Will time-outs hurt my child's psyche?
Only if you shame your child while you do them. Try to avoid intensifying her resentment with phrases like "You go to your room immediately! Do you hear me?" It may help for you to see a time-out like a time-out in sports—a short break in the action. Say, "Sorry, buddy, but I think you may need to cool off a little."

Some parents do choose to sit their toddler on their lap and hold them tightly as a type of punishment. That's fine if it works for you. But I find that for more spirited toddlers it only turns a time-out into a power struggle.

What if my child resists going to a time-out?
Then escort her there or even pick her up and carry her. You can expect younger toddlers to resist. For children older than two and a

half, many people add some extra time to the time-out for thrashing and excessive resistance.

What if I end up doing time-outs ten times a day?
When Trevor, then 18 months old, threw a ball at the plants, his parents gave him a time-out. As soon as it ended, he threw the ball at the plants again—and got another time-out. How many time-outs do you think Trevor should get?

This may sound like a school math problem, but it's really a question of common sense. Do what you have to do. But if you find you're giving your child time-outs more than two or three times a day, something needs to be changed. Ask yourself: Does she need more time outside or with other kids? Are there too many temptations in your house? Are you giving her enough warm attention and kind words? Are you rewarding her when she is being good?

Spanking: Real-Life Questions

If my son doesn't respond when I say no, my husband gives his hand a little swat. Is that okay?
Here's the problem with swatting: As your child grows older, that "little swat" will no longer intimidate him. When he rebels, he will require a harder and harder spanking.

It's especially inappropriate to use spanking to punish your toddler for hitting. You don't teach your child not to spit by spitting in

---

Hitting: How NOT to Punish Your Toddler

Violence is obviously a huge problem in our country—and it has its roots in the home environment. That's why it's so important for us to treat our children with kindness, respect, and self-control. That will help them learn better ways to express their feelings so they don't end up picking on the little guys.

When you are really feeling irritated put your hands together and—clap. Don't slap. Show your frustration with growling or stomping, not with shaking and spanking.

---

her face, do you? Some parents eventually find themselves using a belt, coat hanger, or stick. Later, children get so big that even those things don't work.

In short, spanking is a dead-end street that sends a giant wrong message: that it's okay for big people to hit little people. Is that really what you want her to learn?

My father was spanked, and it made him behave, and he spanked me, and I behaved too. So what's the problem with me spanking my son?
Many parents say, "I was spanked, and I turned out okay." It's true that corporal punishment doesn't always leave permanent scars, but many adults still feel humiliated, resentful, and angry because they were spanked.

Most family traditions have value and should be upheld, but spanking is not one of them. In your grandfather's day, children were paddled and whipped with switches and belts, and they had their ears pulled, faces slapped, mouths washed out with soap, and knuckles rapped with rulers. Let's leave forcing kids to cooperate by threats and fear back in the horse-and-buggy days.

No offense, Grandpa, but there *is* a better way!

PART THREE

Pushing Aside
Troublesome Boulders

How Prehistoric Parenting can
help you get past some
common toddler problems

Chapter 12

Boulders That Trip Up One-Year-Olds:
Tantrums, Public Meltdowns, Sleep Problems, Biting

Main Points:

- Tantrums: They first appear at 12 to 15 months when emotions run high but self-control is low.

- Public meltdowns: Outbursts where there's an audience have to be tamed.

- Sleep problems: One-year-olds hate giving up the excitement of exploring—even when they're exhausted!

- Sleep training relies on routine and limit setting. Be soothing and nurturing before bedtime, and firm and consistent afterward.

- Biting: Nip it in the bud by growling.

Now let's see how to use some of the advice discussed in Part Two to help remove some common obstacles that trip up our primitive little toddlers. The next three chapters are not an exhaustive catalog of every tough situation you may face with your child. But they highlight many of the most common problems, and through them, I will show you exactly how to put the Prehistoric Parenting principles into action.

The challenges I will address in this chapter especially affect children under two, but they may occur in toddlers of all ages.

Tantrums: When Mount Toddler-Suvius Erupts!

> *"What makes me mad? Days when buttons won't go straight and I want to stay up late and I hate what's on my plate . . ."*
>
> —Catherine and Laurence Anholt, "What Makes Me Happy"

Tantrums and toddlers go together like firecrackers and the Fourth of July. They can occur at any time during these three years—and beyond. But they first rev up at 12 to 15 months—the real beginning of the "terrible twos."

Why Do Toddlers Have Tantrums?

It's no accident that tantrums debut in one-year-olds. That's exactly when young toddlers start developing the explosive combination of increasing independence and the typical Neanderthal-like traits of intensity, stubbornness, rigidity, aggressiveness, and impatience. Just mix together some of your child's passionate *wants* with your increasingly vocal *don'ts* and—kapow!

As Ted said of his spirited 20-month-old, "Tess is bilingual: she either talks or screams." Here are a few things that may push your little one over the edge:

His life changes unexpectedly. Keeping in balance is tough enough for your toddler when his life is running smoothly. But adding a big change on top of that—such as the absence of one or both parents, a new baby, or a trip—may tip the scale and lead to a meltdown.

Internal stresses trip him up. What's going on inside your child can be as upsetting as the stresses on the outside. Common tantrum triggers are hunger, fatigue, sweets, TV, exposure to angry fights in the house, caffeine (chocolate, tea, cola, cold remedies), overstimulation, and frustration (the inability to say or do what he wants). Fortunately, if you can find a pattern, you may be able to stop tantrums before they occur.

He's been cooped up too long. Toddlers aren't meant to be indoors. They thrive on fresh air, chirping birds, squishy mud, other kids, and 1,001 other treasures of Nature—so it's no wonder they get bored in our stuffy four-walled rooms!

He's painted himself into an emotional corner. The number-one misconception parents have about toddler tantrums is that they're a form of manipulation. Actually, when your little Neanderthal goes bonkers, he is just as much the victim of his passions as you are. Tantrums are like quicksand—the more he struggles, the deeper in he sinks!

As I mentioned earlier, more than anything (even the thing he's yelling for) your tot craves your understanding and attention. But because of his primitive sense of pride, the more upset he gets, the more he suddenly finds himself painted into a corner. That's when he needs your diplomatic assistance to help him recover *without feeling humiliated.*

They get him what he wants. Like whining and screaming, tantrums can also be learned behaviors. If your toddler likes your response, whether it's you giving in or losing your cool, bingo! He'll make a subconscious note about how well his tantrum worked. (This is mostly true after two years of age.) This is not exactly a conscious manipulation—it's more like a habit he keeps finding himself falling back into.

He has the "temper" temperament. Intense and spirited toddlers tend to melt down more because—well, they do *everything* more intensely. Michele used to marvel at her son Harrison's fits for their sheer gusto: "They put his sisters' mini-tantrums to shame!"

Why Do Older Toddlers Get Tantrums?

Parents often expect their more verbal and capable older toddlers to outgrow tantrums. But bigger kids go ballistic too! That's why child development experts Louise Bates Ames and Frances Ilg named their terrific book about older toddlers *Your Three-Year-Old—Friend or Enemy*. Here are three good reasons you may continue to see occasional fireworks:

1. Your three-year-old is still struggling with impulse control. Yet he's increasingly in situations where he's expected to be good (preschool, Grandma's house, play dates, etc.). By the end of the day, he may have so many bottled-up impulses inside that the moment he's back to the safety of your home, he shoots off a tantrum with the force of Old Faithful.

2. He feels very off balance—not quite baby, not quite big kid. Sometimes that emotional whiplash may be overwhelming and push him into the danger zone.

3. He's suddenly realizing how the world works. More than ever, three-year-olds use tantrums to get attention, help, or revenge.

Taming Tantrums the Prehistoric Parenting Way

All toddlers have tantrums—it's normal! So don't think you have a troubled toddler or that you're a poor parent. The good news is that once you know how to handle tantrums, you can often defuse them faster than a bomb squad.

Prevention strategies: Help keep your toddler on an even keel by lavishing him with lots of little time-ins; fresh air; sleep; good food; praise (many understated tidbits said directly to him as well as through his "side door"); and patience- and confidence-strengthening exercises (discussed in Chapter 9). Prepare him for what to expect each day, and provide clear consistent limits. Remember, each of these techniques is like putting another coin in the parking meter, buying you longer periods of calm and cooperation.

Containment strategies: If your toddler is getting increasingly upset, you may be able to head off a full tantrum if you immediately start narrating your child's feelings back to him using the Fast-Food Rule and Toddler-ese.

Too often, inexperienced parents comment on their toddler's actions without first mirroring his feelings:

"I'm cold!" "You can't be cold."

"I'm hungry!" "You just ate."

"Mine. Mine!" "No, honey, it's Tommy's."

"Cookie! Cookie!" "Hey, look over here, an anthill!"

If you skip the Fast-Food Rule, the more you try to calm him, the more upset he may become. Pretty soon the conversation becomes an argument, and then the argument turns into a prehistoric shouting match. You say, "You don't understand, son." And he yells, "WHAAAA!!!!!" (which loosely translated means, "No, *you* don't understand, Mom").

Your first goal is to connect with your little friend's wild spirit, not to set up a roadblock to stop him from expressing his upset. Use Toddler-ese to narrate what you think your child would say if he could state his feelings. Don't yell back, but try to mirror some of his intensity. Feel it from your heart. (With a little practice, most parents find that Toddler-ese has a calming effect in a minute or less.)

Save your reassurance and distractions for after he winds down. Once your child begins to settle, *then* it's your turn. Try to think of a win-win solution: "You want cookie! Let's pick two cookies to eat *after* lunch!" Or you might start playing the Boob—perhaps "tripping" as you stand up, or dropping something. This is a funny distraction and also helps him to save face by lessening his feeling that he is the only person who makes mistakes.

What if your toddler escalates the tantrum with kicking and screaming despite all your efforts? As long as he's not being destructive or aggressive, you might hold off on the time-out and first try ignoring him with a cold shoulder.

For example, you might say, "You're so mad! You're mad! Mad! MAD! You don't like it! You don't like it! I'm so sorry, sweetheart! You can keep kicking if you want, Mommy is going to the kitchen. I'll be back very fast." Remove yourself from the situation for thirty to sixty seconds. With his audience gone, your toddler may lose the incentive to be loud and dramatic. And because you're gone and the spotlight is off him, it may be easier for him to quiet down without losing dignity or feeling defeated.

When all else fails: If simple ignoring doesn't halt your toddler's tantrum, and he's being destructive or aggressive, he needs you to take control. Try giving him a bear hug from behind (restraining his arms) while you keep whispering in his ear that everything will be fine and you love him. If he resists, it's probably time for the help of a time-out.

Rubbing Your Child the Right Way

One unusual calming technique comes from John and Elise. "We have discovered an amazing way to soothe our two-year-old foster child, Matthew, when he goes into one of his wild tantrums. One of us strokes the sole of his foot or his palm with our fingernails or a toothbrush. It works in seconds!"

Tantrums: A Real-Life Question

My toddler got so upset, he passed out! What was that all about, and how can I stop it from happening again?

Breath-holding during a tantrum can be scary, but it's pretty common in 15- to 30-month-olds. They get mad, scared, or startled, and they try to cry, but no sound comes out! They stay like that for thirty to forty seconds, getting bluer or paler until they pass out. In essence, your child simply "forgot" to breathe! As soon as he passed out, his automatic breathing kicked in. (Sometimes there's a little twitching in his face, too.) Most breath-holding little Neanderthals revive within a few seconds.

If you catch your child in the middle of one of these bouts, sprinkle him with water or blow right at his face. This may make him gasp and start breathing.

There is no risk of brain damage from simple breath-holding spells; but if your child has such an episode, immediately call your doctor to make sure the fainting spell wasn't due to a seizure or some other medical condition.

Public Meltdowns: How Not to Panic in the Streets

Sandy brought 22-month-old Corey along to the toy store when his older sister, Chrissy, had to buy a birthday present for a friend. It was their third stop that morning, but Sandy hoped it would be fast. She set Corey down at a display of toy trains and watched him play while she helped Chrissy.

When it was time to go, Corey refused Sandy's cheerful requests to leave. When she tried to pick him up, he collapsed to the floor, kicking.

The salesclerk frowned, Chrissy moaned and Sandy checked her watch. Corey should have had lunch and started his nap an hour ago.

Ignoring the stares of the other shoppers, Sandy knelt next to her son and in a passionate voice said, "You say, 'NO!! No, no, Nooooo!!!' You say, 'NO go home! NO! Corey like train!' Corey say, 'NOOOOO go home!'" Corey kept crying. Sandy persisted, stomping her feet, shaking her head, and waving her arms with renewed intensity to match her son's. "You say, 'No! No, no, NO!!! NOOOOOOOO!!' You say, 'NO go home!'" Corey paused for a nanosecond.

"You say, 'NO go home! NO . . . NO!!! Corey not ready, Mommy!!!'" Sandy continued this Toddler-ese a little longer as Corey stopped crying. Then she lowered her voice to a whisper. "Hey! Psssst! Hey!! Let's play train. Choo-choo! Choo-choo! Let's choo-choo all the way to the car!" Chrissy was so embarrassed that she pretended she didn't know her chug-a-chugging mother and brother, but Corey was thrilled to make train noises holding on to his mom's hips all the way out the door.

Public tantrums are especially tough because they are so . . . public. It feels like you're under a spotlight and the whole world is "staring at your warts"! What's more, your shrieking toddler may cry even harder if he feels you're embarrassed or confused about how to respond.

Planning ahead goes a long way toward avoiding meltdowns in aisle three at Wal-Mart. If possible, time your trip around naps and meals. Make your excursions short and organized. Do only one or two errands at a time—meandering through a mall is a sure recipe for sensory overload in a toddler's Stone Age brain. Bring along a snack or a small treat such as stickers, a pen and paper, or a special toy carried only on errands to help make your toddler's waiting easier.

When your toddler does erupt, you have three options:

1. You can ignore him, which is hard to do because public outbursts usually escalate—he's playing to a large audience.

2. You can use Toddler-ese to show empathy, as Sandy did, and then offer a detour (a compromise or distraction).

3. You can count to three, remove him from the scene, and do a time-out in the car. Here's how to do that: Put him in the car, roll down the windows a little, lock the doors, and then wait right outside with your back turned to him. If he calms in a couple of minutes, take him out and either give him a small reward to "grease the wheels of cooperation" so that you can quickly finish your shopping, or go home, which is probably where he needs to be anyway. *Warning:* Do not strap your child in his car seat. You don't want him to identify this safety device with punishment. And never put a child in a hot car, or a car that's in the sun.

Sleep Problems: Now You're Getting Sleepy . . . Not!

Gigi was always a great sleeper. By five months, she conked out for twelve straight hours, from seven P.M. to seven A.M. "We were the envy of all our friends," Gigi's mom, Anita, wistfully reminisced. But at 18 months that wonderful pattern came to a screeching halt. Gigi started to wake two, three, and four times a night. And scream! Anita or her husband, Paul, would get up and rock her to sleep, only for her to awaken from a deep slumber just a few hours later. Even when they rocked her to sleep, Gigi jolted awake the instant they put her down. Some nights Anita and Paul started at seven P.M. and didn't get her down until nearly eleven P.M. Soon Gigi began to resist going to bed altogether!

"She just keeps going and going," Anita confessed wearily. "But I'm a goner!"

Why Toddlers Resist Sleep

The typical toddler sleeps for twelve to fourteen hours a day, counting naps and nighttime sleep. And he needs every bit of that sleep to recharge his brain and file away the hundreds of new experiences he has each day. So why do some toddlers resist sleep so stubbornly?

He's in love—with walking! Your toddler may develop sleep problems because he loves exploring the world so much that he can't bear to give it up. No wonder he fights going to bed even though he's totally pooped. If he accidentally awakens during the night, he might even feel refreshed enough to want to start the day!

He misses you. You may have noticed that your toddler is getting more and more upset when he has to separate from you. This is normal, especially after a trip, an illness, or a big change (like the birth of a sibling). But separation is particularly tough in the middle of the night because your dark, quiet house feels lonely (or even scary), and your little one may insist that you come to save him from the isolation.

He's teething. The throbbing of new teeth increases when a child lies down and may be just enough to rouse him from a light sleep.

He's getting nosy. Your little explorer is interested in what's going on in his world (your home). Now when he hears talking or other kinds of noises from another room, it piques his curiosity. He doesn't want to miss a thing.

He's a creature of habit. Be careful about what sleep habits you allow your toddler to form. If you always rock him to sleep, he will expect to be rocked even when he gets up in the middle of the night; if you sleep with him when he's sick, after a few nights he may start to expect that every night too. (Of course, if he's sick you may decide to do it anyway and retrain his sleep habits after he recovers.)

Sleep-Training the Prehistoric Parenting Way

Although tantrums are common, sleep problems bring out the most complaints from parents of toddlers. That's because they affect the quality of life of everybody in the house. After Jennifer saw her friend Janice turn her car into oncoming traffic (she was so tired, she didn't know what she was doing), she sent Janice to see me to learn how to sleep-train her 14-month-old "night owl."

Here are some of the suggestions I made to her:

Reduce stimulants. Lower the excitement level before bedtime. An hour before bedtime, turn down the lights. (Nightlights are fine.) Avoid roughhousing, TV, loud music, and all internal stimulants, such as cola, iced tea, chocolate, and decongestants.

Make sure he's sleeping during the day. Contrary to what most parents think, keeping a child awake later into the night does *not* make him sleep longer. In fact, he will usually sleep less well! What most sleep specialists say is that if you want your toddler to sleep more at night, encourage him to sleep *more* during the day!

Give a little pain medicine. If you think your toddler is teething, ask your doctor about giving ibuprofen at bedtime to prevent the annoying throbbing.

Make sure he's not hungry. If your young toddler wakes you with his crying at two A.M. and then drains your breast or a bottle, try waking *him* up to feed him a little earlier in the night. What's the difference? Giving him sweet, delicious milk when he awakens is like rewarding him for getting up. ("My mom's so happy when I wake up at night, she gives me a *present!*") On the other hand, if you wake *him* to eat, he'll get the calories he craves without encouraging his self-waking.

If your child is getting up in the middle of the night, try waking him sometime between eleven P.M. and midnight to fill his stomach for the long sleep ahead. If he still awakens hungry at four A.M., I'd feed him, but the next night I'd wake him for a meal thirty minutes before he got up the previous night (in this case, at about half past three). Don't talk or cuddle during this feeding.

Then every three or four nights shorten the middle-of-the-night nursing by a couple of minutes, or replace two ounces of the milk with two ounces of water. Within two weeks you should be able to stop the early-morning feedings altogether.

Another trick that can work to keep a toddler sleeping at night is to load him up with a calorie-rich meal right before bedtime (like avocado mashed with a little olive oil).

> *Daniella, the mother of 13-month-old Skyler, found that he slept all night when she gave him an egg just before bedtime.*

Develop a perfect bedtime routine. A consistent, unchanging bedtime routine is the perfect signal to your toddler that it's sleep time. (And using one now paves the way for easier bedtimes at age two, when Cave-Kids are *really* routine-dependent.)

- Dim the lights, and play white noise one to two hours before bedtime. (You can play white noise all night long.) White noise has two benefits: First, it imitates the sound your child heard in the womb and gets him calmed and into a deeper level of sleep; second, it drowns out disturbing noises from within and outside your home.
- Give him a warm bath, then rock him or give him a massage (Chapter 10) to soothe him.
- Stroke his forehead from the eyebrows to the scalp, pulling

the eyes open a tiny bit with each stroke. Your child's automatic response will be to want to close his eyes!

■ Other soothing sleep aids include lullaby music (in addition to white noise), nightlights, soft singing, affirmations, and of course a sweet, cuddly lovey.

If your child falls asleep with you next to him, jostle him and wake him up a tiny bit when you leave. This may sound odd, but the more chances he has to practice putting himself back to sleep, the more likely it will be that he can do it if he wakes in the middle of the night.

Get serious about training your toddler to sleep through the night. The bad news is that your toddler's sleep habits can be easily disrupted, but the good news is that new ones can be easily learned.

If you have tried all of the above and your little Neanderthal is still fighting bedtime or waking in the middle of the night, you may need to set firmer limits. Here are three useful approaches:

The "I Am Here for You as Long as You Need Me" Technique
Toddlers can be demanding and tenacious, and they often need many repetitions of the rules to finally realize that they have no choice but to give in. This technique consists of three steps:

1. Go to your toddler as soon as he cries, and hug him in the crib or pick him up. Tell him you love him, but don't say much more; the more you talk, the more you're rewarding him for waking up.

2. Put him down as soon as he quiets. (Sit down right by the crib.)

3. Hug him or pick him up the moment he starts crying again.

The lesson you're teaching him is "I love you, and I'm here for you, but once you're calm, I want you to sleep on your own." This technique works best on toddlers who are more easygoing and less stubborn. Don't be surprised if it takes twenty to fifty repetitions to get your child to finally go back to sleep and if this has to be repeated a couple of times a night for several days (or even a couple of weeks).

The "Teach Him to Put Himself to Sleep" Plan

This is the traditional sleep-training idea. It's terrible to let a child cry at night if he is truly fearful. (See Chapter 14 for more about fears.) But more often than not, nighttime crying is just a habit. Your child just can't bear seeing the day's party come to an end. This crying is very similar to his screaming in protest to other limits you set. ("No! You can cry all day, but there's no way you can have those scissors!") This technique also consists of three steps:

1. Go to your toddler after three minutes of crying.

2. Pop your head in the room for a couple of seconds, just long enough to see if he vomited or caught his arm in an uncomfortable position. Only say, "I love you. Go to sleep, sweetheart," then leave.

3. If he keeps crying, return in five minutes, then ten minutes after that, and then every fifteen minutes to check on him and let him know you haven't left the planet. Each time you come in, stay for only three to four seconds and repeat the line, "I love you. Go to sleep, sweetheart."

The first night will be tough! Your toddler may cry for up to one hour, occasionally longer. And you will need to repeat this whole process with any further wakings that night (this often happens one to three times). Usually the next night will be about the same, but the third night will be much better. By the fourth night, most toddlers begin sleeping all the way until morning!

Resist the temptation to pick your toddler up or talk too much. The more you say or do, the more you're giving him hope that you'll change your mind and rescue him. Even going near the crib may be "putting gasoline on the fire." It may feed his hope that his crying is working and that you'll soon pick him up.

Letting your toddler cry himself to sleep for a couple of nights won't scar him. He may be upset in the morning, but his momentary hurt and anger will be more than balanced by all the love and attention he gets from you all day long. And besides, you'll be able to give your child so much more affection during the day if you're not perpetually exhausted.

If your toddler is no longer in a crib when you do the training, you'll need to put up a barrier to keep him from leaving his room at night. If he can climb over a gate, I recommend putting a hook-and-eye latch on the outside of the door. During the day show your child that when the door's locked, it won't open. At night leave a blanket and pillow next to the door, because some children leave their beds and fall asleep on the floor once they realize they can't get out.

With both sleep training techniques, a lovey and white noise can help the process go faster. White noise mutes outside sounds that may awaken him and also tends to put children into a deeper, more lasting sleep.

If your child shares a bedroom with a sibling, it's usually best to let the sibling sleep in your room or the living room while the sleep training is taking place.

Twinkle Interruptus: A No-cry Way to Get Toddlers to Sleep

This is a great approach to help toddlers (close to age two) who're having difficulty falling asleep. Twinkle Interruptus can be a no-cry, painless way to train your child to fall asleep quickly. Aaron, the father of Emma, named this method after the song "Twinkle, Twinkle, Little Star" because his daughter used to make him sing it over and over, for thirty to forty minutes, until she fell asleep.

Here's how it works.

Do your usual bedtime routine. Sing "Twinkle, Twinkle" or another favorite song twice, and as you start the third round, stop and act as if you're a Boob who suddenly remembered something important. Say, "Oh, oh, oh, I forgot to kiss Mommy. Here, you hold teddy. I'll be *RIGHT* back." Come back fast—after a few seconds.

Then settle in again. Start to sing the song from the beginning, but after another minute go through the same departure routine. This time wait about ten seconds before you come back. Sing for a few minutes, then repeat the same routine, but return in thirty seconds and stay with him until he falls asleep. The next night go through the routine again but have him wait ten seconds, then thirty seconds, and finally a minute. The third night stay outside the room for thirty seconds and then a minute and ultimately three minutes. Pretty soon your toddler will fall asleep waiting for you after just your first or second departure.

Of course, this is a manipulation of sorts—but so is much of being an ambassador. There's nothing devious about it—it's a plot for good, not evil! You're merely using your diplomacy and advanced intelligence to outsmart his worries.

Avoiding Crib Falls

Before doing sleep-training, remove the bumpers in the crib to keep your athletic little child from climbing out. Even with this precaution, however, make sure there's something soft on the floor around the crib. You never know when your intrepid toddler will make that first crib escape. Fifteen-month-old Will climbed out of his crib while his mom, Sue, was doing sleep-training. "He was okay," she said, "but I got completely spooked because I suddenly heard his crying getting closer and closer!"

If you think your toddler is just about ready to climb over the crib (he can get one leg up on the railing), it's time to transition to a big-kid bed, to prevent possible accidents.

Sleep Problems: Real-Life Questions

What if my toddler keeps crying and crying?

There's no magic amount of time to wait out your toddler's cries. If you're sure he isn't sick or afraid, you may allow him to cry for up to an hour (some incredibly persistent kids can even go longer than that!). You should check him very briefly every fifteen minutes just to be sure that he's okay, but avoid accidentally giving him a mixed message by talking too much, staying too close to the crib or lingering too long in the room.

The bedtime battle is one thing. But then my son wakes up crying in the middle of the night!
For a toddler who wakes up in the middle of the night, do the same thing you do at bedtime. Briefly check to see if he is okay and then do the five-minute, ten-minute, and fifteen-minute visits. Usually, the more times you repeat this exercise, the sooner he will learn to fall asleep on his own.

David and Catherine were exhausted. Until their daughter Chloe was two, she slept with them. Then they wanted her to be in her own bed, but they wanted to avoid having to endure what they had been warned would be two weeks of screaming at night. So, when they moved her they made up a great bedtime routine: saying goodnight to all of Chloe's toys, giving her a massage, cuddling with her and her lovey, and singing lullabies. It didn't work. Chloe demanded her parents stay with her for hours, and they were frustrated and exhausted. Finally, they decided to do a "let her cry" sleep routine to save their own sanity. The first night Chloe cried for an hour and then slept till morning. But that was it for crying. Since then she's fallen asleep quickly and slept from eight P.M. to seven A.M. every day!

Biting: My, What Sharp Teeth You Have!

Diana was trying to tie Lucas's shoes, but he kept waving his feet around. So she held his foot between her knees long enough to allow her to make the knot. That's when Lucas, 16 months old, bent over and bit her hand—hard! "Oww!" she gasped. Then, struggling

to compose herself, she mildly scolded him, saying,
"Please Lukie, no biting!"
　　But Lucas didn't stop biting. In fact, whenever he
got mad, it became his favorite response.

Why They Chomp

Neanderthals used their teeth so much, they wore out in front! It's little surprise that our younger toddlers tend to bite more than older ones. For primitives who don't yet talk well, biting is a way of expressing anger or frustration. (Even mild-mannered toddlers sometimes bite playmates when they feel cornered or threatened.) Young toddlers also bite as a way of saying they're hungry or teething.

Some toddlers bite once and never do it again. But with others it becomes a bad habit. Often this occurs because, like Lucas, they enjoy the response it brought. Whether you're a parent or a playmate, it can be hard not to shriek when little Dracula sinks his baby teeth in. The fussing that may follow a biting incident can also serve as a great diversion. If his buddy Sally drops the toy rake he wanted, the biter may strike again the next time he wants to get a similar result.

Fortunately, kids generally outgrow this behavior by the end of toddlerhood, when they learn more appropriate ways to express themselves.

Reacting to Biting the Prehistoric Parenting Way

Your primary goal is to prevent biting from occurring, but if you can't do that, your next two goals should be to stop the biting as it is happening or quickly thereafter.

Preventing Bites
The right prevention efforts can help you avoid ever having to deal with biting, or turn a one-time incident into a one-time-*only*.

- *Respond to hunger and teething.* If your toddler is hungry, feed him. If he is teething, provide him comfort with a pain reliever like ibuprofen or a teething toy. (I prefer washcloths and cloth toys—they have no plastic residues.)
- *Remember the need for outdoor play.* Whether he's teething or not, make sure your toddler isn't cooped up for long stretches. That will relieve some of the frustration that naturally builds up all day.
- *Use side-door messages to explain the rule.* If your toddler has witnessed a biting incident, gossip to one of his toys that you don't like biting, or tell a fairy tale in which a frog bit everyone he met instead of kissing them and soon had no friends. (Don't forget the happy ending: He learned that he could bite his shirt instead of other kids, and magically he had all his friends back again!)
- *Minimize conflict opportunities around other kids.* If your child is in a day-care setting or playgroup, be sure there are plenty of age-appropriate toys to go around. Another way to minimize conflicts is to have several small play zones within the room that focus on different activities—for example, art activities in one corner, a pretend kitchen in another, blocks in the middle, and so on.

In the Heat of the Moment

When your toddler looks like he's about to nip, remind him that you don't like it: "No bite. No biting allowed!! Biting is for food." Notice that this is a time when you can skip the Fast-Food Rule and jump right to *your* more urgent message, in Toddler-ese.

Tone is everything. If you mildly say, "Mommy doesn't like biting," as Diana did in the example above, your message will be as lost as a whisper in a storm. Make your words firm and forceful, like you mean business. Your expression should be stern and serious. Most toddlers will get the message and put their teeth into retreat. Don't keep staring at him after you give your warning. Some kids intentionally disobey when they are stared at.

After a Bite

What if the chomper strikes before you can stop him? In a stern voice, say, "NO!" and growl, frown, clap, and stomp, then use the *cold shoulder* to give this strong message even more power. This does two things: It teaches that biting is not acceptable, and it models growling as an alternative way to express strong feelings.

If your toddler makes another nip attempt right after you've done this, it's reasonable to do a time-out for biting. You have already communicated your displeasure, and your toddler now knows there is a no-bite rule. Because he violated that rule, he needs a stronger response to underscore your message.

If it was another child who was nipped, turn your attention to him, while ignoring your own child for a minute or two. You don't want to reinforce your toddler's misdeed by giving him too much attention after his attack. (Remember the Law of the Soggy Potato Chip—see page 203.)

What If Your Child Is the One Who's Bitten?

As mortifying as it can be to be the parent of a biter, it's of course very upsetting to watch your child get bitten. It may be that the biter was hungry or didn't have enough fresh air or active play, or that there just were not enough toys to go around. Sometimes there's a rash of biting in a day-care room or playgroup as toddlers copy this behavior from one another (like sticking out tongues).

Interestingly, it's often not the meek child but the aggressive one who is bitten. In his exuberant play style, he might unwittingly invade another toddler's space, triggering a bite done in self- defense.

It helps to know what was going on when your toddler was bitten. If you weren't there when it happened, ask your toddler's babysitter or day-care provider to clarify, and look for steps you can take to prevent future nips.

Chapter 13

Boulders That Trip Up Two-Year-Olds
Separation Worries, Picky Eating, Toilet Learning

Main Points:

- Separation worries: Even independent toddlers sometimes experience deep worries. This push-pull is often at the heart of separation troubles.

- Rather than sneaking away, gradually shorten your good-byes (Mommy Interruptus) to make partings less abrupt.

- Picky eating: It's a normal tendency at age two as your toddler's growth slows and she needs fewer calories.

- Toilet learning: Cave-Kids love the potty—if you approach it diplomatically.

Separation Worries: "Mommy, Don't Go!"

"Parting is such sweet sorrow."

—William Shakespeare, *Romeo and Juliet*

Frogs and lizards happily hop and slither away from their families the instant they're born. But we are social animals. Our tight bond to our mothers has been a hallmark of mammals for tens of millions of years! At the same time, humans are programmed to reach out and explore. That's why much of toddlerhood is a game of "two leaps forward, one step back." Like a scouting party that rushed too far ahead of the wagon train, your independent toddler may suddenly feel exposed and vulnerable—so she backtracks (regresses) to a more immature time to recharge her comfort level with a little no-pressure "baby love."

Why Toddlers Have a Hard Time Separating

It's not really surprising that separation worries usually peak between 15 and 30 months. As your child toddles away from you and begins exploring the wide world, it's exhilarating—and more than a little scary. Here's why separation fears are often a problem at this age:

It's their nature. Separation worries usually start around 15 to 18 months as toddlers enter the Neanderthal phase (rigid, impulsive, and passionate). When they get upset or scared, many of them experience a tidal wave of alarm knocking their world into chaos. A simple thought like *Where's Mommy?* can snowball into a sudden desperate fear: *Where's MOMMY?!!!!*

Your young toddler's primitive attention span tends to concentrate on one thing at a time—therefore she may get so engrossed in what she's doing that she doesn't hear you leave the room. Suddenly she looks around, and—oh no!—her great protector is suddenly gone. She feels abandoned—all alone in the world! Even if you're just in the bathroom.

By 24 months, your toddler adores sameness, and any disruption of the normal routine may intensify her anxiety. So she may separate well at day care every morning if Daddy customarily takes her there, but she'll cling and cry if Mommy brings her or if there is a substitute teacher. Cautious young toddlers have an especially hard time with change.

Separations may also be tough for older toddlers. Some three-year-olds temporarily regress (move backward) in their development as they begin comparing themselves to everything else in their world. Suddenly, they realize that they are small and vulnerable. (To learn more, see the discussion of fears in Chapter 14.) These children cling tightly to their mommies and daddies.

Circumstances make them feel vulnerable. Expect more separation worry if you are anxious. Because toddlers are so attuned to non-verbal messages, they can sense your stress and sadness over a death, illness, marital disagreement, or financial crisis. Ditto if your toddler is feeling insecure by too many changes, such as a new home or school; a sibling's birth; illness or hospitalization; loss of a close family member, nanny, or pet; travel; or even such everyday stresses as hunger, fatigue, or overstimulation.

Handling Separations the Prehistoric Parenting Way

You need to approach potential separation problems with your prehistoric buddy using all your ambassadorial tools:

Build confidence to "inoculate" against painful partings. Use the confidence-builder tactics to build up her strength and resilience (see Chapter 9). And rely on lots of praise, time-ins, little rewards, and the comforts of routines to help your child weather the stress of time apart (see Chapters 9 and 10).

Practice saying farewell through play. Hide-and-seek is a fun way to teach your child that when you go away, you always come back. You can also use gossip and role-play with dolls or pretend games (see

Chapter 9). Let your toddler be the mommy while you play the worried baby. Say, "I miss Mommy. Mommy! Mommy! Mommy!!!! I want Mommy!!! Oh! There you are! I knew you always come back!"

Make up fairy tales (also discussed in Chapter 9). Tell your child, "Once upon a time there was a little girl froggie who was worried when her mommy hopped off their lily pad, but she had a talking teddy bear who sang songs with her and kept her happy and safe until her mommy came back with kisses and big juicy flies to eat!"

Transfer your power. Remember that blankies and loveys are called "transitional objects" because they allow your toddler to transition away from being so attached to *you*. Your toddler at two and three is trying to make sense of the world and believes in the power of objects and magic. So she will feel more brave if you give her a trinket that's a special reminder of you, like a bracelet, a special hankie, a face drawn in ink on her hand, a locket of your hair, or a photo—something she can keep with her and touch or look at whenever she needs to feel that you're near.

Practice calming breathing. Make breathing exercises a part of your good-byes (see Chapter 10).

Never sneak away. Sure, you avoid seeing her pained reaction. But doing so only confirms her worst fear that the world is unpredictable and unsafe. When your toddler gets upset as a parting nears, use lots of nonjudgmental Toddler-ese. Repeat her pleas of "No! No! Don't go, Mommy! You say, 'No no NO!!! No go!!!'" Then work toward finding a win-win solution by saying, "Mommy go work and come back. Then we'll have another big hug just like this and take a bike ride!"

If she's still upset, you can start teaching her Mommy Interruptus.

The Art of Mommy Interruptus

This is basically a way of teaching patience to worried toddlers. It uses baby steps of progress to make separations less abrupt.

Take, for example, being dropped off at day care. When your pre-historic pup says, "No! No school!" and clings to your legs outside the classroom door, she's probably not really saying that she hates school. She simply lacks the brainpower to recall the past (that she had a blast yesterday) or to see the future (that it will be fun today too). She's stuck in the present, and all she can see is you *abandoning* her. Your task is to help her remember that you always come back.

Here's what to do:

Use your best Toddler-ese to let her know you get her message. "You say, 'No! No, NO! No school! No Mommy go!'"

Once your child calms a little, go inside and try to get her interested in doing something with you. After a few minutes, casually say, "Oh, I have to check something. I'll be back in one second." Leave the room, even if your toddler is crying, but come back in just three to five seconds. Reflect her feelings again, using a few short phrases with the right body language, tone of voice, and hand gestures, and then play a little more. After she calms for a few minutes, go out again, saying, "I have to go pee-pee. Here, hold my magic princess bracelet (or lovey), I'll be right back."

Over the next half-hour, repeat this process three or four times, leaving for gradually longer periods, for example, thirty seconds, forty-five seconds, and two minutes. Finally, when you're leaving for good, give a big wave and cheerfully call out, "Good-bye, I'll see you after your nap. Whenever you want me you can look at the funny face I drew on your hand. And don't forget we're going to the playground when school's over!"

By now, your toddler may be thinking, *Okay, Mom, get out of here already!* But if she still cries at this point, be reassured that all the preparation you've done will make her distress briefer. Call in an hour and ask the teacher how she was after you left. Usually, the answer will be, "Oh, she calmed down and happily joined in a minute after you left." (Meanwhile, your guilt haunted you!) If, however, your toddler continued crying for an hour after you left, something else is going on. If you can't identify the probable cause (sickness, for example), you need to consider other solutions, like staying with her at day care for a couple of days. Or even changing schools.

> **Mari handles her son's separation worries using the Fast-Food Rule:** "My two-year-old, Aidan, goes to school twice a week. When we get there, he usually starts to shriek that he doesn't want to get out of the car. He wants to stay with me and our new baby, Nate. I narrate his feelings and mirror his tone of voice: 'I don't want to go to school today!!! No teacher Chris!!! No teacher Cindy!!! No friends!!! I want Mama and Nate!! NO SCHOOL!! NO!'

"By then, he's usually calmed a little, and I make a respectful compromise with him: 'It's okay, it's okay, but we have to go in and tell Chris that you won't be at school today. If you really don't want to stay, you'll come with Mama.' At this point he gets out of the car happily and proudly swaggers down the walkway with me. Once he gets inside the preschool, he immediately gets interested in the buzz of activity and his old friends, and he kisses me good-bye in less than five minutes!"

Excellent Toddler-ese and baby steps allowed Aidan to get used to the separation rather than making him confront it all at once by crying it out. But if, unlike Mari, you don't have the option of *not* dropping your toddler off, you could say, "You say, 'No, no, NO!!! No school!!! Don't want it! Don't want it!!'" When your toddler calms, suggest to her, "Let's go inside, and tell the teacher you say 'No, no, NO!!'" You're not saying she *can* stay home; you're only respectfully mirroring her feelings. This little detour helps delay the conflict, increasing your odds of getting your child in the building and involved with something, so you can then use the graduated good-byes of Mommy Interruptus to part gently.

Congratulate her successes. When you are reunited, ask with interest about her day, and later use your child's "side door" by telling a fairy tale, or by gently gossiping to her dolls about her courage and success: "Darcy told me, 'No, no. Don't go . . .' but then she was a big girl and played with her toys all by herself. Then Mommy came back, and we had a treat and hugged, and we were all happy."

Separations: A Real-Life Question

Doesn't Mommy Interruptus make a child feel ignored?
No. Two-year-olds take things at face value. If you say you have to go for a few seconds, and you really do come back quickly, they think that's reasonable. They can tolerate tiny bits of frustration.

Here's one way your child is not like her uncivilized ancestors: appetite. Cave dwellers would eat whatever they could get their hands on, but toddlers often have skimpy appetites. As Shana, the mom of two-year-old Danny, put it, "I swear to God, he may only eat one cracker, and that's it for the day!"

But don't allow your fear to blow the problem out of proportion. Picky eaters are less likely to become obese adults. And even the poorest children in the United States get enough protein. As I will soon discuss, it's vegetables, iron, and calcium that you may need to pay a little attention to.

Why Toddlers Are Uninterested in Eating

Here are the reasons that what seems finicky to you is often perfectly normal behavior:

Your toddler really isn't hungry. Shortly after their first birthday toddlers suddenly shift gears from their fast baby growth to their slow toddler growth pattern. The resulting slowdown in appetite can be shocking compared to your twenty-four-pound one-year-old guzzling almost a quart of milk a day. But kids simply don't keep that pace up forever. It would be like a 120-pound woman downing more than a gallon of whole milk every twenty-four hours! (That's more than three thousand calories a day—from milk alone.)

By 18 to 24 months, toddlers have usually become "grazing animals," eating several small snacks a day and often going days without eating an actual meal with vegetables, fruit, or meat. It sure doesn't seem like a balanced diet, but as I always tell parents, you have to add up all the foods eaten over one to two weeks to really know if it's in balance.

A meal isn't just a meal to a toddler. We sit down to chow down. But to a toddler, a meal is about more than nourishment—it's science time. Your little cave-girl may ponder, *If I fling the peas with my spoon, where will they land?* or *What does applesauce feel like—on my hand? In my hair?* No wonder she may regard you with indignation as you try to shovel an extra spoon of yogurt into her mouth, as if to say, *What do you mean, you want me to eat more? I'm too busy!*

Green is yucky: an ancient protective mechanism kicks in. By age two, toddlers often develop rigid food preferences. White, yellow, and red stuff—yes. Green stuff—no! (Even when it comes to lollipops—they'll pick red over green almost every time!) It's quite smart to be attracted to reds and sweets. These characteristics indicate what's ripe and safe to eat. Even animals use sweetness to judge the ripeness of fruit. It's also smart to avoid green food, which in Nature is often bitter.

So don't push your toddler too hard to try any food adventures at this stage. You will be most successful at meals if you appeal to her sweet tooth with carrots, yams, corn, and other sweet vegetables, or by making sweetened greens, like broccoli with teriyaki sauce.

She may have "temperamental taste buds." Some toddlers are simply more sensitive to strong flavors and prefer bland foods. Toddlers with tentative personalities may be even more resistant than most to trying something new.

Handling a Picky Eater the Prehistoric Parenting Way

Your focus has been feeding, feeding, feeding for so long, it's hard to stop thinking this way, especially since we all feel like such good parents when our kids clean their plates! Don't see fussy eating as a struggle between you and your toddler—see it more as a challenge to you to be creative and figure out how to make food fun.

Try the following tips for a month or two. One or more of them will help you turn your no-win confrontations into win-win successes. (Although in truth, some toddlers tenaciously refuse anything other than pasta, dairy products, pizza, and buttered bread.)

Barter in baby steps. If you want your toddler to eat a veggie, the least successful tactic is to threaten or be pushy. Instead, try bargaining: "If you eat a green bean, I'll let you have another French fry." Be prepared for your Cave-Kid to drive a hard bargain. She may eat only half the bean or have just a nibble. But even this much is a victory. It's a baby step in the right direction.

Make the food seem very desirable. Use reverse psychology. When two-year-old Celia didn't want to eat, her parents, Mark and Karen, removed bits of food off her plate in a sneaky, sly way. They would pretend they were greedy and wanted all her food for themselves. "We appealed to her basic sense of possessiveness," says Mark. "It only works about half the time, but a fifty-fifty success rate ain't so bad."

Even better, when your toddler reaches for the food, give her only a tiny piece of it. You know the old saying, "We always want what we can't get." A variation on this theme: Say with pretend indignation, "Hey, don't eat that broccoli—it's mine! Mine!" and protest meekly if she disobeys you and eats it.

Be a Master of Disguise

Okay, this section may sound like you're being a spy more than an ambassador, but here are my favorite tricks for getting nutrients and veggies past your toddler's lips:

- Appeal to her "sour tooth." Cut vegetables into French-fry-size strips, cook them, then marinate them overnight in pickle juice or Italian dressing.
- Blend veggies into a soup.
- Blend and bake veggies into batter bread. Use a recipe for zucchini bread, but use pureed broccoli in place of zucchini and double the amount the recipe calls for.
- Make yam chips by baking or broiling them in an oven with a little salt and butter.

- Dip lightly steamed veggies into ranch or creamy Italian dressing.
- Grind zucchini or carrots and put them into pancakes and serve them with syrup.
- Give fresh carrot or carrot/apple or carrot/orange juice.
- Iron is important for blood, muscle, and brain growth. You can add a lot of iron to your child's diet just by cooking in a cast-iron pot or skillet. Add lemon juice or vinegar, and the acid will really help bring the iron out of the metal and into the food.
- Your toddler needs about 12 mg. of iron a day. Iron-rich foods include black beans (1 cup has 8 mg.), liver (4 oz. has 7.9 mg.), lentils (1 cup has 6.6 mg.), beef (4 oz. has 3.6 mg.), blackstrap molasses (1 tablespoon has 3.5 mg.), raisins (8 oz. have 3.2 mg.), prune juice (8 oz. has 3.0 mg.), and cooked greens (½ cup of mustard greens, dandelion greens, or collards has 2.6 mg.). Squeeze a little lemon juice over iron-rich foods—you'll increase iron absorption severalfold. (But beware, dark grape juice cuts iron absorption by over 50 percent.)
- Your toddler needs 700 to 1,000 mg. of calcium each day. Some powerhouse sources of calcium that are easy to sneak into your toddler's diet include skim milk powder, which is easy to mix into foods (2 oz. contains 400 mg.), blackstrap molasses (1 tbsp. has 290 mg.), sesame seed butter (tahini), sold in health-food stores (2 oz. has 270 mg.), yogurt (8 oz. has 270 mg.), grated parmesan (2 oz. has 260 mg.), and broccoli (1 stalk has 160 mg.). You can give your child a further calcium boost simply by letting her play outside! Just fifteen to thirty minutes of sunlight a day will help her body make vitamin D, which is essential for her to fully benefit from the calcium in her diet. (Don't forget to put on the sunscreen if your toddler is going to be out in the sun for over thirty minutes.)

Be careful about what your face says. Your Cave-Kid can't read labels, but she's an expert at reading your face. If you look disgusted by spinach, she's sure to pick that up.

Don't get into a fight you can't win. You can't force your toddler to eat. If you try, you will turn her against food—and you! Remember, food fights are not battles you can win. So if your tot digs in and refuses, back down and ignore her for a minute or two to show her that you won't pay attention to her if she's uncooperative.

Let your toddler leave the table when she says she's finished—even if she hardly ate. If she returns to the table just for milk, try this negotiation: Acknowledge her desire in Toddler-ese, then ignore her for a few seconds, reach for the milk, and right before you give it to her, withdraw it and bargain with her to eat a *tiny* taste of dinner first. If you are successful, she will take only a minuscule bite, but it's a beginning! It's an important first baby step toward cooperation.

Consider a children's multivitamin every day. Ask your doctor if she thinks this is a good idea. If your tyke is a very picky eater, it will probably help your peace of mind in addition to your toddler's health. Just be sure to keep the vitamin jar out of reach. Remember, at this age toddlers can open childproof containers, and vitamins look like candy. Be especially careful with vitamins containing iron. Vitamins with iron are highly *poisonous* if your child gets into them and takes several at once.

Toilet Learning: Good-bye Diapers

Is it potty time? One-year-olds won't sit still long enough to try. Eighteen-month-olds won't take orders; their interest in poop, if any, is limited to sticking a hand in the diaper and squishing some. The two-year-old Cave-Kid stage is the earliest age that toddlers show readiness to learn that pooping and peeing and toilets go together. (This fits perfectly with the idea of Prehistoric Parenting. Cavemen living about 150,000 years ago were the first to use "indoor plumbing"—a pit in a distant cave corner.)

Cautious, fastidious Kyle, age two and a half,
color-coordinates his clothes at night. He hates water
play because it leaves little droplets on his shirt. He

was so resistant to trying the potty that his parents, Sondra and Martin, offered him a present if he pooped in it. When that didn't work, I advised them to take the spotlight off his pooping. I told them it was just too much of a challenge for him and instead to reward him with a little treat just for <u>sitting</u> for a minute on the potty (using a timer) while they read him a book.

At first Kyle balked at this. Sondra responded perfectly. She said, "No problem," then gave him a little cold shoulder for a minute. She didn't mention it again that day. Two days later when she asked, Kyle agreed to try the potty at storytime. Sondra set a timer, did a dramatic book reading for one minute, and gave him two animal crackers afterward. They repeated this a couple of times every day.

Soon Kyle wanted to do more! He didn't want to get off the potty! It was fun!

Next Sondra began giving Kyle a poker chip for doing something good during the day. Each chip could be redeemed for—an extra minute of storytime on the potty! Sondra also let Kyle overhear her gossiping to Martin about what they read and how happy she was that Kyle sat there until the dinger went off.

The next day Kyle began to pee on the potty, and within a week he was starting to poop there. He was very excited and proud, and although Sondra was supportive and positive, she was careful to keep her praise subdued. "Good job," she said. "You are so happy. We can tell Daddy tonight. Okay, let's clean up and finish reading the book."

Sondra knew that if she reacted with too much excitement it might make Kyle feel pressured.

Why Toilet Learning Can Take Time

Just because elimination is a natural act doesn't mean toilet learning will be a smooth process. It often goes more slowly than parents would like, for several reasons.

Parents' timetables and toddlers' aren't always in sync. Maybe other moms in your playgroup are already free of the hassle and expense of diapers, and you wish you were too. (I can't blame you, although mom-of-four Gretchen notes, "Being toilet-trained is such an overrated accomplishment. Diapers are so easy in comparison to cleaning up after accidents and reminding them to go!") Or maybe you're hoping your toddler will be potty-trained by a certain date for the start of preschool or day care. However convenient that would be for you, most young toddlers lack the impulse control and attention span needed for toilet training.

The golden opportunity really comes after the second birthday, when your toddler becomes more verbal, eager to please, and fascinated by doing things in the right order.

Time to Learn About the Potty?

These are the five classic signs that a toddler is ready for potty training:

1. She is saying yes in more and more situations.

2. Walking is no longer new and exciting, and she's willing now to sit still in one place.

3. She has words for poop and pee.

4. She likes to imitate you.

5. She's interested in neatness, organizing things in groups, and cleaning up.

Parents try too hard. Even two-year-olds who are ready for potty learning may still have the Neanderthal tendency to be negative, defiant under pressure, and they're also becoming easily embarrassed by toilet functions. That's why too much pressure and too much focus on the potty may backfire and make them more resistant. This is a battle you can't win and don't want to get into.

It's a confusing process to learn. You can't exactly explain the bladder or the rectal sphincter to a toddler. It's truly one of life's "learning-by-doing" experiences! For example, Micah, age two, loved watching his daddy flush the toilet, so he went to the bathroom—where he peed on the floor and then flushed the toilet all by himself!

Toilet Learning the Prehistoric Parenting Way

Knowing your little time-traveler and what makes her tick makes all the difference!

Don't try too early. Wait until your child is showing two or three of the potty readiness signs (see box).

Make the potty a fun place. The control over this process is all in your toddler's court, and force or pressure will only make him resist. So your best course is to make the potty a destination he enjoys visiting. Bryn, age two, was so obsessed with reading her special potty books with her mom that she'd beg "Tinkle now!" all the time—just to read!

Use the baby steps approach:

1. **Start with a little "no pee, no poop" routine.** First use the potty as a place to read a fun book together, whether your child is dressed or in a diaper. (Eventually, you'd like her to sit bare-bottomed, but if she'll only sit clothed, that's okay—at least it's a beginning.) Every day, at about the time she normally poops, say something like "It's time for the potty book!"

This will appeal to your toddler's growing love of routine by making potty reading a familiar, regular thing. Set a timer for one minute. (Later you can gradually increase it to two or three minutes.)

2. **Reward her for sitting there—even if nothing happens.** When the time's up, give her a reward, such as making a check on the hand, a sticker, or animal crackers—whether or not she "produces." You could also use a star chart—but again, the stars are earned just for *sitting on the potty.* Be sure you give stars for other positive behaviors during your child's day, too, so the focus isn't *all* on the poop.

3. **Here's the hard part: Be low-key.** If she does actually pee or poop—and eventually, she will—*don't make a big fuss about it! Use big praise for sitting but understated praise for pooping.* Applause and celebrations about using the potty usually backfire with toddlers. Shy kids may become hesitant to try, because they feel like they're pooping under a spotlight. Worried kids may become hesitant; they don't want to accidentally disappoint you. Spirited kids may see how important their potty training is to you and stop doing it when they're mad at you!

For months, Ethan, two, had been using the potty.
But when he was visiting his grandparents, they
made big celebrations the first two times they saw this
miracle in action. As soon as he was back home again,
this overwhelmed little boy started asking for his
diapers again.

Instead of setting off verbal fireworks, say in a pleasant but mild voice, "Oh, you peed. Good job. Let's clean it up and flush, and then we'll finish reading the book!" Later in the day, express your pleasure the side-door way: Let her hear you gossiping to Dad about her success.

Make sure your child's poops are soft. At around two, toddlers often become constipated because they're finicky eaters, preferring too much white food (milk and starchy foods like bread and pasta). Offer whole grains and plenty of fresh fruits and vegetables. Fresh carrot juice or prune juice mixed with orange or apple juice or dried fruits are also helpful. (Speak to your doctor for more dietary advice.)

Use the Fast-Food Rule if you run into snags. Daniel, two, loves to pee in his potty, flush the toilet, and wash his hands, but he hasn't been able to master pooping. That embarrasses him, so he has begun retreating to a closet to poop and then resisting having his diaper changed.

Pressuring or ridiculing a child like Daniel would be cruel and counterproductive. Instead, empathize with him and respect his decision. Narrate back his reaction when he's being changed: "You say, 'No, no, no, no!' and push me away. No like diaper change. No diaper change. NO!' I'm so sorry. Mommy says, 'No more poop diaper,' but Daniel says, 'NO!! NO!! Noooooo!!'" (Meanwhile, you are changing the diaper while you distract him and narrate his true feelings!)

Backsliding: Kyle Revisited
When Kyle was almost three, Sondra gave birth to
twin boys. Not long afterward Kyle had a very hard

poop. He became terrified of the toilet. His parents tried to reassure him. They reminded him that he used to go without any problem. Their logic was perfect. But Kyle didn't give two poops about their logic.

He held his stool for a week. Using the potty became increasingly painful. Even after receiving medicine to soften his stool, he still refused to use the potty. I encouraged Sondra and Martin to give him diapers, ease all pressure off him, give him fiber to keep his stool soft, and reward him once again if he simply sat on the toilet (with his diaper on). I also had them encourage Kyle to do messy play like finger painting and working with clay to help him relax and "let go" of his hesitation to "make a mess" in his potty. This continued for about two months.

One day Kyle said, "Okay, no diapers." He pooped three times in the toilet and was very proud of himself. After that he had no stools for four days. But with continued low-key encouragement, he gradually improved, and after a few weeks of practicing sitting on the toilet every day and eating high-fiber food, he finally quit diapers for good.

If your child is withholding, there could be many reasons:

- A painful elimination, which has made her afraid to poop again. This is common after a child has had constipation, diarrhea, or a rash.
- Anger, sibling rivalry, or some other strong emotion she's trying to contain.
- Fear of failing to poop and disappointing you.
- Lack of privacy (often a problem at school).
- Fear of being flushed away. (Remember, your toddler's spatial reasoning is poor. That's why she's always trying to crawl into places that are too small for her body. Since some things can go down the toilet and disappear forever, she may think, "Maybe I could too?")

■ Unsteadiness on the toilet because her feet don't reach the ground. Use a child-size floor-model potty, or give her a footstool to rest her feet on when she's on the big potty. (It's also hard to push to get the poop out if your feet are dangling in the air—you try it!)

There are some very rare medical problems that can also cause a child to suddenly withhold. Speak to your child's doctor if the withholding is lasting more than three or four days or if your child is not acting normally.

Potty Training a Three-Year-Old

Not rushing to potty train a resistant or uninterested Cave-Kid does have one up side: After three they are easier to reason with, as Sam's story shows.

Sam didn't want to use the potty for pooping, but he did want to be a Jedi Knight and get a light saber. His mom, Heidi, said, "I'd love to get you a light saber. You'd be a great Jedi Knight. Oh, but I just remembered: Jedi Knights pee-pee and poo-poo on the potty." She didn't say anything to threaten or force him. She said everything in a nonchalant, no-big-deal way. Then she added, "Someday soon, I bet you'll be ready to be a Jedi Knight. Then we can pick out that light saber. What color would you like? Red? Green?"

Later that day, when they were drawing pictures, Mom drew a Jedi and said, "Sam, I forgot to draw a diaper on that Jedi. No, that's silly. Jedis don't wear diapers!" She gossiped to Dad later, saying, "When Sam's a big boy, he will be a big Jedi and have a light saber and even some Jedi underpants!"

Within a day, Sam was a Jedi *potty*-master.

Toilet Learning: Real-Life Questions

My 27-month-old won't have anything to do with the potty no matter how hard I try to entice him. He just runs away or ignores it. What should I do?

When your toddler shows the signs of readiness but still resists toilet training, he may be showing you his defiance. Another possibility is that big changes at home are throwing him off-kilter. For example, does he have a new sibling? Has he just left the crib? Changed schools? Moved? Has there been a death in the family? Quarreling in the house? Did he see a scary TV show?

I recommend that you back off from any talk about poop or pee. See if you can start rewarding him just for sitting there, fully dressed, to read a book with you for just a minute. Make it fun!

Help! My son stays dry all day but wets his bed every other night!
Don't worry. Nighttime dryness often takes a while longer, especially in boys. It's beyond their conscious control. Even by age five, about 10 percent of boys are still wetting (as are 5 percent of girls). The tendency runs in families.

Chapter 14

Boulders That Trip Up Three-Year-Olds
Fears, Stuttering, Medicine Taking, New Siblings

Main points:

- The many new ways your three-year-old sees the world may make his fears seem very, very real.

- Fears: Here are successful ways to fight them, designed for a Villager's level of understanding.

- Stuttering: How to help kids whose mouths stumble while trying to keep up with their brains.

- Medicine taking: Using bartering (and sneakiness) helps the medicine go down.

- New siblings: It's your toddler, not your newborn, who needs all that extra TLC.

Fears: A Powerful Part of Our Self-Preservation That Goes a Little Haywire

> "Along came a spider and sat down beside her and frightened Miss Muffet away."
>
> —Nursery rhyme

Stella, three, was a smart and confident child who always looked before she leaped. So her hysterical crying came out of the blue the day she spied an ant crawling up her leg. Her mom, Fran, removed the tiny bug, reassured her, and thought no more about it.

The next day, however, Stella was afraid to sit in the grass because of the "buggies." Fran persuaded her to play outside by tucking her pants into her socks (a simple, logical solution that would make sense to any Versatile Villager). But that night things got worse. Shortly after going to bed, Stella started to cry out for help in a very agitated voice, "Go away! GO! GO!! Mommy, M-O-M-M-Y!!!!!" When Fran arrived seconds later, Stella clung to her for dear life, saying, "Buggies, Mommy! BUGGIES!"

Fran turned on the lights and inspected the bed for insects, but there were none there. She tried simple logic again. "See, honey? No bugs, everything's okay. See? No buggies." Stella calmed and Fran left. But a minute later came the cries again about "buggies." That night Stella's parents let her stay in their bed, where she was calm and quiet the whole night.

This scenario continued for three nights, with Stella getting more and more panicky the moment the lights went out. (We'll revisit Stella and learn how her bug-aboo was resolved after I explain why fears are so typical for our prehistoric Villagers.)

Why Do Toddlers Develop Fears?

Fears thrive in a deep, primitive part of our minds: fears of snakes, falling, spiders, rats, isolation (abandonment), loud noises, and bright lights. It can be impossible to know what provokes a particular fear in a toddler. Triggers can include stresses in the family (a new baby, parents fighting, illness or death or a move), an injury or a scare (such as an earthquake or a car accident), something in a TV show or movie, being teased ("The moths are going to get into your hair and fly you into the trees"), or accidentally overhearing and possibly misinterpreting something ("At the picnic the ants carried everything away"). Often the cause remains a mystery.

Toddlers of any age can develop fears. Younger ones tend to fear sudden distressing things like thunder, firecrackers, or big dogs, and the fears tend to disappear with a little cuddling. But around age three toddlers develop fears—of bad men, monsters, and witches— that are less easily soothed away. These fears, irrational as they may seem, pop up in this age group for two main reasons:

Three-year-olds feel more vulnerable. Major changes occur in your toddler's Stone Age brain that may make him feel more vulnerable at this stage. First, he is now constantly comparing himself to other people. The realization that he's bigger than a baby ("a big boy") but small compared to everyone else is a pretty scary new awareness. Second, he is trying so hard to distance himself from his unacceptable primitive impulses that he may unconsciously project them (like his desire to bite and hit) onto the shadows, strangers, and scary animals of the world around him.

They believe in magic. Another dramatic advance in your toddler's way of thinking is his new ability to figure out how things work. It now makes sense to him that milk comes from cows and that rivers come from melting snow. And what can't be explained from his own experience, he's now very able to explain with *"magic!"* Like the earliest villagers tens of thousands of years ago, he now believes that anything's possible, and his mind can concoct plenty of spooky "anythings," including monsters under the bed and armies of tiny ants out on a mission to get him.

Handling Fears the Prehistoric Parenting Way

Left unattended, the angst kindled by fear can lead to a smorgasbord of different behaviors: acting out, aggression, clinginess, and anxiety symptoms such as nail biting, stuttering, masturbation, phobias, regressions, toilet troubles, sleep problems, nightmares, and night terrors.

It's normal for you to want to quickly reassure your child when he is panicked by thoughts of dinosaurs or angry bees. But as you may know from friends who fear driving or flying, dismissing these concerns or labeling them illogical is worse than useless. It doesn't lessen the fear, and it makes your child feel terribly alone—like you really don't understand or respect his concerns! So what should you do? Here are some ways you can become your toddler's ally by using his own unique ways of understanding the world!

Don't immediately try to dispel the fear. I often explain to the parents in my practice that when it comes to reassuring a frightened toddler, "The shortest path between two points is not always a straight line." In other words, even though it might seem that all you need to do to end the fear is just show him "there are no witches," being so direct and logical usually doesn't work. A frightened child's mental images of monsters or "bad men" seem every bit as real to him as this book you're holding in your hands!

In my experience, the fastest way to lessen a toddler's fear is to patiently acknowledge his concern with love and respect and then to use primitive logic to reassure him (as described below). This slower journey of taking baby steps *around* the deep chasm of his fear is always safer and more successful than minimizing his fear and trying quickly to dispel it!

Outsmart his fear using primitive logic. The more you rationally discuss fears and try to talk your toddler out of them, the more fearful he'll get. To him, it's real, period! That's because toddlers are very

literal, and they truly believe that *anything* is possible. ("Your boss *exploded* at you today? Yikes!")

So rather than insisting, "There are no monsters," use explanations that will make sense to *his* level of logic. For example, say, "Mommy monsters don't let baby monsters go out at night. They have to eat dinner and go to bed! But anyway, let's do something *secret* and *powerful* to make sure those monsters go somewhere else, not here." Or "You know what I just remembered? Dinosaurs hate the smell of garlic. So let's rub some on this little piece of paper and keep it by the window. That will keep them away!" (Take your job seriously. It may seem silly to you, but to your toddler it's a life-and-death issue! If you chuckle while you're trying to reassure him, he'll feel patronized or ridiculed.)

Here are some great ways to reassure your fearful toddler that three-year-olds love:

- Use a protective talisman like a special bracelet; a dolly; a blanket; a dream catcher (for bad dreams); a bedside photo of his "protectors"—Mom and Dad; and/or a spray bottle of "magic water."
- Pretend to slide an imaginary "protective suit" on him each night. Massage it on from head to toe so it'll keep him safe once he's in bed.
- Draw a picture of the fear, then let your child crumple it, stomp on it, and tear it up.
- Read books about his fear. (See the story of Fran and Stella on page 278.)
- Role-play that you and he are battling the fear, but don't be surprised if your prehistoric buddy has very graphic bloody fantasies.
- Ask your toddler what he thinks might help.

> When Tess, three, became very fearful of the smoke alarm after it went off accidentally, her parents named it—Fred. Then they attached a smiley face to it that Tess had drawn. They all said good morning and good night to Fred and offered "him" cookies. Within a few days, Tess's fear was just a distant memory.

> Suddenly Jaymie, almost three, refused to bathe. She was cautious by nature, and her dad had been away a lot on business. She wasn't afraid of going down the drain, like some kids, but she was afraid of having an "accident." "I don't want to pee in the water," she complained (she had finished toilet-training only a few months before).
> So when Jaymie began to freak out at bath time, her mom, Barbara, used the Fast-Food Rule to let her know she understood. "No bath! No bath! No, no, NO!! You say, 'NO bath! No like water!'" she said vigorously

in a serious voice, shaking her head no and waving her hands no as she pointed to the tub. "No water! No bath! Might pee-pee!"

She could have suggested that Jaymie pee first and empty her bladder, but that's adult logic and it probably wouldn't have persuaded her. She could also have tried some baby steps: "Okay, let's not even go all the way into the bath. You're in up to your toes. See if you can push the duckie!" This approach might have worked after two to three days of gradual progress. First toes, then feet, legs, bottom, and finally the whole body. But Barbara chose to use magic instead. She told Jaymie: "Let's pee, then I'll put magic cream on you so you won't pee till bedtime." She also gave Jaymie a Pull-Up just for the bath, along with lots of gossiping to her duckies, some extra time-ins, and Special Time. Jaymie complained a little at first, but Barbara noticed that her cries were more protests than screams, so she just mirrored them back and then kept on gossiping to the duckies. Within a few days, she was back to bathing without the soggy Pull-Up.

Try not to fuel the fear. When something is going to happen that you know will be frightening to your toddler, don't tell him too far in advance, especially if he has a cautious temperament. For example, wait until the day before a doctor's appointment to inform him about it. If he asks about shots, don't say he *will* get one; instead, say, "You *may* get one. I'm not sure." It may be a little white lie. But believe it or not, doctors' offices do actually run out of vaccines from time to time, so you leave him a little wiggle room for *hope*. Saying it as a certainty may only make his fear get bigger and bigger!

Also, remember that fears are especially tough on a toddler when his parent seems afraid too. If you are nervous about something that frightens your child, like thunder and lightning, try to look calm. Your toddler reads your fear like an open book, making him feel all the more vulnerable and afraid.

Handling Fears: A Real-Life Question

Why do fears get worse at night?

Even grown-ups feel more uneasy after nightfall. Our minds often fill the darkness with worried thoughts and fearful fantasies. Kids feel this way too—especially at night, when they have to be on their own!

Among the bolstering tactics you can use: confidence-builders, gossip, role-playing, time-in, increased physical touch (hugs and massage), breathing exercises, praise (all in Chapter 9), and the prevention advice on separation worries in Chapter 13, since this behavior too is really a kind of fear.

Prehistoric Parenting in Action

Let's check back on Stella, the little girl who was afraid of ants. After four nights of growing increasingly panicky at bedtime, and four nights in her parents' bed, her mom, Fran, called me for advice. Here's what we did:

- *Role-play.* During the day Fran played bug games with Stella. She played the "mean bug" who couldn't find his favorite toy, and she also played the scared little bug who was lost. Stella played the girl who told her to "Go away!" and go out and play with her own brothers and sisters.
- *Villager-level logic.* Fran found a library book for children about bugs. She and Stella read it to learn where bugs live (in the dirt, *not* in people's houses or beds) and what they eat (leaves—they don't like the taste of kids! Phooey! Kids taste yucky to them!). The book showed how tiny a bug is and how big a kid is.
- *A calm bedtime.* I urged Fran to lower the lights and sound level for the hour before bed, then to try a soothing nightly massage, during which they talked about the fun things Stella did that day and those to be done tomorrow. After a

lullaby, they said goodnight to all the dollies, calling them "Stella's big protectors." A nightlight helped cut the vastness of the dark.

■ *The power of magic.* Fran ended the night routine by putting on Stella's protective "superclothes." These would protect her from *anything* scary. (I told Fran not to even mention ants. Why bring it up first?) Starting at the feet, Fran firmly rubbed her daughter's skin as if she were putting on a tight invisible suit all the way to the top of her head while singing a special little song: "Mommy loves you, Daddy loves you, Stella, Stella is safe, safe, safe." Then she made the room extra-safe with a few squirts of "secret superspray"—a little spray bottle filled with water that Fran had drawn a smiley face on.

The first night Stella was fine for about five minutes, but then she got worried. So her parents came in and sang their song again and "reapplied" the protective suit and sprayed the secret superspray, and that was it for the night. The next night she slept beautifully after her whole routine. After five more days they shortened the routine. After two weeks they went back to the short routine they had before. By then she loved buggies again! That Halloween Stella asked to dress up as an ant!

Stammering and Stuttering

Polly, three, was proud of her many recent accomplishments, including learning to get herself dressed and filling the dog's bowl with food. She saw herself as a "big kid" and seemed to be trying hard to do all the things her older siblings could do. So her parents, Thomas and Hope, were startled when she began having trouble getting her words out. "It's my tur-tur-turn to feed the dog! Not Pe-Pete's tur-tur-turn!" she'd stutter.

Night Terrors: A Cousin of Sleepwalking

Some toddlers wake up crying in the middle of the night because they are having bad dreams. When your toddler is having a night terror, however, he will cry, scream, and otherwise act like he just woke up from a frightening dream—but he is still asleep! He will totally ignore your reassurance, touching, or hugging. Night terrors occur about two to four hours into sleep, as your toddler switches from deep sleep to a lighter REM (rapid eye movement) stage. They are related to sleepwalking and talking in one's sleep.

Even though he's not awake, he's not comatose either. So if he is in the throes of a night terror, I suggest you try to connect with his subconscious mind to reassure him. Turn on a low light, rock him in your arms, and sing any quiet lulling song that he loves, or just repeat calmly in a singsong way, "Mommy and Daddy love you" over and over again.

If night terrors are frequent, I recommend you do a calming routine with him every time you put him down to sleep. Pick a calming little lullaby song, and as you sing it to him, make believe you are putting a protective suit on him. Each night apply this magic suit from head to toe. Pretend that you have to pull on it "because it's a little snug in spots" and make sure you get it on completely like a real, invisible suit. The more times you do this song/magic suit routine, the more you are giving a little magic message to his subconscious mind that everything will be okay. And if he does happen to get a night terror, you will probably be able to reassure his subconscious mind (remember, he is still asleep) by reapplying the magic suit and singing the lullaby.

Sometimes reflecting and being thoughtful are good things. They can help your toddler stop himself from climbing onto a dangerous counter or hitting his sister. But sometimes three-year-olds think too much. When they do so while speaking, the result can be stuttering and stammering—an alarming sound to parents who were just months earlier thrilled by their amazing child's first words and sentences. But don't worry. Fortunately, this problem is usually much less serious than you think.

Why Some Toddlers Stammer

They think too much. Around the third birthday, most toddlers become much more conscious about speaking. They start thinking about what they are about to say, and this can disrupt the flow of how words come out. The same thing happens anytime you try to think too consciously about an automatic behavior. Take skipping, for example. If you focus on "lift right foot, throw it forward, hop," and so on, you'll definitely slow your actual skipping and maybe even stumble.

Talking—like walking, riding a bicycle, or playing a piano—is best done with your unconscious brain in control (the cerebellum). Your conscious brain should act only as a senior supervisor, making some of the big decisions like where to walk and what to say, but not how to walk or how to correctly pronounce each word.

So while in rare situations stuttering and stammering may be a sign of emotional stress, most of the time when it happens during toddlerhood, it's simply a sign of thinking too much!

They think or talk too fast. Sometimes it may seem to you like your toddler's brain is working so fast that his mouth is having a hard time keeping up with it! In his eagerness to communicate with you, he may trip over his words or have them come out a little scrambled.

On the other hand, your toddler may sometimes use a stammer as a mental way to hold a thought while his mind figures out exactly what he wants to say. The result is a kind of jerky repetition. "After lunch can I—, can I—, can I—, can I watch a movie?"

They saw someone else do it. Toddlers can be great little mimics (monkey see, monkey do). Sometimes their stuttering is just an imitation of someone they saw at school or on TV.

Responding to Stuttering the Prehistoric Parenting Way

Most toddlers who stutter do it only for a couple of weeks (or a couple of months) and then it just disappears. But here are a two things you can do to make it go away even faster:

Don't make a big deal about it. As with any mistake your toddler makes when speaking, it's best not to shine a spotlight on it. Remember, this is an area where he's still a novice. Help your toddler save face by treating stammering the same way you would treat a grammatical error: Ignore it. In fact, if you have a particularly sensitive child, he may notice your lips purse or your eyebrows rise in concern even when you don't make a peep about the stuttering. So I find that the best way to ignore stuttering is to stay engaged yet to casually turn your face and look the other way as you listen.

Boost him up and lessen his anxiety. Another way to help your toddler relax, let his words flow, and stop trying so hard is to do other things to boost his confidence and lessen his anxiety. Try increasing your use of confidence-builders and gentle praise (see Chapter 9); add in a few more fun time-ins like Special Time affirmations and outdoor play (see Chapter 10); help him lower his anxiety with some loving massage and calming breathing in Opening and Closing Ceremonies (also in Chapter 10).

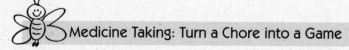

Medicine Taking: Turn a Chore into a Game

When your doctor hands you a prescription for your child, ask him how it tastes. Unfortunately, the answer is often "Yucky!" That's when most parents try a few common tricks like mixing the medicine into some juice or food. This trick sometimes works, but all too often clever two-year-olds and even smarter three-year-olds see right through this ploy, because mixing medicine with juice usually ends up making the whole glass of juice taste wretched. You might have better luck mixing it into a serving of something dark with a strong flavor—uncaffeinated cola or grape soda. But don't be surprised if your sensitive, cautious, or defiant toddler takes one sniff and says, "No thanks!"

Instead, try Dr. Harvey's Famous Switcheroo. Before you call your toddler in to take his medicine, pour one-ounce portions of uncaffeinated cola into two small glasses, and mix a dose of the medicine into one of them. Then call your toddler, put some more medicine into a spoon, and tell him, "Take your medicine, and then you can have some soda to wash it down."

If he says, "Okay," just give him the spoonful of medicine and then the glass with just the soda. If he refuses, just repeat your offer again: "Drink your medicine, and then you can have soda." *Then* if he still refuses, pretend to pout and complain: "Okay, you win!! Ugh!! You *always* win! I never get to win! Okay, go ahead, you can have the soda, and I'll put this medicine away." Sigh and look pained, like you've been hoodwinked again, and hand him the soda that's mixed with the medicine and busy yourself poring the medicine from the spoon back into the bottle.

At this point, your toddler will feel he's won and is likely to guzzle the soda greedily. He doesn't know that you've already mixed the medicine into it! Don't gloat or say "Gotcha!" when it's over. Let him feel he's won, and then you can try to "win" again when the next dosage is due.

A New Sibling: A New Playmate or a Challenger to the Throne?

Stephen and Nicole's three-year-old son Sam had his first meltdown in public right after his baby sister was born. "With the baby he has a 'good angel, bad angel' side," Nicole explains. "He'll start touching the baby gently, then grit his teeth to a tense smile—and suddenly pinch her!"

Imagine your husband came home one day and said, "Look, honey! I've brought home a new wife for you to play with! She's going to take up a lot of my attention for a while, but eventually you're gonna have so much fun together!" What would your response be? *Um, I don't think so!*

The arrival of a new baby is usually the most disorienting and shocking to your firstborn (or if you have several children, your other kids under five). I'm sure you felt exhausted and stretched thin, but at least you kind of knew what you were getting yourself into. For your child, however, this was all new.

Many parents feel guilty that they can't give their new baby the same undivided attention they were able to nurture their first child with. *Don't spend a second fretting over that!* Sure, your older one got more attention from *you,* but what your new one doesn't get from you, he will receive five times over from your older child. No one else will make your baby laugh or learn as much as his older sibling—his superhero in the flesh! I always like to remind parents that *a first child lives in an adult world, but a second child lives in a child's world.* After you have two, they mostly just keep you around to provide them with a steady supply of love, kisses—and *hot food!*

Why Toddlers Have Trouble Becoming "Big Bro" or "Big Sis"

Put yourself in your toddler's tennies, and you can see why he's probably the least joyous person around when a new baby comes home.

Toddlers are self-centered and have poor impulse control. As the "new wife" scenario shows, who wouldn't feel competitive in this situation? Your toddler is so self-centered, it's normal for him to feel like you're putting salt in his wounds whenever you tend to the baby and ignore him. What's more, the immature impulse-control center in his right brain makes it hard for him to restrain his competitive outbursts. So your "big boy's" feelings of resentment may well be displayed by a steady flow of pinches, slugs, slaps, and bites!

Their feelings are in terrible conflict. Your toddler's growing understanding of the rules means that he "knows" biting and hitting are wrong. In addition, his desire to please you is strong, and he now understands that he may be punished if he is rough with the baby.

Nevertheless, his aggressive desires may be very hard to suppress. Sometimes these strong feelings sneak out in the form of worries about scary monsters or nervous behaviors like stuttering, nail biting, nightmares, separation difficulties, masturbation, or fears. And don't be shocked if there are times when your toddler (who ought to know better) just won't be able to stop himself from pinching the baby or kissing her a little too hard.

Before the Baby Arrives

Don't talk up the new baby the minute your pregnancy test turns positive. At best, your toddler will get bored waiting for the baby to arrive. (Remember, he doesn't have a great sense of time.) And at worst, it will only provide him with many months during which his green-eyed monster of jealousy and fear of abandonment can grow. Wait until about two months before your due date to start talking about the "baby in Mommy's tummy." Here's what I tell parents in my practice to do to prepare their kids for a new sibling:

- Give your toddler (boy or girl) a small, easy-to-hold baby doll so that he can practice feeding, changing, and good handwashing.
- Gossip by talking to the baby inside you (and to the baby after he's born) about his big brother/sister's great accomplishments.
- Prep your toddler by teaching him deep calming breathing (see Opening and Closing Ceremonies in Chapter 10).
- Time your crib move carefully. If your toddler hasn't given up the crib at least two or three months before your baby's arrival, postpone any plans to get him to do so until two to three months after the birth, so he won't feel displaced.
- Buy a nice toy that will be a present from the baby, and some little toys that can be "from" visitors who come to your home and bring gifts for the newborn but not for your firstborn.
- Make sure your toddler is up to date with his shots.

Helping Your Toddler Adjust to a New Sibling the Primitive Parenting Way

Play to your firstborn's strengths, and you'll have less trouble with his weaknesses.

Rely on Special Time. Now is the time to beef up Special Time (see Chapter 10). Do it at least twice a day. It's a great way to teach delayed gratification, which your toddler will need when you are preoccupied with feedings and diapering. If you can, give your toddler both Dad Special Time and Mom Special Time. Occasionally do a *special* Special Time, such as an outing for ice cream with no rivals—I mean babies—allowed!

Catch 'em being good. Villagers love to be noticed and to get rewards (Star Charts, hand checks) when they are good.

Be generous with "extras." Create a more elaborate nighttime routine, and give plenty of affirmations and strength-builders.

Roughhouse! Not only do wrestling and pillow-tossing help your child vent aggressions in an acceptable way, but also these are "big kid" behaviors that he knows little babies are "too tiny and weak" to be able to do! Don't forget to connect roughhousing with the calm breathing exercises of the Opening and Closing Ceremonies, so your toddler gets extra practice learning how to settle down as well as rev up!

Redirect aggression. Rather than criticize your toddler when her baby-play gets too rough, show her a better way. Be positive, saying, "Your little sister loves to be touched softly like this—you're good at that!" Later, gossip about the good touching with Daddy.

If your Villager is pretty verbal, let him know he can teach, soothe, and entertain the baby with his words. I love it when an older sib talks Toddler-ese when the baby cries, imitating how his mom uses it with him!

Will, three, was having a rough time with his baby
sister, Estelle. She would cry if he held her too tight

or accidentally bumped her. But the first time she laughed at his funny faces, he was totally delighted!!

Enlist their help. Villagers love role playing. Give your new big sibling a job, like getting you a diaper when you need one. Another great job for a toddler over two is to make him a little cardboard badge and call him the "tiny-toy police." Let him know what a big help it is to have him pick up little toys. Teach him how to put a toy through an empty toilet-paper roll to check the size to be sure it isn't a choking hazard. Even though your baby won't be crawling for months, it's good practice. Moreover, it makes your toddler feel more important!

Don't tempt fate. Even if your toddler seems protective of a younger sibling, he may have a hard time restraining his impulses and hit or scratch. What's more, he may want to carry the baby—without any realistic sense that a real baby is heavier and wigglier than a baby doll. Never leave your toddler alone with a baby under one year old. Better safe than sorry.

Let your toddler regress. You may be more ready than ever for your toddler to exhibit big-kid behaviors like using the potty and sleeping in a real bed. But he needs a little leeway right now. Ask, "Do you want to be a big boy or my baby now? Come in my lap, you big strong baby, and you can hug me for a little while."

Set the appropriate expectations. Remind visitors to pay attention to your toddler before ooing and aahing over the baby. Above all, don't feel guilty about giving your baby a little less attention than your older child. Your toddler is the one who has lost the most.

Keeping Everybody Well

To prevent illness, change your toddler's clothes when he comes home from playing with other children. And make sure he washes his hands several times a day. You don't need antibacterial soap, just make sure he rubs his hands vigorously as he's washing and drying.

You can't prevent rivalry—it's a simple fact: You have two little people who see you as the center of their universe, and they both want as much of your attention as they can grab. Hopefully, however, by using the tips and tactics described in this chapter, you'll be able to help keep the peace in your house until your kids get a little bigger and can start working things out between themselves.

Epilogue
Civilization, Ho!:
Your Happy, Confident
Four-Year-Old

"The journey is the reward."

—Taoist saying

Congratulations! You've made it. You've just watched millions of years of history unfold before your very eyes and ears. And, you've guided your toddler through some of the most miraculous, fast-paced, and challenging developments that she will experience in her entire life!

Your toddler has transformed from a one-year-old Charming Chimp-Child gleefully practicing her first steps and words . . . to an 18-month-old Knee-High Neanderthal alternately swaggering with the new thrill of freedom and falling victim to wild tantrums . . . to a two-year-old Clever Cave-Kid beginning to learn the simple rules of language, hygiene, and social cooperation . . . to a three-year-old Versatile Villager fascinated by people, play, art, humor, and friendship.

Whew!

At times during these past three years, I bet a single day dragged so slowly that it felt like a month. Toilet learning alone may have

seemed to take a million years! But now that all those millennia of development are behind you, don't you feel like it all happened in the blink of an eye?

Here you are on the brink of your child's fourth birthday, ready to leave toddlerhood behind as your child knocks at the gates of childhood . . . and the civilized world.

Of course, there's still lots of work ahead. Your child can now pass for a "big kid" at least for short bursts of time or until she's overtired, hungry, frustrated, or mad. But she's not quite there yet. And, she still has to navigate the challenges of another ten thousand years of human evolution on her way to reaching the level of Modern Man. That journey will occupy her for the rest of her childhood.

But she's no longer truly primitive. She's now more like the queen of her rustic kingdom. Four-year-olds know their own little worlds perfectly and are ready to tackle exciting new cultural refinements: learning written language, the rules of right and wrong, patience, and responsibility. If you found toddlerhood fun, just wait. In the next year alone, your child's sense of humor will blossom. (Uh-oh, barf and poop jokes are coming!) Her curiosity about the world will explode. ("Why? Why? Why?") And she won't be able to get enough of friends and family ("Mommy, please can we have a tea party for my birthday? *Please!?*").

At four your child:

- Begins to decipher and use symbols. Eight thousand years ago man invented the earliest writing, making marks on paper and using pictures to represent things (hieroglyphics). As a preschooler, your child will learn to count and identify the whole alphabet, and even learn how to spell or write her name.
- Deftly uses both language and logic. Four-year-olds can say some 1,500 words and understand another 3,000 to 4,000. They speak so well and think so clearly now that they can figure many things out and make up complex and interesting stories. In the playground four-year-olds who are smart and funny often become the most popular.
- Develops a more sophisticated sense of humor. She begins to learn that one word can have two meanings—one of which bends a rule of logic. This is the beginning of puns (and knock-knock jokes!).
- Develops confidence. Bossy and boastful, four-year-olds try to impress using the power of language and their new understanding of rules, including lying and cheating! (Once you know the rules well, you can bend them.)
- Loves friends and is interested in what people think of her. For many four-year-olds, the first big insult isn't "You're a poo poo head!" it's "You're not my friend!" For the first time the opinions of others besides Mom and Dad matter, namely those of other kids!
- Tries to figure out the meaning of things. Everything!
- Becomes acquisitive. She wants what she sees on TV, in stores, at preschool, in friends' houses. She wants.

Will your amazing, ever-more-sophisticated former primitive out-grow Prehistoric Parenting? Yes and no. The basic ideas I've presented will serve you well throughout childhood. They're the foundations of Modern Parenting: having realistic expectations, understanding temperament, inventing loving routines, teaching a child to wait patiently, mirroring and acknowledging the feelings of an upset child, using positive ways to shape behavior, setting loving limits, looking for win-win compromises, and so forth. The specific issues you face will change, as will the language you use to address them. But these basics should serve you well.

Speaking of language, by age four your child may want you to stop talking Toddler-ese. She may begin to feel embarrassed by it. She may even say that it sounds like baby talk. "Stop talking that way," Liam, four, would say to his mom, Beth. That makes sense, since your child's brain is so much more mature now. But don't store Toddler-ese away on a shelf the minute your ex-toddler blows out the four candles. Toddler-ese will still come in handy for several more years when your child is really emotional and upset. Remember, we all slide a few rungs down the evolutionary ladder when we're frustrated and angry.

One basic concept your child will never outgrow is the good old Fast-Food Rule. All of us—older children, teenagers, and adults alike—need to hear our feelings reflected back to us in order to feel heard and understood, and safe and loved.

As your child gets older, you'll still have to be an ambassador. That's a good analogy for all of parenting. Only now you'll be serving as a representative to a land that's not quite so distant and whose inhabitants speak a language much like your own.

And as you face this latest visitor from the exciting frontier of Big-Kid Land, I hope you'll be able to look back fondly on the days when you had the happiest toddler on the block. I hope my advice helped make these amazing years less puzzling and combative and more loving and fun. Now the best news: You will have a breather until adolescence! The next ten years or so have their own unique challenges, but if you've made it smilingly through toddlerhood, I'm sure you've also got what it takes to help your child become the happiest kid on the block!

1. **It helps to think of your toddler as sort of a . . . caveman.** With all their grunting and grabbing toddlers often seem quite primitive. In fact, as amazing as it sounds, developmentally, they have a lot in common with little Neanderthals! Between one and four years of age your talented child will zip through 5 major achievements that it took prehistoric cavemen (and women) the past 5 million years to accomplish: walking, talking, manipulating things with the hands, figuring things out, and forming friendships.

2. **Be an "ambassador" to your prehistoric little child.** Once you realize your toddler has a lot in common with a Stone Ager (especially when she's mad), it becomes clear that your job is trickier than just being a "parent." You are an *ambassador* from the 21st century to the Neanderthal people! And as a great ambassador you must guide your child with respect and love; being neither too pushy or a mushy pushover.

3. **Follow the Fast-Food Rule.** This rule is simple: When your child is upset you should take a lesson from the order-takers at a burger joint—always repeat back his *"order"* (what he wants) before you tell him your *"price"* (what you want). Toddlers in the middle of a meltdown are incapable of hearing our message (our reasons, reassurance, distraction, or warning) until they're sure we understand and respect their message. So when your tot is upset, before you mention *your* ideas, take a minute to sincerely describe what he's doing and how you think he feels.

4. **Speak Toddler-ese.** Toddlers are pretty immature to begin with but they get downright primitive when they're upset. So, when you're talking to your cranky little cavegirl, always translate your words into Toddler-ese (her basic, almost prehistoric language). You can translate anything into Toddler-ese simply by using:

   - Short phrases.
   - Tons of repetition.
   - A passionate tone of voice.
   - Lots of exaggerated facial expressions and body gestures (like big smiles, frowns, and vigorous pointing).

5. **Know your toddler's temperament.** Although all toddlers go through the same phases of development, they each have a unique way of approaching the world. Is your child easy? Cautious? Spirited? Knowing who you're dealing with can help you tweak your parenting tactics so they work best for *your* toddler.

6. **Keep your cool.** Just because your prehistoric little pal goes ballistic doesn't mean you should too. Stay calm even if you're facing one of these common parenting dilemmas:

   - *Frustration:* All toddlers make their parents mad sometimes.

- *Feelings of failure:* All parents get discouraged (or feel temporarily overwhelmed) in the face of frequent daily clashes.
- *Whispers from the past:* Your toddler's behavior may awaken forgotten and disturbing feelings from your own childhood.
- *A mismatch between your toddler's temperament and your own:* Like stripes and polka dots, your personality may totally clash with your child's.
- *Little family or community support:* Too many couples are isolated and living without family or friends nearby.

7. **Encourage good behavior with "respect and rewards."** These gifts are guaranteed to bring out your toddler's best behavior:

- *Respect:* This is the key to a great relationship with your toddler. Showing respect and helping your child "save face" are very important when disciplining him (to avoid accidentally causing the destructive feelings of shame, embarrassment, or humiliation).
- *Believable praise:* Nourish your child's self-esteem with a balanced diet of praise—some wild applause and celebration mixed with lots and lots of gentle attention and loving comments describing her activity. The best compliments praise a child's specific deeds rather than making general remarks about his personality. And once you give praise don't take it back (praise spoiling).
- *Side-door messages:* Your toddler believes what he overhears even more than what you say directly to him! You can use this powerful secret in the following three ways: 1) "Gossip" (let him overhear you whispering some loving praise about him to someone else), 2) telling fairy tales (entertaining stories that have important hidden meanings imbedded inside), and 3) using reverse psychology (encourage good behavior in a defiant child by playfully telling him to do the *opposite* thing!).

- *Confidence-builders:* Help your child develop pride by using "strength-builders" (simple ways to demonstrate your belief in him) and by "playing the Boob" (silly ways to teach kids confidence by poking fun at yourself).
- *Rewards:* Little rewards such as hand checks, stickers, and tasty treats can help grease the wheels of cooperation.

8. **Rely on lots of time-in.** Time-ins are little tidbits of attention and routine that help your toddler feel valued. Some of the best time-ins are:

- Cozy massages.
- Cuddly blankies and loveys.
- *Special Time:* A great way to pack a ton of love and attention into just five minutes.
- *Affirmations:* Sharing positive words and hopes with your child at bedtime.
- *Opening and Closing Ceremonies:* Calming, healthful breathing exercises.
- *Play:* All sorts of play, but especially outdoor play, creative play (like art and pretend), and reading.

9. **Use gentle discipline to steer your child's behavior in a better direction ("detours").** Your toddler's job is to push the limits; your job is to enforce them.

- Start with appropriate expectations for her behavior.
- When possible side-step struggles by using distractions and compromising.
- Pick limits you know you can enforce.
- State the limits briefly, in a serious voice . . . and in Toddler-ese (avoid comparing, exaggerating, and name calling).

10. **Don't be afraid to use punishments as needed ("road-blocks").** When detours don't work to keep your child from misbehaving, it may be time to use a toddler-appropriate punishment. Those that work best are:

- Ignoring (giving your child "the cold shoulder").
- Loss of privileges (taking away the thing your child wants).
- Toddler time-outs.

Index

Page numbers of illustrations appear in italics.